Praise for *The Holy or the Broken* by Alan Light

"Thoughtful and illuminating . . . [Mr. Light] is a fine companion for this journey through one song's changing fortunes."

—*The New York Times*

"A combination mystery tale, detective story, pop critique and sacred psalm of its own."

—*Daily News*

"Brilliantly revelatory. . . . A masterful work of critical journalism."

—*Kirkus Reviews* (starred review)

"A deeply researched mixture of critical analysis and cultural archaeology."

—*Los Angeles Times*

"Keeps the pages turning. . . . A well-constructed, consistently enlightening book, which should have Cohen devotees and music fans alike seeking out their favorite version of the song."

—*Boston Globe*

"Fresh and compelling."

—*Entertainment Weekly*

"Reverentially details every stage in the [song's] evolution—and along the way, he reveals the compelling stories behind some of its most iconic interpretations."

—*The Atlantic*

"Absorbing. . . . Eloquent. . . . Light expertly unpacks the song's long, strange journey to ubiquity."

—*The Village Voice*

"A must for music fans."

—*Booklist* (starred review)

"Captures the essence of a song and of the culture it was reflecting. . . . It's just so well done."

—*Christian Science Monitor*

"[A] charming ode to a pop-culture phenomenon."

—*Publishers Weekly*

ALSO BY ALAN LIGHT

The Holy or the Broken: Leonard Cohen, Jeff Buckley and the Unlikely Ascent of "Hallelujah"

The Skills to Pay the Bills: The Story of the Beastie Boys

My Cross to Bear by Gregg Allman (co-writer)

LET'S GO CRAZY

Prince and the Making of *Purple Rain*

ALAN LIGHT

ATRIA PAPERBACK
New York London Toronto Sydney New Delhi

ATRIA PAPERBACK
An Imprint of Simon & Schuster, Inc.
1230 Avenue of the Americas
New York, NY 10020

First Atria Paperback edition October 2015

ATRIA PAPERBACK and colophon are trademarks of Simon & Schuster, Inc.

For information about special discounts for bulk purchases, please contact Simon & Schuster Special Sales at 1-866-506-1949 or business@simonandschuster.com.

The Simon & Schuster Speakers Bureau can bring authors to your live event. For more information or to book an event, contact the Simon & Schuster Speakers Bureau at 1-866-248-3049 or visit our website at www.simonspeakers.com.

Interior design by Meryll Rae Preposi
Cover design by Lucy Kim
Cover photograph by Ebet Roberts Photography
Author photograph by Mary Ellen Matthews

Printed and bound by CPI Group (UK) Ltd, Croydon, CR0 4YY

10 9 8 7 6 5 4 3

Library of Congress Cataloging-in-Publication Data

Light, Alan.
Let's go crazy : Prince and the making of Purple rain / Alan Light.
pages cm
Summary: "A new book on the unlikely coming-to-be of Prince's now legendary album. Purple Rain is a song, an album, and a film--each one a commercial success and cultural milestone. How did this semi-autobiographical masterpiece that blurred R&B, pop, dance, and rock come to alter the recording landscape and become an enduring touchstone for successive generations of fans?" — Provided by publisher.
1. Prince. Purple rain. 2. Rock music—United States—History and criticism. I. Title.
ML420.P974L44 2014
781.66092—dc23

2014026430

ISBN 978-1-4767-7672-9
ISBN 978-1-4767-7675-0 (pbk)
ISBN 978-1-4767-7677-4 (ebook)

For Suzanne and Adam, always

ONE

We Are Gathered Here Today

The stage is dark. A chord rings out.

It's an unusual chord—a B flat suspended 2 with a D in the bass. A year from this night, the sound of that chord will be enough to drive audiences into hysteria. But right now, in this club, the crowd of 1,500 or so people listen quietly, because it's the first time they are hearing the song that the chord introduces.

A spotlight comes up, revealing a young woman playing a purple guitar. She is dressed simply, in a white V-neck tank top, patterned miniskirt, and white, metal-studded, purple-trimmed high-top sneakers. Her asymmetrical haircut is very much on trend for 1983, the year this show is taking place. Wendy Melvoin, the girl holding the guitar, is just nineteen years old, and this is not only the first time she is performing this song in public, it is also her first appearance as the new guitarist in Prince's band, the Revolution. So far tonight, they have played nine songs; this one is kicking off the encore.

She plays through a chord progression once, and the rest of the five-piece band falls in behind her. They go through the cycle again, and then again. The fifth time around, you can hear a second guitar coming from somewhere offstage. On the ninth instrumental go-round, Prince strides out, wrapped tightly in a purple trench coat. He plays a few fills, moves his head to the microphone as if he's about to start singing, then pulls back again. Finally, three and a half minutes into the song, he begins his vocal, reciting more than singing the first line—"I never meant to cause you any sorrow . . ." The performance would yield what would soon become his signature recording and one of popular music's greatest landmarks.

When he reaches the chorus, repeating the phrase "purple rain" six times, the crowd does not sing along. They have no idea how familiar those two words will soon become, or what impact they will turn out to have for the twenty-five-year-old man onstage in front of them. But it's almost surreal to listen to this performance now, because while this thirteen-minute version of "Purple Rain" will later be edited, with some subtle overdubs and effects added, this very recording—the maiden voyage of the song—is clearly recognizable as the actual "Purple Rain," in the final form that will be burned into a generation's brain, from the vocal asides to the blistering, high-speed guitar solo to the final, shimmering piano coda. As the performance winds down, Prince says quietly to the audience, "We love you very, very much."

In the audience, up in the club's balcony, Albert Magnoli listens to Prince and the Revolution play the song. Magnoli, a recent graduate of the University of Southern California's film school, has just arrived in Minneapolis to begin work on Prince's next project, a feature film based on the musician's life, which will start shooting in a few months. He thinks that this grand, epic ballad might provide the climactic, anthemic moment for the movie, an element that he hadn't yet found in the batch of new recordings and work tapes Prince had given him. After the set, Magnoli joins the singer backstage and asks about the song.

"You mean 'Purple Rain'?" Prince says. "It's really not done yet." Magnoli tells him that he thinks this might be the key song they are missing for the film. Prince, the director recalls, considers that for a minute, and then says, "If that's the song, can *Purple Rain* also be the title of the movie?"

This launch and christening of *Purple Rain* occurred on August 3, 1983, at the First Avenue club in downtown Minneapolis. The show—with tickets priced at $25—was a benefit for the Minnesota Dance Theatre, where Prince has already started his band taking lessons in movement and rehearsing in preparation for the film. The sold-out concert, which raised $23,000 for the company, was his first appearance in his hometown since the tour that followed his breakthrough album, *1999*, ended in April, during the course of which he reached the Top Ten on the album and singles charts for the first time, and made the hard-won leap to becoming an A-list pop star.

The event was significant enough that *Rolling Stone* covered the show in its Random Notes section. Noting that "the mini-skirted Wendy" had replaced guitarist Dez Dickerson, the item said that Prince and the band "swung into a ten-song [actually eleven] act, including new tracks entitled 'Computer Blue,' 'Let's Get Crazy,' [*sic*] 'I Will Die For U,' [*sic*] 'Electric Intercourse,' and a cover of Joni Mitchell's 'A Case of You.' Then he encored with an anthemic—and long—new one called 'Purple Rain.' . . . Prince looked toned up from workouts with Minneapolis choreographer John Command, who's plotting the dance numbers for the film Prince has dreamed up. The new songs, which may appear on Prince's next LP, are to be part of the movie's sound track. . . . Filming is slated to start November 1st."

The location for this concert was no accident. First Avenue, a former bus station that reopened as a discotheque in 1970, was familiar, comfortable territory for Prince. "It was his venue of choice to try material out," Revolution drummer Bobby Z (Bobby Rivkin; his stage moniker was derived from "Butzie," a family nickname) has said. Grammy-winning megaproducer James "Jimmy Jam" Harris, whose career began as a member of Prince's protégé band, the Time, noted how the venue was an exception to the de facto segregation of live music: "A lot of clubs wouldn't let us play because we were a black band, and they were one of the first to really give us a shot." Indeed, First Avenue would practically function as a full-fledged character in the *Purple Rain* movie, and on this night, its hospitable confines served as the perfect place to introduce not only new material but a new configuration of the band.

Looking back, Wendy Melvoin claims that she didn't feel nervous about her first show with the Revolution. "From eat-ing and drinking to singing and playing and choreography, everything had a desperate importance, and nothing took priority over the other," she says. "Every moment that you were in Prince and the Revolution had to be like your last day on earth. So when we were doing that show, it seemed just as important as making it to rehearsal on time the day before."

The crucial decision to record the benefit was made in a bit of a scramble. Alan Leeds, who had worked as a longtime employee in the James Brown organization, had recently been brought on board as a tour manager for Prince. After the 1999 dates ended, Prince's managers asked Leeds to stay on as plans for the film developed. "By default, I ended up as the production manager," he recalls. "Honestly, I was in over my head . . . so I was nervous from a technical standpoint. . . . I had to find a [remote recording] truck, and I finally got a guy named David Hewitt, who had access to trucks, and he found the right truck and we had David Z [engineer David Rivkin, Bobby's brother] in it. So there was a lot of last-minute running around to pull that show off. It was also ridiculously hot and humid.

"The place was just absolutely packed to the rafters," Leeds continues. "Steve McClellan, who ran First Avenue, was afraid that the fire marshals were going to come and close us down. Half the problem was the last-minute guest lists from Prince and Warner Brothers; we had, like, two hundred people we hadn't anticipated, and no one knew where to put them in a small venue. All of a sudden, my friends in the industry were like, 'Yo, can you hook me up?' *USA Today* was there. It's like, 'Oh, shit! I guess we're doing something.' "

Still, for the members of the Revolution, the fact that the show was being recorded wasn't such a big deal. "I wasn't really aware that Bobby's brother had been brought on board to engineer what was coming into the live truck," says keyboard player Matt Fink. "When they told me that, I thought, 'Oh, he's recording this for posterity.' He didn't say to us, 'Oh, by the way, we're trying to capture this for the sound track.' "

"We were recording all along, as we always did," says the band's other keyboard player, Lisa Coleman. "We felt really good about the songs, we really liked the set, and we knew the trucks were there recording, but it was just another show."

But the show was evidently important enough to Prince that Melvoin remembers him talking to the band before the set, to calm their nerves. "When we were getting ready to go onstage, he said, 'If you feel nervous, slow your body in half. So if you're playing at 100 bpm, slow your body down to 50 bpm. Cut everything in half while you're playing. Everything—every move, every thought you make, just cut it in half.' It was an incredible piece of advice, because you know how long those jams can go, and if you get too excited and someone's rushing, that's one of the worst mistakes you can make in his band."

Prince hadn't necessarily planned on using the First Avenue recordings on the actual album, but when he listened to the tapes, he found that some of the new songs sounded good, in both performance and audio quality. Incredibly, not only "Purple Rain," but also two other songs that were debuted that night—"I Would Die 4 U" and "Baby I'm a Star"—wound up being used on the final *Purple Rain* sound track (though the others were reworked more extensively than the title song was). The show gave a major running head start to a film project that continued to seem like a pipe dream to most of the people involved. To the musicians, it still wasn't clear where the whole thing was headed.

"The reaction to the new material helped," says Fink, "but we didn't know what was going to happen with the movie. That concert was a lot of fun and went well, but on some of the new songs, the audience was just listening. They didn't react in the strongest sense of the word, because that's what happens with new material at a lot of shows—they want to hear the hits. So even being onstage at the time, I just couldn't tell."

Almost exactly one year later, on July 27, 1984, *Purple Rain* opened in nine hundred theaters across the United States. It made back its cost of $7 million in its first weekend, and went on to clear nearly $70 million at the box office. The sound track album has sold more than 20 million copies worldwide, and spent twenty-four consecutive weeks at number one on *Billboard*'s album chart. It won two Grammys and an Oscar, and included two number one singles ("When Doves Cry" and "Let's Go Crazy") and another, the title track, that reached number two.

It seems like anytime there's a "best of" list or a countdown, *Purple Rain* is there. In 1993, *Time* magazine ranked it the fifteenth greatest album of all time, and it placed eighteenth on VH1's 100 Greatest Albums of Rock & Roll. *Rolling*

Stone called it the second-best album of the 1980s and then placed it at number 76 on its list of the 500 Greatest Albums of All Time, saying that it is a record "defined by its brilliant eccentricities"; the magazine also included both "Purple Rain" and "When Doves Cry" high on its list of the 500 Greatest Songs of All Time.

In 2007, *Vanity Fair* labeled *Purple Rain* the best sound track of all time (ahead of some serious competition: the sound track for *A Hard Day's Night* was number two, followed by those for *The Harder They Come, Pulp Fiction, The Graduate,* and *Super Fly*). In 2008, *Entertainment Weekly* listed *Purple Rain* at number one on its list of the 100 best albums of the past twenty-five years, and in 2013 came back and pronounced it the second-greatest album of all time, behind only the Beatles' *Revolver,* adding that *Purple Rain* might be the "sexiest album ever."

The Purple Rain tour, which ran from late 1984 into the spring of 1985, saw Prince and the Revolution perform just shy of a hundred shows in five months, and sold 1.7 million tickets. They played multiple nights in many arenas, and even filled a few football stadiums, including the Superdome in New Orleans and Miami's Orange Bowl.

In retrospect, maybe the *Purple Rain* phenomenon seemed inevitable. Prince was the greatest pop genius of his time—on a very short list of music's most gifted and visionary figures—and it was just a matter of his finding the vehicle that would translate his incomparable abilities to a wide audience. Yet in truth, when you look closer, the fact that the *Purple Rain* movie got made at all is hard to imagine, difficult to explain, and the result of many extraordinary leaps of faith on the part of virtually everyone involved in the production.

Prior to this release, Prince was nowhere near a household name: while he had established himself in the R&B community, he had just one album that could be considered a mainstream hit, and no singles that had peaked above number six on the pop charts. He was also shrouded in mystery, surrounded by rumors about his ethnic background and sexual preference, and had completely stopped talking to the press as of the release almost two years earlier of his previous album, *1999*.

The film had a rookie director, first-time producers, and a cast that, with only a few exceptions, had never acted before. The star and most of the featured players were black, and most of the footage was shot on location in Minneapolis, about as far away from the coastal entertainment industry as you can get. On top of all of these strikes against popular acceptance for the movie, the road was already littered with failed vanity projects by singers attempting to make it as movie stars—artists who were a lot better established, including folks like Bob Dylan, Paul Simon, and Mick Jagger.

But Prince's unwavering focus on the project was vindicated, to the shock of many in Hollywood. And he maintained his seemingly illogical faith because he knew—or sensed, or divined—that there were people like me out there. At a suburban Cincinnati high school, my friends and I were already nothing short of obsessed with Prince, whose music felt like the culmination of all the sounds and styles we loved—dance beats, rock guitars, provocative lyrics, passionate vocals, style, glamour, intrigue. There was an extra locker in our senior class hallway, and we dedicated it to Prince, hanging the poster that came with the 1981 *Controversy* album (of Prince in a shower, posed in front of a crucifix, wearing nothing but bikini briefs, which I'm sure delighted our teachers and administrators) inside the door. We sent him a letter welcoming him to the class of 1984 and got back a postcard with the handwritten words LOVE GOD stamped across his photo.

Purple Rain was released just a few weeks after our graduation. Earlier that spring, we had all stayed up until midnight, cassette recorders at the ready, for the radio premiere of "When Doves Cry." On this mesmerizing, churning single, and then on eight more album tracks, we heard that he had modified his sound—focused and sharpened it, became a guitar god fronting a true rock 'n' roll band. Oddly, the aura of apocalypse and religious salvation that had already begun to turn up in his work was, if anything, pulled even further forward; yet during the heart of the Reagan era, with the nuclear arms race at the top of everyone's mind, this didn't make his lyrics any less accessible for new listeners.

The album seldom left our turntables in the weeks after it came out. We lined up to see the movie on opening weekend in late July. And we saw it over and over again for the rest of the summer, mesmerized by the stunning performance sequences, repeating the campy but irresistible dialogue to one another. If any of our other friends weren't previously on board with our Prince fixation, now the word-of-mouth street team was in full effect, and they simply couldn't avoid hearing about him everywhere. And once their curiosity got the best of them and they took a chance on the movie, any lingering resistance was futile as soon as an offscreen voice intoned the first words—"Ladies and gentlemen, the Revolution," and a backlit Prince recited the opening words to "Let's Go Crazy."

When I got to college in the fall, I discovered that many of my new classmates were equally obsessed with *Purple Rain*—which meant that now we all had to go see it together, repeatedly, as part of the new bonds we were creating. (A few months later, my closest new friend and I took turns sleeping on the sidewalk in the snow to purchase tickets for the nearest stop on the Purple Rain tour.) Perhaps affluent, mostly white and mostly male kids weren't initially the target audience for a Prince film, but what the world soon realized was that a $7 million investment gets paid back pretty quickly when groups of teenagers go to see a movie six or seven or eight times.

The 1980s were all about big-bigger-biggest blockbusters and sequels and expensive music videos, and Prince was going head-to-head with some of music's most towering icons at their peaks of popularity—Michael Jackson, Bruce Springsteen, Madonna. But in that moment, no one understood the potential of the new scale for media and harnessed it for his own purposes as effectively as Prince did. He shook the culture, musically and racially, sexually and spiritually, transforming possibilities and ignoring rules. And if he never reached those heights again, and in many ways never recovered personally or creatively from the *Purple Rain* juggernaut, he still took us all to a place we had never been.

• • •

Rocketown is an unassuming, warehouse-sized club just a few blocks from the Bridgestone Arena in downtown Nashville. Geared to Christian teenagers, it's adjacent to a skate park; there are pool tables upstairs, and the marquee lists a bunch of bands you've never heard of. It is now May 2004, twenty years after the release of *Purple Rain*, and Prince has already finished a sold-out performance at the arena (which was still called the Gaylord Center at the time), followed by an additional ninety-minute set on Rocketown's stage, after which he has an almost three-week break in his touring schedule—"I gotta go home and water the plants," he tells the crowd of five hundred or so with a laugh.

Prince is in the midst of one of his periodic resurgences in popularity, spurred by both music and strategy. After a series of experimental and even surly records, released in the midst of his ongoing battles with the music industry, his new album, *Musicology*, is accessible and funky; not a breakthrough or a true classic, it's still a fully realized collection of satisfyingly Prince-style songs. He made some high-profile media appearances (opening the Grammy Awards broadcast performing a medley with Beyoncé, singing for Ellen DeGeneres), delivered a knock-out mini-set at his induction to the Rock and Roll Hall of Fame in March, and concocted a plan in which everyone who bought a ticket for the tour received a copy of *Musicology* on his or her seat—each of which counts toward SoundScan's bestseller lists. Since the ninety-six-date run would prove to be the top-grossing tour of the year, earning $87.4 million, this meant that the record would go gold and stay in the Top Ten for the whole summer, even if not one person bought a copy in stores.

So Prince is happy. He has also recently become a Jehovah's Witness, and his conversation is now laced with frequent biblical references and allusions. The after-show performance at Rocketown offers the musical manifestation of this new Prince. Where these intimate, late-night gigs used to be cathartic, virtuoso displays, this time he leads his band through a set of loose funk jams. He bops through the crowd to listen from the soundboard and roams the stage cueing the players through a mash-up of Led Zeppelin's "Whole Lotta Love" and Santana's "Soul Sacrifice." There's no tension, all release.

I'm there to interview him for a cover story for *Tracks,* a magazine I founded and edited in the early 2000s, and after the show, I observe something even more unlikely: At 2:30 A.M., Prince can be found standing outside the stage door, hanging with his band members and talking to fans. The thirty or so clustered civilians are breathlessly excited to be in his presence, yet seem understanding when he tells them that he doesn't believe in signing autographs. He is, as always, shy and quiet, listening more than talking, but he actually seems to be enjoying the chance to mingle.

One young woman tells him that *Purple Rain* was the first album she bought when she was in the first grade, but that her mother wouldn't let her see the movie because it was too risqué. "Just think about what 'too risqué' means today!" Prince responds.

Material from *Purple Rain* had provided the focus for the

arena concert earlier in the evening. He performed seven of the album's nine tracks during the thirty-song, two-hour greatest-hits set, closing with the title song. In the grimy Rocketown dressing room, though, he claims that the twentieth anniversary of the project is of little consequence to him.

"I was there," he tells me. "I did it, it was my baby. I knew about it before it happened. I knew what it was going to be. Then it was just like labor, like giving birth—in '84, it was so much work."

In fact, he says, just a few nights earlier in Atlanta, the Time—the Minneapolis friends/rivals/contemporaries who played his nemeses in the film, and sometimes in real life—came out and performed during his show. "We never got a chance to do the real *Purple Rain* tour, because the Time broke up," he says. "But then, there they were, onstage last week, and people started tripping, and I was watching my favorite band. So there's no anniversary, no dates; we just have to have faith in Jehovah and lay back and ride it." (The fact that Prince became a Jehovah's Witness may also explain some of his attitude toward the anniversary of the album, since members of the religion do not celebrate birthdays.)

Ten years later, his feelings about such milestones seem even more detached. In February 2014, Prince played a super-intimate performance in London for ten people, held in the living room of his friend, singer Lianne La Havas, as part of a press conference to announce a series of upcoming "hit-and-run" UK shows. Matt Everitt of BBC 6 *Music News* was one of those in attendance, and he noted that Prince seemed surprised when he was asked about *Purple Rain*'s impending thirtieth anniversary. "I hadn't even realized," he said. "Everything looks different to me, because I was there. I wrote those songs; I don't need to know what happened."

A few weeks after that, he appeared as the only guest for an hour of the *Arsenio Hall Show*—yet another in a series of odd media visits without a tour or new release to support. An audience member asked him when he last saw *Purple Rain,* and what he thought of it. "I was in the living room three days ago," said Prince, "and it came on television, and I watched 'Take Me with U.' " He did not address the second part of the question. (On July 27, 2014, the actual anniversary of the movie's release, Prince did play a surprise show at his home base of Paisley Park: he opened the show with "Let's Go Crazy," and at one point slyly noted, "Thirty years ago today . . ." but he didn't close the loop by playing "Purple Rain.")

Every pop star presumably has some feelings of ambivalence about his or her biggest moment or defining hit. It immediately becomes both an obligation whenever you perform and the marker of a career pinnacle that, by definition, you can never match. Prince had a long run as one of the most successful musicians in the world, and can still sell out an arena pretty much whenever he wants to. He's had an impressive half dozen records certified two- to four-times platinum, with *1999* (which predated *Purple Rain*) highest on that list, but he has never had an album with sales close to *Purple Rain*'s 13 million in the U.S. Indeed, he once described *Purple Rain* as "my albatross—it'll be hanging around my neck as long as I'm making music."

His work in film has suffered a more troubled fate. Each of his subsequent efforts—the features *Under the Cherry Moon* (in 1986) and *Graffiti Bridge* (in 1990), and the concert documentary *Sign o' the Times*—has flopped. *Sign,* which chronicled performances from the magnificent 1987 album of the same title, earned some critical praise, but it was a production disaster and did minimal business. The other two movies were ravaged in the press, and the common belief is that Prince's insistence on directing played a big part in his fall from the peak of the pop world.

Whatever his feelings about the legacy of *Purple Rain,* though, Prince has always kept its songs front and center in his shows—especially the title song. It has served as the climax of most of his concerts, including his 2007 Super Bowl halftime show in Miami, which was seen by 93 million people in the U.S. alone and is generally considered the gold standard of all performances at sporting events. (Over the years, "Purple Rain" has also been covered by a wide range of artists, from LeAnn Rimes to Foo Fighters, Etta James to Tori Amos, Phish to Elvis Costello, while other songs from the album have been recorded by everyone from Mariah Carey to Patti Smith.)

A December 2013 concert at Connecticut's Mohegan Sun Arena saw Prince at his latter-day loosest; he introduced the night by saying, "We're gonna just jam tonight—it's just an old-school party," and largely stayed away from the hits, digging deep into his catalogue (including quick runs through "Jungle Love" and "The Bird," the two songs by the Time featured in *Purple Rain*) as he alternated between a twenty-one-piece, horn-heavy funk ensemble and his stripped-down, all-female rock trio, 3rdEyeGirl. Still, the inevitable closer, as a second encore, was a heartfelt rendition of "Purple Rain," with a tender vocal and a winding guitar solo that saw him exploring the indelible melody as if it were a brand-new composition. As he had that night at First Avenue thirty years earlier, he stood in the spotlight, and an audience stood thrilled and riveted by what it heard—despite, or because of, the fact that this roomful of middle-aged, mostly white concertgoers was able to sing every note and anticipate every turn of the song, and had been able to do so for the majority of their years on earth.

Prince's reluctance to look back at his career in more comprehensive ways is a mixed blessing at best. An artist can't be faulted for wanting to keep moving forward, for making all best efforts not to be weighed down by a legacy that, if he's lucky, eventually and inevitably turns him into a reliably bankable oldies act. The fact that Prince keeps making new music after all this time, that he refuses to coast on his back catalogue, is admirable, and whatever it takes for him to do that is understandably a priority.

At the same time, though, we are at serious risk of watching one of music's all-time greats erase his own legacy. For years, Prince has talked about his vault full of hundreds of unreleased songs—many of which have made the bootleg rounds among his superfans, while others circulate only as rumors or whispers. He constantly scrubs the Internet of unauthorized video footage and even his own official music videos, recently going so far as to file a lawsuit against twenty-two individuals, for $1 million each, who "engage in massive infringement and bootlegging of Prince's material." (The suit was dropped a few days later.)

Where Bob Dylan's authorized Bootleg Series or the Beatles' Anthology discs represented attempts by these artists to control and codify their unreleased material, improving the sound quality for fans and editing to help present their own versions of their histories, Prince has run in the opposite direction; in fact, the two primary documents capturing him live in his mid-'80s prime (the 1985 Syracuse concert that was released as a home video and the *Sign o' the Times* film) are both out of print and were never transferred for official DVD release in the U.S., leaving the immaculately choreographed and lip-synched performance sequences in *Purple Rain* as the only real evidence of what he was capable of onstage. And, as cultural critic Greg Tate wrote in *The Village Voice* when the movie came out, "Those of y'all going gaga behind *Purple Rain* and never seen the boy live ain't seen shit."

Following the bewildering announcement that Prince would make a guest appearance on the Zooey Deschanel sitcom *New Girl,* Ahmir "Questlove" Thompson, drummer for the Roots (and such a superfan that he taught a course on Prince at New York University in the spring of 2014) posted on Facebook, begging that Prince just "make it count," since it was a rare opportunity for people beyond the dedicated fan base to see him, and saying that he was tired of needing to explain Prince's greatness to a new generation without having any material to show them to prove it. It was a thoughtful plea from a true believer, and concisely presented the very real challenge Prince has created for himself by moving only forward. (The amiable, slight *New Girl* guest shot, in which he offered romantic advice to Deschanel and then had her sing with his band at a party, didn't wind up helping matters much in the end.)

Yet a surprise announcement in April 2014 suggested a long-awaited change in Prince's thinking about his own musical legacy. Just a few weeks after he revealed that he now controlled the publishing rights to all of his music, a new deal with Warner Bros. Records, his initial champions and longtime adversaries, was unveiled, which would lead to the release of "previously unheard material . . . a veritable gold mine," while also giving Prince his hard-fought, long-desired "ownership of the master recordings of his classic, global hits." A statement from Prince said that "both Warner Bros. and Eye [*sic*] are quite pleased with the results of the negotiations and look forward to a fruitful working relationship."

The deal is potentially a landmark in the recording community. An often overlooked change in copyright law allows musicians, writers, and other artists to exercise so-called termination rights. The provision, which took effect in 2013, enables the creators of music to win back their U.S. rights after thirty-five years, so long as they can show that they weren't employees of the record label, even if they signed a contract that transferred all the rights to their work. These rights, though, are not automatically awarded, and to obtain them usually requires extensive litigation.

That thirty-five-year window reaches back as far as 1978,

when Prince signed with Warner Bros. No further details of the deal or of future plans were announced—except that the first fruit of this agreement would be a newly remastered, deluxe thirtieth-anniversary version of *Purple Rain*. (His actual enthusiasm about this, however, still remains to be seen: the dates marking the anniversaries of first the sound track and then the movie release both came and went, and still no date had been announced for the reissue.)

Regardless of any anniversary, of all of Prince's groundbreaking work, it is *Purple Rain* that endures first and foremost. It will always be the defining moment of a magnificent and fascinating—if often erratic—career. It carries the weight of history. Its success, on-screen and as a recording, was a result of the supreme confidence, laser-focused ambition, and visionary nature of the most gifted artist of his generation.

Dancing on the line between fact and fiction, Prince utilized his mysterious persona to hypercharge the film's story with tension and revelation. He let us in—only partway, certainly not enough to rupture his myth, but more than he ever did before or since. Defying all odds, a group of inexperienced filmmakers and actors, working against the clock and the brutal Minneapolis weather, clicked for just long enough to make a movie that the public was starving for, even if they didn't quite know it at first.

"We just wanted to do something good and something true," says director Albert Magnoli. "The producer was on the same page, and we had an artist who wanted the same things, a group of musicians who felt the same way. It was one of the very few times when everybody actually wanted to make the same movie—which sounds obvious, but is actually very, very rare in the movie business."

"I think part of the success of *Purple Rain* was that [Prince] did open up and examine himself, and that it was real," says Lisa Coleman. "It was an authentic thing; you could feel it, and there was all this excitement around it. And I don't think he's ever done that again."

Purple Rain came along at precisely the right moment—not just for Prince, but for the culture. The summer of 1984 was an unprecedented season, a collision of blockbuster records and the ascension of the music video that created perhaps the biggest boom that pop will ever experience. It was also a time of great transformation for black culture, when a series of new stars, new projects, and new styles would forever alter the racial composition of music, movies, and television. While the magnificence of the *Purple Rain* songs remains clear thirty years later, the album and the film were also perfectly in tune with the time and place in which they were created, and their triumph was partly the result of impeccable timing and circumstances that could never be repeated or replicated.

The first time we heard the songs on the radio, the first time we put on the album, the first time the lights in the movie theater went down, we all did just what the man told us to do: we went crazy.

TWO

Alone in a World So Cold

"Can you keep a secret?"

These—I kid you not—are Prince's first words to me when I meet him in April of 1993. (And since the answer is yes, all I can tell you is that you really wouldn't be all that interested.) I had received a call in New York on Friday saying that Prince had read something I wrote about his tour's recent opening shows. He wanted to see me in San Francisco on Saturday, the first step in feeling me out for what would eventually become an interview that ran in *Vibe* magazine, his first lengthy on-the-record conversation with a journalist in over four years.

The driver who picked me up from the airport showed me the erotic valentine his girlfriend had made for him, then told me about the work he and his wife were doing for the Dalai Lama. It was time to wonder: *Is this whole thing a put-on?* But no—I arrive at the Bill Graham Civic Auditorium and there is Prince, sitting alone in the empty house, watching his band, the New Power Generation, start its sound check. He's fighting a cold, so we speak quietly back and forth in our seats for a while, and then he leads me onstage to continue the conversation while he straps on his guitar and rehearses the band.

Mostly, Prince talks about music—about Sly Stone and Earth, Wind & Fire, and other classic soul favorites we share. The NPG plays "I'll Take You There," and we discuss the Staple Singers and Mavis Staples, whose new album he has just finished producing. He is talkative as he jumps from guitar to piano to the front of the stage to listen to his group, with that surprisingly low voice that loses its slightly robotic edge when he's out of the spotlight.

As all reports indicate, he is indeed tiny—what's most striking isn't his height but his delicate bones and fragile frame. He is also pretty cocky, whether as a defensive move to cover his shyness with a new person or with the swagger needed to keep a performer going during a tour. Underneath the onstage roar of the NPG, he leans over to me, his fingers not leaving his guitar, and says, "You see how hard it is when you can play anything you want, anything you hear?"

Which is, in many ways, the question underlying Prince's lifelong creative journey, from his days as a prodigiously gifted high school student leading a band on the weekends to his years spent fighting the conventions and restrictions of the music industry. First came the years of striving for maximal communication through music, then came the efforts to keep up with the constant flow of creativity that resulted.

Prince Rogers Nelson was born in Minneapolis on June 7, 1958, to pianist and songwriter John L. Nelson, whose stage name was Prince Rogers, and singer Mattie Shaw. In a 1991 television interview with *A Current Affair*, his father said, "I named my son Prince because I wanted him to do everything I wanted to do."

Let's get this out of the way right now, since it would later come to dominate so many conversations about *Purple Rain*: both of Prince's parents are black.

Not that he was always forthright about that fact. Early in his career, eager to avoid any possibility of being pigeonholed as a "black" artist with a limitation on his potential audience, he was quoted as saying that his mother was white, and also that she "is a mixture of a bunch of things." Even after *Purple Rain* was released, *People* magazine referred to him as a "mulatto." He told *Rolling Stone* that he was the "son of a half-black father and an Italian mother." (Former girlfriend/protégée Jill Jones claims that he borrowed this mix from her: "When we met, he was like, 'You're half what?' and I was like, 'Oh, I'm half Italian and black,' and it was like, 'Oh, okay, I can see that—I can make this work.' He went on tour, and when he came back, he was Italian and black.")

Regardless, what is clear is that the racial composition of the Twin Cities, and the pop and rock music he heard on the radio (there wasn't even a round-the-clock black station in the city with a strong signal—just the low-wattage KMOJ), made for a complex blend of influences on the young Prince. "I was brought up in a black-and-white world," he said to MTV. "Black and white, night and day, rich and poor. I listened to all kinds of music when I was young, and when I was younger, I always said that one day I would play all kinds of music and not be judged for the color of my skin, but the quality of my work."

Prince's family obviously made a powerful impact on his budding relationship with music. "Who said I was supposed to be a musician?" he said to me in a rare moment of openness in 2004. "I just watched my father, and saw that when he played it pleased my mother."

Howard Bloom was Prince's publicist from 1981 through 1988. He also worked with such other superstars as Michael Jackson, John Mellencamp, and Bob Marley before developing chronic fatigue syndrome and not leaving his Brooklyn apartment for years. When he recovered, he quit the music business and returned to a career focusing on his early training in the world of science. I meet Bloom on a blustery winter night at the local café that he uses as his office, and from there we head back to his cluttered walk-up to talk about his time working with Prince.

Bloom says that during his publicist days, he always searched for an artist's "imprinting points . . . the moments when your brain opens up and you look for something with certain characteristics, and when you find it, you seize on it, and your brain is wrapped around it for the rest of your life." He maintains that Prince's first such imprint came when he was five years old and his mother took him to watch his dad rehearse: "He steps into a theater and there are all these chairs aimed at the center of the stage, and there's his dad in the center of the light with five beautiful women behind him. And that was it."

But the eccentricities and struggles of his parents, which

would later be used so effectively in fictionalized form for the songs and story of *Purple Rain,* didn't make for a stable household. (In 1996, he told Oprah Winfrey that the most autobiographical scene in the movie was "probably the scene with me looking at my mother crying.") John and Mattie separated when Prince was ten years old, and in the years that followed, he was constantly shuttling between different homes. Sometimes he lived with his father—who worked for Honeywell Computers during the day and played gigs at night, so was seldom around—and sometimes with his mother and a stepfather he didn't much like (but who did take him to a James Brown concert where, according to legend, Prince got onstage and danced). He tried living with an aunt for a while. Eventually he moved into the home of a neighboring family, the Andersons, who had six kids, one of whom was André, a friend of Prince's from church who became known as André Cymone when he was a member of Prince's band. At one point, in fact, André's bass-playing father was in a band with Prince's father.

The time he spent living in André's basement became a big part of the Prince mythology. He spoke about it at some length to journalist Barbara Graustark in 1981 in an interview that was initially planned for *Newsweek* but eventually appeared in *Musician* magazine. As long as he continued attending Central High School, he said, "I could come in anytime I wanted; I could have girls spend the night. . . . I think it had a great deal to do with me coming out into my own and discovering myself." He was also creating a community of other musical and sexual explorers: "One time [André's mother] came down and saw a lot of us down there, and we weren't all dressed, and stuff like that . . ."

This, says Bloom, was Prince's next defining point. "He was imprinting on the hippie movement," he says, "and started his own community, with the idea that if we indulged all of our sexual desires, then we wouldn't make war. Prince was building a little tribe around this basic idea."

Prince (guitar) and Anderson (bass) were joined by Prince's cousin Charles Smith (who was later replaced by Morris Day) on the drums and André's sister Linda on keyboards in a group they named Grand Central, playing Top 40 and funk covers at local clubs and parties. "I was into Kool and the Gang," Cymone told writer Michael A. Gonzales in 2014. "Morris introduced us to Tower of Power, while Prince was into Chaka Khan and Earth, Wind and Fire." The group played house parties and local clubs ("places where real pimps were the patrons"), and numerous battles of the bands. "We were playing against guys who were older," he said, "but we were fearless and cocky." Grand Central later changed its name to Champagne and started performing original music. While booking and playing frequent dates, and recording on his own at night in local studios, Prince kept up his grades at school and played basketball—apparently quite well, though his small stature limited his playing time.

Prince would later say that growing up in Minneapolis was "kinda sad . . . the radio was dead, the discos was dead, ladies was kinda dead, so I felt like, if we wanted to make some noise, and I wanted to turn anything out, I was gonna have to get somethin' together." Eventually he grew so frustrated that in the autumn of 1976 he moved to New York, where he stayed with his sister. He had hoped that some of his bandmates would want to move, too, but they resisted: "I don't think they really liked the idea of me trying to manipulate the band so much," he said, "[but] I was always trying to get us to do something different."

Though he would say "I never wanted to be a front man," he found that there actually was some interest in his music in New York, and he was offered a few production and publishing deals. What he was looking for, though, was an actual recording deal, and the creative freedom that he felt his music required. "Any fifteen-year-old on Planet Earth, having an offer of any kind, is going to imagine that the minute he signs, he's a superstar," says Bloom. "But Prince did not take those offers. I've never seen anything like it in my life. He had what we call in neurobiology 'executive control'—the ability to inhibit his brain and maintain discipline in pursuit of what he wanted." And so, after a few months, he moved back to Minneapolis.

"When I was sixteen, I was completely broke and needed to get a job," he told Arsenio Hall. "So I got the Yellow Pages out, and I couldn't find one thing that I wanted to do. So I decided I was going to push as hard as I could to be a musician, and win at it."

While he was in New York, a demo tape that Prince had recorded with producer Chris Moon in Moon's studio caught the attention of Minneapolis businessman Owen Husney, who signed Prince to a management contract. He financed a higher-quality demo, recorded by producer/engineer David Z. Cliff Siegel, a regional record promoter and a former bandmate of Husney's (and a cousin of the Rivkins, just to show how close-knit the local music community was), recalled that as far back as those first sessions, Prince's goals were "to do films, be number one, and produce other groups."

Husney began cultivating Prince's image as a brilliant, enigmatic cipher, a virtuoso on dozens of instruments who barely spoke or looked anyone in the eye. His ad agency created a press kit for Prince, which helped get the demo noticed by a number of major record labels, including CBS, A&M, and Warner Bros.—the last of whom eventually signed Prince to an unprecedented three-album deal in which he retained an unusual degree of creative control, producing his own recordings and even having approval over all photographs and album packaging. Prince also insisted that he sign and be treated as a regular Warners pop act, and not just be assigned to the black-music department, where budgets were smaller and influence was limited.

"When we signed Prince, he was nineteen years old," says Mo Ostin, who at the time was chairman at Warner Bros. Records. "We all felt very strongly about him as an artist. A&M insisted on his publishing as part of the deal, and he wouldn't give that up; Columbia made him an offer of a two-album commitment. So we said that we would not take publishing and would make a three-album commitment, to show our faith in his future.

"Maurice White [from Earth, Wind & Fire] was willing to produce the first album, and he was a huge star at the time. Prince had never produced anything before but insisted that he would produce his own albums. [Warner executives] Lenny Waronker and Russ Titelman went to the studio to watch him do his thing, and they were so impressed [that] they said he didn't need anybody; he could do it himself."

He went to Sausalito, California, to record his first album in the celebrated Record Plant studio. The sessions did not go smoothly; though he had won the right to produce himself, he wasn't really trained for the job (and would always be a self-taught producer with his own working language, for better and for worse). Playing all the instruments and singing all the vocal parts himself, and butting heads with Tommy Vicari, the executive producer whom Warners had assigned to oversee the project, Prince had trouble finding the sound and style he wanted. He ended up taking three months and spending almost $170,000 of the $180,000 that had been allotted for all three of his albums on the record that would be released in 1978 as *For You*. The title track included no fewer than forty-six vocal overdubs. "I was a physical wreck when I finished," he said.

The album is mostly keyboard-based, bouncy post-disco that's lacking in fire; the most fully realized track is probably the plaintive "Baby," with classic, almost doo-wop harmony parts, while the closing "I'm Yours" displays some guitar flash in the album's final minutes. The single was "Soft and Wet," which grazed the pop charts, reaching number 92, though it fought its way up to number 12 on the R&B charts. It didn't cross over to the wider audience Prince craved, but it did make an impression on some of the people who would later be among his key collaborators.

"I was thirteen years old, underage, at the Starwood dance club here in Los Angeles," says Wendy Melvoin. "I heard 'Soft and Wet' and I went up to the DJ, asking, 'Who's this girl? Who's this girl?' And the DJ said, 'It's this young kid named Prince.' I was fucking floored by him."

"I lived in West Hollywood," says Susan Rogers, who would later serve as Prince's recording engineer for much of the 1980s, "and I was on the bus, and there was a kid sitting in the back with a boom box. I heard 'Soft and Wet,' and I remember thinking, 'Whoever that artist is, I want to know more.' I became a fan from that first record."

To the extent that the rock-critic establishment noticed *For You*, the response was summarized in *The Village Voice* by Robert Christgau, who described the album as "lots of chops, not much challenge." A follow-up single, "Just as Long as We're Together," stalled at number 91 on the R&B chart. Prince fell out with Husney, and the high-powered team of Bob Cavallo and Joe Ruffalo—who managed such acts as Earth, Wind & Fire and Ray Parker Jr.—bought out his deal for $50,000. (One of their employees, Steve Fargnoli, made a strong impression on Prince because he had previously worked as Sly Stone's road manager; Fargnoli was soon promoted to partner in the company and would handle Prince's day-to-day business.) They arranged for Prince's first concert appearances on January 5 and 6, 1979, at the Capri Theater in Minneapolis, as a one-off showcase for the label to determine whether he was ready for a tour. The conclusion was that he needed more seasoning, which began his dedication to constant, almost obsessive rehearsal with his touring musicians.

Matt Fink and I are sitting in the control room of the recording studio in the basement of his comfortable home in suburban Minneapolis. (Outside, not surprisingly, snow is falling with increasing strength.) Down here, the former keyboard player in the Revolution keeps busy recording local bands and commercial work, as well as his sons' various groups over the years. While he drove me around town pointing out some of the local Prince-related landmarks, he also ran through his upcoming travel schedule for shows with several different bands, including his Prince cover band, the Purple Xperience. It's not a bad lifestyle, all essentially a direct result of the bet that he placed by signing up with Prince more than thirty-five years ago.

"Just to be involved with an artist signed to Warner Brothers was enough for me when I joined the band," says Fink. "In those early years, there were a lot of skeptics around me. 'Ah, he's a flash in the pan. What are you doing? It's never going to work.' I got a lot of that. And I'd just look at them and say, 'I think you're wrong. I believe in Prince. I think he's gonna break through; this guy's gonna be huge someday.'"

Prince had assembled a group of local musicians—Cymone, guitarist Dez Dickerson, keyboard players Fink and Gayle Chapman, and drummer Bobby Z—which was then being called the Rebels, a name later modified to the Revolution. (Resentment from Morris Day may date back as far as this first band configuration: "I could play ten times better than Bobby Z, but we ain't gonna get into that," he said in 2012.) But he still worked alone on his second LP, which would be recorded in six weeks during the spring and released under the title *Prince*. Aware that he needed to make a strong impact this time around, this collection was a major step forward from *For You*, and included his first number one R&B hit, the bright post-disco "I Wanna Be Your Lover," as well as the convincing rocker "Why You Wanna Treat Me So Bad?" and "I Feel for You," a bouncy little number that become a major hit when it was recorded by Chaka Khan a few years later, at the height of *Purple Rain* mania. He sounded more relaxed, more confident, and while his singing voice remained firmly planted in his falsetto over too many of the songs, he was finding his way toward a style that was genuinely his own.

This would be the album that truly announced Prince's arrival, complete with music videos and (uncomfortable) appearances on *The Midnight Special* and *American Bandstand*. This time, Christgau raved in the *Voice* that "this boy is going to be a big star, and he deserves it," though he did also note that he felt Prince "does leave something to be desired in the depth-of-feeling department—you know, soul." Prince was subjected to his first intense round of talking to the press, something he was never at ease with. "His early interviews were really awkward," says Bob Merlis, a former Warner Bros. publicist. "We thought maybe he just shouldn't do them—they were bizarre, risqué. I remember he asked one writer from *Record World* magazine whether her pubic hair went up to her belly button, stuff like that."

After the sessions for *Prince,* he worked on a band-based project, but never completed or released that album. Prince and the group started their first tour on November 26, 1979, at the Roxy in West Hollywood. They played eleven club dates before moving into bigger theaters and arenas in February as the opening act for forty-two stops on a tour by "the king of punk funk," Rick James. James would become a bitter rival in the years ahead, later telling *Rolling Stone,* "I can't believe people are gullible enough to buy Prince's jive records." He complained that Prince was stealing his stage moves, and according to Teena Marie, who sang with James, James retaliated by stealing Prince's equipment. "Back then people weren't really programming their own synthesizers," she said. "Prince . . . and Stevie [Wonder] were the only ones really doing it." At the end of the tour, according to Marie (who would in turn take the opening slot on Prince's own next tour), James simply took Prince's synthesizers and used them on his pop breakthrough album *Street Songs*—"and then he sent them back to [Prince] with a thank-you card." (In his posthumous autobiography, *Glow,* James wrote, "When I saw that Prince was stealing from me, I stole from him.")

It was during this time that the band was becoming a formidable unit. "As that original lineup came together, we felt like Transformers, that all the parts had come together," says Dickerson. "We thoroughly believed that we were supposed to be the biggest band in the world." Presumably emboldened by the nightly spectacle of James's leather-clad, pot-smoking onstage persona, Prince began pushing his writing into the territory he had explored during his days and nights in André's basement. In 1980, he blindsided the music world with *Dirty Mind,* a near-perfect, thirty-minute manifesto of sexual liberation and broken taboos. Between the album title and the cover photo (a black-and-white shot of Prince in a trench coat, open to reveal that he was wearing only briefs underneath), the packaging couldn't have made the new direction more obvious.

The sound of *Dirty Mind* was more rock than funk, heavy on spiky, new wave–inspired keyboards. The subject matter was outright shocking: "Head" saw the singer ejaculating on the wedding dress of a bride headed to her nuptials, and the frantic "Sister" offered an ambiguous account of incest. (In 2013, at a Carnegie Hall concert paying tribute to the songs of Prince, Philadelphia-based singer Bilal delivered a slowed-down version of the song that drew out the harrowing emotions at its center.) "When You Were Mine" was an irresistibly hooky, classic pop song about a ménage à trois. The outrageous image, combined with his growing reputation as a live performer, piqued the attention of the rock establishment, and Prince landed a story in *Rolling Stone* and a booking on *Saturday Night Live.*

There was truly something distinctive about Prince's conception of sexuality. Traditionally, black artists—many of whom had started out singing in church—struggled with the tensions between the flesh and the spirit. You could make an argument that before Prince, that dichotomy defined black pop music, as it played out in the work of giants like Sam Cooke, Little Richard, Marvin Gaye, and Al Green. But Prince didn't seem to recognize a distinction or a conflict between these two forces. In his music, sex and salvation were often the same, and, as for the most hedonistic and simple-minded rock singers, any sense of guilt was absent from the equation.

"He didn't have any boundaries," says Wendy Melvoin. "He didn't have any margins when it came to separation between what a hard-on he had and that five seconds before his hard-on came, he was praying to God. There was no dividing, nothing. He didn't have a guilt syndrome for that; it all worked for him."

"There was no apology for his expression," says singer/songwriter Tori Amos, calling from her dressing room before a show in Vienna. "People work and play with the whole idea of the sacred and the profane, but he was holding both at the same time, in a new way. It seemed to be this completely Dionysian energy, but it wasn't segregated, and it wasn't just to be shocking—sexuality can be forced, crass, gimmicky, but this was just who he was as a performer. He reminded me of Rimbaud and Baudelaire, this passionate kind of fire that always seemed to have intention."

After years dedicated to the idea of pure independence and

self-sufficiency, Prince also now seemed interested in the idea of a band. He ran a moody photo of the touring group, with their names graffitied on the wall, on the album's inner sleeve. *Dirty Mind*'s centerpiece, "Uptown," titled with the nickname Prince gave to the Minneapolis community he was building, offered his vision of an urban utopia: "White, black, Puerto Rican / Everybody just a-freakin.'" Even in the studio, things were occasionally more collaborative, with the album's title song based on a fragment that Matt Fink came up with in rehearsal.

"We were jamming," says Fink (who, after first trying jail stripes as his onstage uniform, switched to medical scrubs and was forever renamed "Dr. Fink"). "I played the main riff, and he goes, 'Hey, I really like that. Remember that one. Let's record that.' So we recorded it on a boom box, and he said, 'I want you to come out to my house tonight and see if we can come up with a song on that one.' On the first two albums, he'd done everything himself—nobody had played on those records with him.

"So he invited me up to the house, and he said, 'Okay, let's lay this groove down. I'm going to help you with the arrangement.' He wrote the bridge section, he played the drums, and then later he laid guitar on it. I got there at about nine at night and was there till midnight, and then after I left, he wrote the lyric and melody and finished tracking the song. He showed up the next day to rehearsal around noon and said, 'Here's the title track of the next album.'"

As the *Dirty Mind* album sleeve also showed, Prince had made a change in the band. Gayle Chapman had decided to leave rather than perform some of the provocative onstage moves he wanted in the show, and Lisa Coleman took her place at the keyboard—the first time anyone who had not grown up in Minneapolis entered the inner circle. A graduate of Hollywood High and the classically trained daughter of a Los Angeles session musician, Coleman introduced some more sophisticated influences into the Prince universe, and was as prepared as anyone could be for the discipline required in his band.

"We would talk about training your body, about practicing an instrument," says Coleman. "We were at his father's house, and he wanted me to play the piano for his dad—it was worse than your mom going, 'Come on, Lisa, play your music for Grandma!' or whatever, it was just like 'Oh, God, Prince wants *me* to play the piano for his *dad*,' a very nervous situation.

"We were playing and then talking about how I had studied classical music and taken lessons and did all those exercises, and we got into a whole philosophical conversation: as a musician, do you really need that? Do you need technique? My argument was, 'Yes, you need technique, because then you can play anything that you hear.' And they both looked at me like that was a revelation."

The Dirty Mind tour took Prince into rock clubs across the country, but he was frustrated by the response. He was a star in Minneapolis, and a small but rabid cult of fans was beginning to form. "Even in the early years, I'd seen girls tear his shirt off leaving a theater," says Fink. "Like, in 1980 that happened in San Francisco—they shredded him; we were barely able to get out the door to the show. So he had those moments of the Beatles/rock star thing, and it would've been more if he didn't have good security."

Elsewhere, though, audiences couldn't quite figure out his rock/R&B hybrid, his mixed-race band, his explosive sexuality. The album sold only half as well as *Prince,* and the singles didn't connect on white or black radio.

"We didn't know what the fuck Prince was," says gangsta rap pioneer/TV star Ice T. "He was like a player, he kept bad bitches, he was little, he was a pimp. He's got a ill hood side to him, too. He was just something else. Prince is dope, he's a motherfucker, but he was really hard to figure out."

As if to balance out the rock orientation of *Dirty Mind,* Prince put together his first side project; he reconfigured his friends in the group Flyte Tyme into an old-school funk band, complete with razor-sharp zoot suits and tight choreography, and dubbed them the Time. "The image was cool," he would say. "That's the key word. That's what we built the Time around. Cool is an attitude, a self-respect thing." His old Grand Central drummer, Morris Day, had essentially traded Prince a track he had written—which would become the basis for the song "Partyup," the closing track on *Dirty Mind*—in exchange for help landing a record deal, so when singer Alexander O'Neal opted not to stick with the new model of the band, Day moved from behind the kit into the lead-vocalist spot.

"Prince took Morris on the road," guitarist Jesse Johnson later told *Wax Poetics* magazine. "When Morris left, he was wearing jeans, sneakers, a regular shirt, and an Afro. When he came back, he looked like the Morris we know today. He was completely different. I never saw him in jeans again."

Prince produced the Time's album and laid down guide versions of the tracks for them, though he denied it publicly, and the album credit was given to "Jamie Starr." It was the first sign that he was struggling to find a way to keep up with all of the music he wanted to make—and with its more easily classified (and masterfully executed) sound, *The Time* sold better than *Dirty Mind* did. With all these forces rattling around in his brain, Prince returned to the studio in August of 1981 and finished his next album in nine days.

Controversy was perhaps the most erratic record of Prince's first decade, but it was also the moment when things started to come into focus. The title track was a guitar-powered statement of purpose, addressing the boldness of his image straight-on ("Am I black or white / Am I straight or gay?"), dropping in a recitation of the Lord's Prayer, and becoming a hit single that effectively defined his identity for the pop world. Elsewhere, he dove even deeper into the erotic ("Sexuality" and "Jack U Off") and put down his first classic bedroom ballad, "Do Me Baby." But *Controversy* also included Prince's first forays into social commentary, with "Ronnie, Talk to Russia," addressed to President Reagan (in March 2014, *Salon* included the song on a list of "17 Songs for the Coming Nuclear Apocalypse"), and "Annie Christian," presenting a disturbing image of a mysterious satanic power. These songs marked the beginning of a fascination with the End of Days that would permeate his next few albums.

If the idea of band and community had reemerged in *Dirty Mind*, that door closed again for *Controversy*, as Prince hunkered down in full one-man-band mode. "I was horrible," he would later say of his resistance to collaboration. "To be perfectly honest, I was surrounded by my friends, but nevertheless, we had a difference of opinion in a lot of situations—musically speaking, that is. A lot had to do with me not being quite sure exactly which direction I wanted to go in."

To Jill Jones, who met Prince when she was singing backup for Teena Marie, the *Controversy* phase was when Prince began to see an opportunity to fulfill his dream of crossing racial barriers with his music and truly locked into that crusade. "I think he was on a mission, because during that time there was black radio and white radio, and he'd been trying so hard to get that opening up," she says. "When he did *Controversy,* he started to see another window. He knew that if he stayed with R&B radio, that's where he was gonna be, so he had to try to figure out how to market it. I don't think any of us were quite clear on what marketing was at the time. He was definitely ahead of his time on branding."

Jones, funny and bright as she looks back at her time with Prince, knows something about this kind of business-speak herself. We meet in one of the conference rooms at the advertising firm where she works in the Westwood section of Los Angeles. Jones grew up in Ohio but then moved to California and into American musical royalty: her stepfather, Fuller Gordy, was the brother of Motown founder Berry Gordy Jr.

After she left the Prince camp, Jones lived in New York with her daughter before moving back to LA.

The relative success of *Controversy* enabled Prince to play bigger venues on tour. André Cymone had left the band to pursue a solo career—he had a hit with the Prince composition "Dance Electric"—and was replaced by another Minneapolis bass player, Mark Brown (alternately known as Brown Mark). The band was now fully focused on all the preparation necessary to take on arena-sized audiences.

"The first time I saw him was on the Controversy tour in Pittsburgh, which I later learned was the opening show of the tour," says Alan Leeds, who would soon step in as Prince's road manager. "A girlfriend of mine who worked for the black radio station WMO begged me to go with her, because the station copromoted the gig. I barely knew who he was—I knew 'I Wanna Be Your Lover'; I'm not even sure I had heard 'Controversy' yet.

"Anyway, I reluctantly went, just so she'd have a date. And of course it was the typical story of 'Oh my God, what did I just see?' I remember saying to her, 'God, I'd love to work with them sometime.' It wasn't just the fact that he was mind-blowing, but the entire production—the lights were not just state-of-the-art technically but were very musical, very artistic. Remember, this is '81, so everybody's still disco crazy, and this was decidedly something else."

The crowd response had not been so positive, though, when Prince was faced with his biggest challenge yet. Mick Jagger had invited him to open two of the Rolling Stones' dates at the Los Angeles Coliseum in October 1981. Almost as soon as he got onstage, the audience started booing and throwing things. He stormed offstage the first night, got directly onto a plane, and flew back to Minneapolis; Jagger reached him on the phone after the Stones' set and convinced him to jet back to LA in time for the second concert—where his reception was even more hostile than it had been the show before. It was a reminder that it would still take a big leap for a white, rock-based audience to accept a sexually provocative black front man with a strong dance beat behind him, no matter how much guitar he played. (Prince would never open for another band again.)

His label still saw growth in his future. "A lot of effort had been put into Prince," says former Warner Bros. publicist Merlis. "Putting him on those Stones dates—we tried a lot of things to keep him relevant to the public. There was always tremendous belief in him."

Prince took the Time out as the opening act for the Controversy tour, which went so well that it created problems. When some reviews said that the opening band outshined the headliner, Prince dropped them from certain dates. The humor and pure pleasure of the Time offered a contrast to the intensity and drama of Prince's set, and he was clearly torn between encouraging them to be great (sometimes showing them footage of Muhammad Ali backstage to inspire them) and wanting to make clear that they were in the support slot. Meanwhile, he began casting his second set of protégées—this time, a hypersexual girl group that he had initially considered calling the Hookers before he found Denise Matthews, rechristened her Vanity, and named the trio Vanity 6.

Through the summer of 1982, he was recording song after song, building up enough material that he told Warner Bros. his next record would be a double album—widely considered a risky move for a rising star, especially a black artist. His management was pleased with the music they were hearing, but felt like the knockout punch was missing, the song that could build on the template of "Controversy." When Prince played the record for Bob Cavallo, the manager recalls saying, " 'This is a great album, but we don't have a first single. We have singles that'll be hits, but we don't have a thematic, important thing that can be embraced by everybody, different countries, et cetera.' He cursed me, and he went away—but he didn't force me to put it out. Two weeks later, he came back and he played '1999,' and that became the title of the album."

The double LP *1999* was released on October 27, 1982. Despite Prince's dreams of a crossover audience for his music, thus far the mentality of the Rolling Stones' audience remained all too representative—and in fact, that exact month represented an all-time low point in pop music integration. Steve Greenberg would later write in *Billboard* that "in 1979, nearly half of the songs on the weekly *Billboard* Hot 100 pop chart could also be found on the urban contemporary chart. By 1982, the amount of black music on the Hot 100 was down by almost 80 percent. . . . Not one record by a black artist could be found in the Top 20 on the Top 200 album chart or the Hot 100 singles chart for three consecutive weeks that October—a phenomenon unseen since before the creation of Top 40 radio in the mid-1950s."

But *1999*'s release also fell directly in between two events that would forever change pop's rules. In September of 1982, the fledgling cable network MTV, which had launched a year earlier, was added to the cable systems in the New York area, followed by those in Los Angeles a few months later, setting in motion its true impact as a national music channel. And one month after *1999* hit stores, on November 30, Michael Jackson's *Thriller* album came out, which would create an entirely new sense of scale for recordings, music videos, and the impact of all musicians.

Critics picked up on *1999*, which had both a stronger focus on guitars and a revolutionary new set of synthesizer sounds. The title song, with its unforgettable call to party in the face of nuclear devastation, made some impact but still came up short of the Top 40. The plans were for Prince to participate in the album promotion, or at least his own version of it, but after his first interview—with Robert Hilburn of the *Los Angeles Times*—he walked out of the room and announced that he would never speak to the press again. It would indeed be two and a half years before he sat down with another journalist.

It was apparently time to truly secure the mythology he had been refining over the years. Prince's band watched him assume a superstar's persona long before he had actually earned the status. "Growing up, like anyone would practice their instrument, he practiced his face; he practiced what he looked like on camera," says Lisa Coleman. "He would videotape himself in his bedroom at night, just talking or doing things, and he'd watch himself to see what he looked like. He really worked on it as if he was a dancer or something, training himself for being a big star—almost the way Motown used to have the finishing school. He just decided, 'I've gotta be famous.'

"One time in Minneapolis, really early on, he was still a cute guy with a 'fro, but some girls saw him walking down the street and one of the girls said, 'Is that Prince?' and the other one said, 'Nah'—like, he didn't look good that day. And that changed his life forever." He saw that to truly fulfill his vision, he needed to be Prince every minute of every day, not have a separate and distinct performing persona.

The 24/7 commitment to being a larger-than-life star eventually extended to the rest of the band, who weren't allowed to appear in public in regular street clothes. "He used to get upset when anyone would refer to the clothes as costumes," says Wendy Melvoin. "He freaked—'Those aren't costumes, those are clothes!'" Engineer Susan Rogers remembered Steve Fargnoli coming to rehearsal and saying to Prince, "Shall I have the band get into their stage costumes?" He responded just as Melvoin indicated. "I knew immediately that he had misspoken, that that was a mistake," says Rogers, "and Prince right away corrected Steve and said, 'They aren't costumes. They're clothes.'" (Albert Magnoli, director of *Purple Rain*, would say that Prince's insistence on using stage clothes conceived by his personal designer, Sorbonne graduate Marie France—later described by journalist Maureen Callahan as evocative of "extravagant romanticism"—as everyday wear throughout the film was one of the greatest challenges of the production.)

"It's like he created a doppelgänger of himself," says Susannah Melvoin, Wendy's twin sister, who would become both romantically and musically involved with Prince. "He didn't want to be the smart kid in high school who played piano in the music room; he didn't want to be normal, and he didn't want anyone around him to be, either. And that could create conflict—if you showed yourself to be broken or fallible, to be weak in some way, he'd be on you, sometimes mad. Like, 'If you fuck it up, I look like I'm not real—I have to believe in it or I'm not going to be able to sell it.'"

Meantime, the Triple Threat tour rolled out, initially in theaters, with Vanity 6 (who had a hit of their own with "Nasty Girl") and the Time (whose fantastic *What Time Is It?* album reached number two on the R&B charts) opening the dates. Now that Prince had used the other groups to help plant the seeds and create the context for his sound, the fate of *1999*, and of his career, changed with the February 1983 release of "Little Red Corvette" as his next single, which found Prince turning his attention from apocalypse back to sex. The slinky, metaphor-laced tale of a promiscuous and irresistible lover shot up the charts, eventually becoming his first Top Ten hit. With a fleet, jagged guitar solo by Dez Dickerson (named in 2008 by *Guitar World* magazine as one of the 100 Greatest Guitar Solos of All Time), the song seemed to connect with white listeners in a new way; incredibly, it was released just a few days before

Michael Jackson issued "Beat It," his own rocked-up track that included an Eddie Van Halen guitar solo, as a single.

"Corvette" was aided immeasurably by MTV's increasing influence. The video, with a memorable, acrobatic James Brown–style dance break by Prince—clad in the familiar purple coat, with a frilly shirt and an increasingly complicated hairstyle piled atop his head—during Dickerson's solo, became a staple on the network. (Rick James believed that this support for his archrival was an act of revenge taken by MTV in response to his criticism of its resistance to giving airtime to black artists.) But Prince's approach to music video was, at least at this point, far different from the narrative clips Jackson and others were pioneering. His videos were really "multi-camera adaptations of his live show," as Nelson George wrote in his 2010 book on the making of *Thriller*, "definitely a reflection of Prince's otherworldly confidence that, in an era of increasingly conceptual videos, his visual expressions were all about capturing his band and himself."

On the heels of the success of "Corvette," the decision was made to rerelease the "1999" single, which this time climbed up to number 12 on the charts; "shut out of pop radio upon its initial release in 1982," *Billboard* later noted, "['1999'] was relaunched in mid-1983, and off the back of its belated MTV exposure became a huge pop radio success the second time around." (*Rolling Stone* pointed out at the time that "Prince's guitar-heavy, synth-fried *1999* had already gone gold before rock stations opened their eyes.") The one-two punch, followed by another Top Ten hit with the frantic electro-dance track "Delirious," marked Prince's entry into the big leagues of pop.

"We were playing in theaters," says Alan Leeds, who had come onboard as the tour manager directly from a job overseeing Kiss on the road, "and during the course of the tour, they broke 'Corvette.' Then they rereleased '1999,' and all of a sudden he was selling out arenas. We saw this happen over a period of three or four weeks, where the audience went from a predominantly black audience in theaters to a heavily mixed audience in arenas."

Dez Dickerson has said that from the stage, you could track the progress of "Little Red Corvette"; that the "impact that the song was having reflected in the makeup of the audience—this tidal wave of white hitting the audience, getting whiter and whiter each night."

Off the stage, Prince was still battling with his need for control. His autocratic side surfaced mid-tour when Jimmy Jam and Terry Lewis of the Time, who had begun doing some production projects on the side, missed a concert because snow kept their plane from taking off following a session with the S.O.S. Band. On the duo's return, he fired them, setting in motion an ongoing and ultimately disastrous tension over whose band the Time actually was—his or Morris Day's. Jam and Lewis, of course, went on to become one of the most successful production teams of the '80s, with their version of the "Minneapolis Sound" powering dozens of hits by the likes of George Michael, Luther Vandross, and, most notably, Janet Jackson.

"Prince had been urging Morris and Jesse [Johnson, guitarist] to find replacements, but they weren't even looking," says Leeds. "I don't know if it was just denial or if it was actually strategic—that if they waited long enough, Prince would have to accept [Jam and Lewis] back. In their mind, Prince had inappropriately screwed up their band. They didn't see it as *his* band; they saw it as *their* band. But if they wanted to really see the truth, they knew they weren't coming back. First of all, those guys had their own ambitions, and I'm not sure they even wanted to come back. So Prince took it upon himself to find the replacements, and basically brought people in and said, 'Hey, fellas, this is your new band,' which of course just made the resentment worse."

Yet at the same time, Prince was opening up his own music, or at least its presentation, to more input from his own band. The videos showcased him not purely as a solo act but as a bandleader; in addition to Dickerson's "Corvette" solo, Lisa Coleman and Jill Jones were placed prominently in the "1999" video and sang on several other tracks; on one song, the soaring ballad "Free," Coleman's girlfriend, Wendy Melvoin (who had been tagging along for some of the tour), even added to the background parts.

For those who were paying close attention, he included a clue about his next direction in the squiggly lettering on the *1999* cover. Written over the *i* in his name were the words *and the Revolution*. Bobby Z has said that "he was setting the public up for something that was yet to come." Prince himself later said, "I wanted community more than anything else."

How much this was a creative desire and how much it was a marketing strategy is unclear, and ultimately unimportant. Certainly, the more Prince seemed like the front man for a badass band, the more context a rock audience would have for his unclassifiable music. "The band was such an important media tool for him," says Lisa Coleman. "*1999* proved that—trading verses, actually having people step up, there was a white girl and a black guy and whatever. His dream was that we would be Fleetwood Mac mixed with Sly and the Family Stone."

After five albums, Prince had reached the mountaintop. It had been a steady build, with lessons learned and refinements made along the way. After multiple hits and a successful tour, *1999* continued to reach new plateaus, and to introduce Prince to more and more new fans. Eddie Murphy, riding high as the biggest star on *Saturday Night Live* and with his film *Trading Places,* titled his 1983 stand-up special *Delirious* after the latest *1999* hit. "I think Prince is five years in front of everybody—he's a fucking musical genius," Murphy said. "He's the only entertainer in the world I would switch places with right now. But he's too short, so I guess I wouldn't."

Prince made the cover of *Rolling Stone* in April—the headline was "The Secret Life of America's Sexiest One-Man Band"—without granting the magazine an interview; by the end of the year, *Rolling Stone* would claim that "the pint-sized founder of the 'Minneapolis Sound' was starting to look like the most influential music man of the eighties so far" (and this in a year when Michael Jackson thoroughly dominated all discussions of pop—or of anything, for that matter). Anticipation began building for his next album; if he could continue this momentum, it could really be his moment. "It was that point in a career where the table was set," says Alan Leeds. "The right record, this kid goes through the roof."

But Prince's ambitions were already getting bigger than just his next album, as his managers would soon discover. Their contract was coming up for renewal after five years. Having broken him through to a multiplatinum audience and developed him into an arena headliner, they assumed that the decision would be a no-brainer. "I thought we did an incredible job, we had a creative relationship, I'm sure he's gonna sign another contract," recalls manager Bob Cavallo. "And he says that he won't sign with us again unless we get him a movie."

THREE

Bring 2 Life a Vision

To those in Prince's inner circle, his fascination with film had long been apparent. "We used to watch so many old films," says Jill Jones. "A lot of Italian films—he loved *Swept Away*—old Cary Grant. He got into David Lynch at one point, so he really started looking at, like, *Eraserhead*; I remember screaming at that little worm-baby or whatever it was. He was looking at European directors, trying to pull all of that in. He was really into the old studio system, too, Louis B. Mayer, he had books on those, looking at how that was structured. Also Elizabeth Taylor films, Marilyn Monroe—he'd look at a person long enough and try to figure out who they related to. Like the concept of giving me the blond hair: he said, 'You're very plain just with your normal hair,' because I looked like I'd come out of some Ralph Lauren catalogue. He cut off all my hair with, like, fingernail scissors and started to Svengali.

"I know he had this idea pretty early on about a film. When

I was touring with Teena Marie and we were opening for him, he said he was going to do a movie, but he didn't really elaborate. He had a pretty clear vision on his road map."

"We were always videotaping rehearsals and shows," Bobby Z said. "We were also doing skits. He was always talking about doing a movie." Lisa Coleman confirms that Prince expressed his ambition to make movies when she first joined the band, during the *Dirty Mind* period. Prince had even attempted a film project titled *The Second Coming* during the 1982 Controversy tour. The March 7 homecoming show at Bloomington, Minnesota's Met Center was shot in full, but Prince drove director Chuck Statler (who had helmed pre-MTV promotional videos for Devo, the Cars, and Elvis Costello, in addition to the Time's clip for "Cool") past the breaking point attempting to film interstitial narrative segments; Statler later described the experience as a "gruesome drill," with Prince demanding take after take of every shot. *The Second Coming* was abandoned before it was ever edited, though stills have turned up on the Internet.

Throughout the Triple Threat tour, though, Prince could often be seen scribbling in a purple notebook that he carried everywhere. Eventually he started letting the band know what his plans were for their next step. "I think it was at a rehearsal where he said, 'Here's what I'm thinking, here's what we're gonna do,'" says Coleman. "Actually, he wouldn't ever say 'Here's what I'm thinking'; that would be way too intimate. He'd just be like, 'We're gonna make a movie.' I remember on a plane ride during the tour, he called me to come sit next to him and told me a lot of the ideas. He would ask me things like, 'Would you kiss Matt if I wrote this scene?' He would describe how he saw the character, who I was. I think he was always aiming at big, 'I'm gonna be a big star,' but to him, a band was much more interesting than just a singer. So he wanted to really feature that, and he wanted to have his philosophy and his politics and his message all be incorporated—on *Dirty Mind,* 'Uptown' was a big thing in his mind. The song wasn't that big, but there was always this utopian thing.

"I remember him saying, 'We're gonna have a director come and meet us, and we're just gonna see what he's about and if he's up to it.' We were little smart-asses, too, so it was like, 'Ha, ha, the director will come, and we'll give him a hard time and scare him away.' "

"I think we were in Cincinnati, maybe a week before the end of the 1999 tour," says Matt Fink, "and he called me and said he wanted to have breakfast with me, just the two of us. He took me to the hotel restaurant and told me about his plans to do the movie, asked what I thought about that and if I was excited about it. I said yes to all of it—I thought it was a great idea to go for; why not? So I said 'Perfect, I'm on board.'

"After the conversation, I did think, 'Now, wait a minute. Do we really have the following to create a movie that's going to generate enough people to come out and see it, create the revenue needed to support something like that?' "

Objectively, the idea of Prince starring in a feature film made very little sense. As of 1983, he had just one album that could truly be considered a major hit. He was still largely unfamiliar to a general pop audience, and, especially since he had stopped doing press of any kind, he certainly did not register as a mainstream celebrity. And other than the Beatles with *A Hard Day's Night* and *Help!*, very few musicians had been able to make a convincing or successful jump to the big screen; most recently, Prince's fellow Warner Bros. artist Paul Simon had just flopped with his 1980 film *One Trick Pony*.

"When I got there, he already had a notebook, and people were saying, 'He's writing a movie,'" recalls Alan Leeds. "The people closest to him were probably in the know about what he was doing; I just knew that he's got this notebook, and he sits on the bus and he writes and he wants to make a movie—you know, like, 'Yeah, so do I.' I didn't take it seriously. I thought he was nuts. I've got to figure that most people around him thought it was nuts, too—even the people who knew how ambitious he was and knew these traits that we now celebrate as being a necessity for success for somebody like him. He was a kid with a very vivid imagination, who was stubborn and angry enough with the world to refuse anybody's no. And you could argue that without all that, he wouldn't have gotten where he got; if he'd have been civil, he wouldn't have ever gotten the movie made.

"Somewhere there's a book to be written about the DNA of guys like Prince or James Brown or Miles Davis, all of whom had mother issues, all of whom had abandonment issues in various ways, and all of whom could be extremely judgmental and difficult to get along with. There's a pattern there; it's not a coincidence. The normal person, if somebody tells you no, you get tired of it or you're needy enough that you want friends or whatever, so eventually you just say, 'Well, yeah, okay, I'll do something else.' Not these guys."

At Prince's label, Bob Merlis remembers that the initial reaction to the idea of a movie was a certain bewilderment. "My own response was, 'Really?!?' I thought it was very bold—it certainly wasn't conventional in terms of the usual sequence for these things. But the success of *1999* was substantial, so he did have momentum, instead of doing it on the downside of a career, which is often when these things are attempted."

To others in the camp, the concept of a movie was less of a shock and more of a tribute to Prince's artistic vision and trajectory. "It made absolute sense to me, because before anybody had heard who Prince was, I read the black charts and other people didn't," says Howard Bloom. "That phenomenon of going platinum when you were buried on the black charts, that says something.

"There are two keys to superstardom—one is an intense work ethic, and it doesn't just come from a work ethic, it comes from the fact that you want to make music more than you want to breathe, eat, sleep, or do anything else in life. When you find a person like that, it's someone worth hanging on to. Prince had that; his entire life was music. And then he had this astonishing executive capacity, this prefrontal-cortex discipline. If you're a soul searcher, which is what I was, you have really found it when you found him. So the idea that he should make a movie was no more outrageous than the idea that the Beatles would write their own songs in 1961—ninety percent of the time when an artist of this caliber makes a decision out of pure passion, he is right, and you have to defend him for all you're worth."

"When he said it was going to be bigger than *Saturday Night Fever*—he had that burning desire—I was like, 'Sure, why not?' " says Jill Jones. "It didn't seem crazy because I had the background, growing up with the Gordys, where anything can happen. But I also really admired the fact that he didn't have any real help, that his mind put all these people together."

"Prince *had* to make it happen, he had no choice," says Susannah Melvoin. "He was compelled, and he knew how to make everyone else feel that compulsion, too—and that was the weird part. How did he make us all fall under his spell? You got sucked in, and sometimes that was great and sometimes it was really crappy. On the periphery, it didn't make sense, but inside this world of his, there were a lot of people who wanted to make it happen."

Whether Cavallo and the rest of the management team really believed in the idea, the ultimatum Prince laid down left them with no choice but to deliver. "It was right out of the blue, but it didn't surprise me," says Cavallo. "It was worth so much money to me, because if he didn't re-sign with us, it would've been a tragedy. We had such a big fucking hit with this guy, and I knew how big he would be. I knew that in person he was unstoppable; he was so good, he works so hard, his shows are so precise. It was something to see."

The marching orders were spelled out very clearly by Prince to Cavallo. "He said, 'It's gotta be a major movie; it can't be with one of [your] gangster friends' or something. I don't have any of those—I went to Georgetown University, I'm not a mob guy! But anyway, whatever his fantasy was, he says, 'It has to be with a major studio, my name above the title'—basically, 'Warner Brothers presents Prince in his first motion picture.' Think how carefully he thought about this."

Dez Dickerson remembers Prince saying, "If it's just me and Chick [bodyguard "Big Chick" Huntsberry] in the snow with a camcorder, I'm going to make this movie."

Meanwhile, at the conclusion of the 1999 tour, Prince decided to make one more personnel change in the band, which would prove to have a major impact on the direction of the movie. His relationship with lead guitarist/primary onstage foil Dickerson was fraying, for a number of reasons: Dickerson didn't want to take as much direction from Prince; he wanted to work more on his own music; he was a Christian and was increasingly uncomfortable with Prince's lyrics. (He was also probably still annoyed that Prince used his home phone number as the title and hook of the Time hit "777-9311.") Prince sat him down and told him about the plans for the movie, and that it would require a multiyear commitment to ride out the project—a commitment he didn't feel he could make. "That was the bottom line," Dickerson says. "I just couldn't see myself doing that for three more years."

"By the time I came on that tour, Dez was on the outs," says Leeds. "The band that I was introduced to when I came aboard was, 'There's the band, and then there's Dez—Dez is a pain in the ass. He's got his wife with him, she stirs him up;

she doesn't like Prince, Prince doesn't like her. He demands his own dressing room; sometimes there's venues where there's not enough rooms to accommodate him and that becomes an issue. He doesn't have to come to sound check, you've got to kiss his ass to get him to do that; it's just bad.' So everybody was fed up with Dez."

"Dez just walked himself out of the job," says Jones. "Dez was the only one who was married at the time—now, after we've all been married, I think we kind of know that those things happen, but it's really no joke how a wife can come in and just wreck your shit. 'You can't be here, you need your own dressing room'—those kinds of things started to really wear on Prince. But I don't think Prince wanted to continue the new wave-y stuff like what he'd done prior, anyway, like 'Head' and those kind of songs; I think he was trying to make it commercial and make a lot of money, because with money, he could do anything, and he knew that."

"I felt bad about the way that Dez was feeling . . . he was super-angry," says Coleman. "His kamikaze headband, white-guy rocker look was kind of cool. But I think he felt what was coming and didn't like what it looked like. I think that he and Prince were mutually done with each other."

Even Dickerson himself ultimately seemed to understand that times had changed. "Prince doesn't need the same kind of band he had when he started out," he said soon after his departure. "Back then, he needed a power band, people who could get him to another level. Now that he's there, he can relax a little." In the end, the blow was softened when Prince helped set up Dickerson and his band, the Modernaires, within his management team. (Later, he even gave them a brief appearance in *Purple Rain*.)

Conveniently, another guitarist was close at hand. Wendy Melvoin, the teenage daughter of an A-list Los Angeles session musician, had grown up with Lisa Coleman, and the two had become romantically involved. Prince had actually gotten close to the couple and to Melvoin's twin sister, Susannah, staying in the apartment in Los Angeles shared by the three women when he came into town to record.

"Wendy and Lisa would pick him up at the airport, and then they'd all just come home and hang out," says Susannah Melvoin. "He would sleep on the living room couch; we had some cats that bothered him in the middle of the night. I had the room in the middle of the apartment with no door on the bathroom. We had no privacy, but we were all having a great time."

Wendy was traveling on the bus with the band for much of the 1999 tour. Prince had overheard her playing guitar—the first time, through a hotel-room door—so when Dickerson wasn't at sound check before a New York City show, he asked if she could fill in and run through "Controversy."

"He was walking around the venue listening," says Coleman, "and he almost ran back up onto the stage and sat at the piano, which was at the middle of the stage at that time, and started jamming. He's like, 'Damn, girl, is your daddy black?' That started this romance; it was like little stars and flowers came out of his eyes."

"I had been a huge Prince fan, so by the time I was on that

stage, I had done my own finishing school," says Melvoin. "I was playing and practicing and knew myself that something would happen. I just kind of knew it."

Coleman and Melvoin, forever joined in the minds of Prince fans as one unit ("Wendy-and-Lisa"), ended their romance years ago, and are both happily settled into long-term relationships—Coleman is married to the duo's manager, Renata Kanclerz, and Melvoin's partner is Lisa Cholodenko, who wrote and directed *The Kids Are All Right*, a 2011 Oscar nominee for Best Picture. But watching them together in the studio they share in Hollywood's Jim Henson Company lot over the course of a rainy Los Angeles afternoon, one can't help but notice that they interact like an old married couple. They finish each other's sentences, trigger memories, laugh easily, bicker over details. Coleman is still and drily witty; Melvoin stays in motion, smoking an e-cigarette, picking up a guitar to illustrate a point. Clearly, one reason they continue to thrive in their work collaborating on scores and sound tracks for movies (*Soul Food, Something New*) and television shows (*Crossing Jordan, Nurse Jackie, Heroes*) after all these years is the strength of their personal bond.

Prince decided to ask Melvoin to join the band, but—in an uncharacteristically deferential move—wanted to clear it with Coleman first. "He was very respectful of me in these times," she says, "so he called me, like, 'How would you feel if I asked Wendy to be in the band? Would that bother you?'—number one, I would no longer be the only girl in the band, and number two, she was my girlfriend, and would I feel weird having my girlfriend in the band? He really seemed to care. I told him I thought it would be great, and it was like a dream come true to me, actually, because Wendy and I had really fallen in love, and it was hard being apart."

To the rest of the Revolution, and the members of the Time, the choice of Melvoin as Dickerson's replacement—rather than one of the "Uptown" mob—came as a shock. "It didn't fly very well," says Jill Jones. "There were new people coming in, and I think the Minneapolis crew felt a little threatened."

"There was some resentment in the band," says Leeds. "That she got it too easy, and the fact that she's a take-charge person just by nature. After a while, if there was a rehearsal and Prince was late, rather than sit around, Wendy would be the one who'd say, 'Let's do something.' And Mark Brown and Fink would look at her like [silent expression of disbelief]—particularly Mark. Bobby Z is the eternal politician, so he always managed to keep the lid on."

"It definitely changed the whole vibe," says Fink. "Dez was, like, a seasoned rock veteran at that point, a rock star in his own right, and he was a very strong element. Wendy came in—she was nineteen at the time—young, albeit very talented. I was worried at first that maybe she wasn't ready or was too green. I tried my best to be supportive of her, but there were moments when technically maybe her playing wasn't quite there for lead playing yet. But then she worked hard and she made it happen, and I've got to give her a lot of credit for that, because it's not easy to come in and be in that role that was suddenly thrust upon her."

"It was more fun to be together with Wendy in the band," Bobby Z has said. "Her personality brought so much to balance the band out and make it the band it became. It couldn't have become the Revolution with Dez. It needed Wendy to bring out that extra oomph!"

"There was a split in the band for a minute there," says Coleman. "Some of the guys really liked Wendy, and some of the guys were like, 'She's fucking it all up.' In the band, Bobby, Wendy, and Lisa became kind of a clique. Wendy and Bobby really became close friends, that was pretty easy. I don't know if people were a little bit freaked that we were lovers."

The addition of Melvoin left only two members of the original Rebels lineup still standing—Bobby Z and Matt Fink. Wendy's new role shook up the band in several ways. Musically, she represented Prince's interest in expanding his sound away from the mix of rock guitars and dance-floor synthesizers that he had been exploring for years and ultimately perfected on *1999*. "He knew that in Wendy he had not only this funky little black girl," says Coleman, "but when she played those chords, it was like, 'That sounds like Joni Mitchell tuning.' So it took the music maybe a little more white in a way, and more experimental. Since I also had a jazz and classical influence, we became like college kids together—sound check started turning into, like, a chord class, of who can play the weirdest, coolest chord, instead of just thumping an E. We were trying all this crazy music, and it was getting harder to tell what fit into this new 'Prince and the Revolution' thing."

Melvoin was a different kind of guitarist from Dickerson.

"Wendy is a great rhythm player but maybe not that great as a lead player," Dickerson says, "whereas lead was really my strength." Whether entirely intentional or not, this cleared the lane for Prince to step out as the sole guitar hero in the group. In addition, the front line of the band no longer consisted of three black males but offered a mix of colors and genders, closer to the arrangements of the Family Stone and Fleetwood Mac, to which Prince aspired. Maybe Melvoin just happened to be in the right place at the right time, but Prince clearly sensed that if he wanted to keep growing his audience, she provided him an opportunity to change his image and his presentation in a way that might resonate with more listeners.

"He wanted her to be the other part of him," says Coleman. "They were the same clothing size, and he'd say, 'Wear this tonight, and I'm gonna wear this.' "

"Wendy brought a vulnerability that he hadn't really been able to show," says Jones. "He was like this dirty little boy onstage before, but she kind of balanced out the animus, the female version—he actually found another mirror that helped the audience to interpret this nice, kindred thing that they had between them. Someone who was very strong, would always have his back, and yet possessed a depth of honesty. Wendy is very confident, and I think he liked that."

"I was young and really excited, and I absolutely loved the role," says Melvoin. "For my own personal growth and how I grew up, I finally felt important; I felt really honored. I was in a band with the love of my life, and because I was such a huge

Prince fan, to be accepted and asked to join that situation was the biggest validation of my life."

Bob Cavallo was pounding the pavement, trying to get a Prince feature film off the ground. The managers and Prince had each agreed to put up $500,000 to start the wheels turning, and the first move was to find someone to take a crack at a script. "I had some kind of a relationship to film," says Cavallo, "because when I had the Lovin' Spoonful, I did Woody Allen's *What's Up, Tiger Lily?*, we put all the music in that, and there was a Francis Coppola movie called *You're a Big Boy Now* that John [Sebastian] wrote all the music for. So I knew directors and producers and stuff, but where the fuck was I gonna get a writer who wants to write a Prince movie?"

He was pointed toward a writer named William Blinn, who had won an Emmy for his work on the *Roots* miniseries and was currently writing for *Fame,* the series based on the movie about a New York City high school for the performing arts. Cavallo arranged a meeting in Los Angeles between Prince and the writer, a dinner at which Prince flummoxed Blinn by ordering spaghetti with tomato sauce and a glass of orange juice. Prince gradually, haltingly began revealing the ideas he had been accumulating in his purple notebook.

Blinn was certainly confused by Prince; he said that the musician's attempts to define the movie's theme were "inarticulate. . . . He is not verbally comfortable. Certainly not with strangers." But he teased out enough of the concepts that he could start to write. "He's a man apart in many ways," Blinn said. "But his whole sexual attitude is positive: this is good, this represents growth, life."

"He was semi-communicative about his dad," Blinn said. "You could tell that his father is very key in what he's about. It was as if he was sorting out his own mystery—[on] an honest quest to figure himself out." Elsewhere, the writer said that Prince's "initial concept, unlike in the finished motion picture, was that his parents were dead. They were the victims of a murder-suicide: his father had killed his mother, and then himself. . . . It was a constant back-and-forth as to whether he was going to embrace life—in the form of the character of the girl, and the substance and form of his music—or, in essence, he was going to be swallowed up by the death that surrounded him." The writer concluded that "this picture was either going to be really big or fall on its ass."

As Blinn was working, he tried to set up a follow-up meeting in Minneapolis, but Prince canceled on him several times. Finally they connected and went to the movies together, but Prince got up and left after twenty minutes. At this point, Blinn announced that he wanted off the project. ("I know he's very gifted, but frankly, life's too short.") He went back to Los Angeles, but Prince called him and asked him to return to Minnesota.

In May, Blinn submitted a first draft of the script, at the time titled *Dreams*. "It's a little TV, it's a little square," Cavallo thought, "but it's a good idea, and I figured the director will rewrite it anyway. But I can't get a director. There was nobody interested."

Sending out the script was getting him nowhere. Awareness of Prince in Hollywood was close to zero. Someone recommended that Cavallo see an early cut of a new movie called *Reckless*, a *Rebel Without a Cause*–style love story starring Aidan Quinn and Daryl Hannah, made by a young director named James Foley. "I go to screen this movie and I'm the only one in the theater," says Cavallo. "I see it, I walk out, and a young man comes up to me and says, 'What did you think?' I said, 'Well, I thought it was pretty good, and that's really all I thought. I thought the editing was good.' He's like, 'Really? Good. I did that.' "

The editor was a recent University of Southern California film school graduate named Albert Magnoli. His final film school project, a twenty-three minute study of musicians titled *Jazz*, won multiple awards, including a student Academy Award. Magnoli remembers that Cavallo approached him after the screening and asked if he thought Foley might be interested in getting involved in Prince's first motion picture. "I was excited to continue editing alongside Jamie, so I told Cavallo that Jamie was a massive fan," says Magnoli, who may not have made a movie in a while but remains a master storyteller, even over the phone during a series of marathon calls. "I ran across the parking lot and called Jamie in New York and said it was great, I had found us our next film. And he said to me, 'Who is Prince?' "

Magnoli got the script from Cavallo and sent it to Foley, who called him the next day and said, "Have you read this? It's terrible, and I will not do it." When he passed that news on to

Cavallo, Magnoli recalls, the aspiring producer "went into a fit of sorts—he said, 'I don't understand, I've sent this script out and they're all passing on it. I thought I was doing everything correctly. Why isn't this working?' He asked if I had read the script, and said 'I really need to understand what I did wrong, and what I'm going to do, and fast.' "

Magnoli read the *Dreams* script and, he says, "Jamie was actually being very nice—it had no relevance to the audience the film was intended for; it was not musical, too cerebral." He called Cavallo and suggested that they meet, telling him, "At this moment, I know way more about the film business than you, and I don't know anything."

The two men met for breakfast at Du-par's restaurant in the San Fernando Valley. Thirty years later, the chronology of this conversation differs a bit, depending on which of them you talk to ("Magnoli completely makes up shit," says Cavallo. "Sometimes he's very flattering to himself, and sometimes he's just wrong"). According to Cavallo, they sat down and he offered Magnoli the chance to direct the movie for $75,000. "Now, he doesn't have a glass to piss in," says Cavallo. "He says, 'I pass.' I fucking went crazy. I lost my cool. I say, 'How the fuck do you pass? Why?' He said, 'Oh, it's so square.' I said, 'I know it's square—can you do something about it? Do you have any ideas?' He says, 'Give me a week.'

"We meet again a week later, and basically, he does the movie standing up, jumping up and down—he's a very athletic kid. [And] we make a deal."

Magnoli's account of his own performance is quite similar,

but he claims there was just one meeting, and that his conjuring of the movie's narrative was much more spontaneous. When he asserted that what the movie needed was a writer/director who would spend time with the musicians and write something more authentic, Cavallo asked him what the story would be.

"It was one of those moments when all the bells go off," Magnoli says. "I looked at him and I just started talking, and in five to seven minutes, I pitched him *Purple Rain*. In elementary and high school, I was a drummer, so that was enough to give me some insight into the troubles and tribulations of a performer. The Blinn script gave me the characters. I had enough information that I could just pitch. And I'm an excitable guy; I was jumping up in the air, getting down on the ground.

"[Cavallo] looked at me and said, 'That's a hell of a story. So now what are you going to do?' I said that the next day I would go to Minneapolis. It was a Friday. I would go and meet Prince and pitch that story. Then Sunday I would come home, and I'll come back with a motion picture or I won't."

They both agree that it was Magnoli's vision of the movie's first scene that helped close the deal. "He got me excited by describing the opening," says Cavallo. "He said, 'Take the ending of *The Godfather* and make it the opening of our picture.' Prince is doing a song, the elevator comes up, the girl is coming from the airport, hustling her way in—all the characters are introduced, and you keep cutting back to the stage. Prince is putting makeup on, getting on his bike, he rides up to the place, the bar scene with the Time, Apollonia pulls a scam and gets in, you see everybody. So he described that scene, and I went nuts."

"I instinctively conceived an opening musical number in which we could introduce other characters and minimize the need for dialogue," says Magnoli. "I mentioned the ending of *The Godfather,* all those cuts to the other characters—moving from Michael Corleone at the church, with those words going all over the other scenes and characters, and that gave him a visual."

(It isn't actually the final scene in *The Godfather* that Magnoli was referencing—that's the famous moment when Michael Corleone denies his involvement in the mob to his wife—but the penultimate scene, often called the "baptism sequence." For five minutes, Francis Ford Coppola cuts back and forth between Michael's godson's baptism and a series of murders of the Corleone family's enemies. It's interesting to note that the director was unhappy with the montage, which used sixty-seven shots, until one of the film's editors suggested he lay an organ track over the entire sequence: in an inversion of the *Purple Rain* concept, in *The Godfather* it took adding the music to unify the scene, rather than the weaving of narrative moments to intensify a song.)

Agreeing that they would move forward, Cavallo sent over Prince's music videos and some concert footage. Magnoli spent the night watching them and felt they were low-quality and didn't reveal much that would translate to a mass audience on a movie screen. He felt uninspired and considered calling the whole thing off—he had an offer from Henry Winkler's production company to write a script, so there was a more secure choice in front of him. But on Friday, he got into the car that would take him to the airport.

"The driver is a black guy in his mid-twenties, and I think, 'This guy is potentially part of my audience,'" he says. "Just before we get to the airport, I ask him, 'Do you know Prince?' And he says yes. I said, 'Do you listen to him?' And he said 'No, the guy's a fag.' I was pretty sure that was not true, but it was another thing that had not gotten over; that was the perception."

In Minneapolis, he was met by Steve Fargnoli and Prince's hulking bodyguard, "Big Chick" Huntsberry. "I hadn't even been told there was another manager," Magnoli says. "And Fargnoli said, 'Understand this—we don't care what you pitched to Cavallo. It's garbage. We're doing the script as written. If you don't understand this, I will buy you a ticket and send you home right now.'"

The plan was to meet Prince in a hotel at midnight and then go to dinner. As the clock struck twelve, Prince walked out of the elevator wearing black pants with buttons up the sides, heels, a trench coat, and a scarf. He walked past Magnoli over to Cavallo and Big Chick, which gave the director a momentary chance to observe him with his guard down. "What I saw was an extremely vulnerable guy who was essentially alone," says Magnoli. "And in that time, I filled in the rest of the pitch—I saw the father, the fragmentation of the family."

They drove to the restaurant and sat in a booth in the back in silence. Prince, once again, ordered spaghetti and orange juice. "He looks at me and says, 'Why do you like my screen-play?'" Magnoli recalls. "This was news to me, suddenly, that it was his script. And I said, 'It sucks. Now let me talk about what I want to talk about.'" Prince reacted—he looked at Fargnoli, looked at Chick. They'd told him Magnoli was coming out to talk about shooting the script as it was, not wanting to make large and dramatic changes. He had been lied to.

Magnoli continues: "I said, 'I want to talk about the story I told to Cavallo; I want to tell you that story.' I gave him my entire rant. He said, 'You guys go home; Magnoli, you come with me.'" Like a true director, Magnoli describes a dramatic scene, in which Prince drives his black BMW to the freeway, then takes an exit that plunges them into complete darkness: "It was like we were in a spaceship. Prince stopped the car and said, 'Okay, what do you know about me?' I said, 'Really nothing.' He said, 'Then how is it that in ten minutes, you told me my life story?'"

The next morning, Fargnoli picked Magnoli up at the hotel and drove him over to Prince's purple house in the Chanhassen suburb. He didn't mention anything about the night before. Prince was going to spend the day playing some new music for Magnoli to consider for the film. The board in the home studio was on the fritz, so they went upstairs and sat on the floor. "We must have listened to about a hundred songs," says Magnoli. "I said, 'I need twelve songs,' and he said, 'You pick them.' I told him that I would come back in August, I'd research and write a script, and then we would make the movie."

Cavallo, meanwhile, had secured the funding needed to

get the production off the ground. He approached Warner Bros. Records chairman Mo Ostin, and they worked out an advance of $2 million against Prince's future royalties. "Bob came to me and said that Prince wanted to make a film and had threatened to terminate their relationship if he couldn't deliver," says Ostin. "The fact is that it was valuable for the record company in terms of potential for Prince as an artist—and it actually seemed incredibly safe from my standpoint: he was already earning royalties."

Ostin is one of the most respected record men from the industry's golden era, and his explanation sounds almost impossibly out of step with the tone of the business today. "When our artists were interested in going into other media, we felt we should support them in terms of facilitating their ability to be successful," he says. "If we saw the possibility of it enhancing their image and making them bigger, and it was something they wanted to do, our responsibility was to create as powerful and strong a creative environment as possible. I thought Prince had a good shot with this, and given the following he had, seeing the audiences he was attracting on the road, the growth in his career, it was a reasonable bet to make."

He may have handed over a huge batch of songs, but Prince didn't stop making more music. The 1999 tour had ended on April 10, 1983; by early June, Prince had set the band up for rehearsal in a warehouse off of Highway 7 in the St. Louis Park neighborhood of Minneapolis. The building has since been torn down, leaving just an empty space next to the electrical towers of a substation in the spot where the *Purple Rain* album came together.

"The whole experience at that warehouse was a really different thing," says Lisa Coleman. "It kind of stands out—it was set apart, away from other buildings. Usually we would rehearse in these industrial parks and they were busy; we would have hours where we couldn't play because there were businesses being run there."

Rehearsal was as relentless as ever—maybe even more intense, because they didn't need to stop. "Prince was such a structured boss, there was no real fun in it," says Susannah Melvoin, who became part of the Minneapolis family in addition to watching her sister work. "If you were five minutes late, he'd dock your pay. You might work on the same groove for five hours nonstop, some three-bar thing over and over. It was like the army."

While Magnoli was refining his choices for the movie, certain songs seem to have risen to the top for Prince. "Baby I'm a Star" was a carefree, straight-up boast. He had started working on the song as far back as 1981, recording a solo piano version while working on remixes for the *Controversy* track "Let's Work."

Its eventual companion piece, "I Would Die 4 U," had a comparably breezy groove, though the lyric was something quite different. The title phrase, which would fill a dramatic moment in the *Purple Rain* script, was something Prince remembered his own father saying, but he transformed it from the notion of surrendering everything to love into an invocation of spiritual salvation; "I'm your messiah," he sings, and "if you're evil, I'll forgive you by and by." Dez Dickerson told Touré, for his 2013 study of Prince, which was titled after this song, that he takes the lyric at face value: "I think Prince had experienced something. I think he had a moving experience with respect to the idea of who Jesus is or was, and he wanted to express it in a song. It's not a very cloaked lyric. It says what it says. He's saying he is Jesus."

Questlove reads the song more metaphorically. "I think in his mind he was lending voice to what he perceived as being the gospel message. I don't think he's literally saying he's the Messiah, but in his own way he's speaking for the Messiah." Years later, after Prince became a Jehovah's Witness, he would continue to perform the song, but would make things much clearer by changing the line "I'm your messiah" to "He's your messiah."

The song contributed to the theme of redemption that would run through much of *Purple Rain*, but it isn't one of the set's most musically challenging tracks. " 'I Would Die 4 U' and 'Baby I'm a Star,' they were fun dance tracks, and he did those things easily," says Susan Rogers, who moved to Minneapolis in the summer of 1983 to help Prince set up recording equipment in the warehouse and at his home. "Just because he does them easily doesn't mean that they're not great, but I would venture to guess that he didn't put nearly as much effort into those."

The most complex piece in this batch was one he had been

working on since the 1999 tour, and would continue to refine until the last minute, well after filming had stopped. "We were jamming one day," says Fink, "and I'm playing something, and he goes, 'Oh, that's nice.' And then that turns into 'Computer Blue,' which became a full-blown collaboration between Prince, me, Lisa, and Wendy, and Prince's father, who wrote the main melody to the bridge section of that song."

"We did the basic track at the warehouse," says Rogers, "but there was quite a bit of editing with that; we brought it to Sunset Sound [in Los Angeles] and made substantial changes to it. The basic piano part was the same, but a lot of overdubbed parts were different." In fact, "Computer Blue" expanded (past the fourteen-minute mark) and contracted significantly over eight months—one instrumental section that was cut turns up in the *Purple Rain* movie, in a scene where Prince is late to rehearsal and Fink, Bobby Z, and Mark are playing a jagged instrumental. A lengthy spoken-word section, known among Prince superfans as the "hallway speech," sees Prince walking down a hallway with a girlfriend and assigning emotions (love, lust, hate) to each room. Vaguely reminiscent of Jim Morrison's recited section in the Doors' epic "The End," this segment would also eventually be dropped.

The members of the Revolution weren't entirely thrilled with the first bunch of songs for the album, or sound track, or whatever it was going to be. "The songs weren't as funky to me," says Wendy Melvoin. "They were pop songs; they were definitely watered down. It was really white, and it felt that way."

"I think that Prince felt that way, too," adds Coleman, "because then he went and did 'Darling Nikki'—which was not necessarily funky, but it was full-out angry energy, something that was missing. He would imitate an old granny, like, 'You could make Granny dance with this one,' but then I think he was just like, 'We're leaning it too far to the granny; we still need danger.' "

Dickerson notes that a new approach was evident from the time Prince was first presenting embryonic new material during the Triple Threat tour. "It was clear that he wanted to write classic pop-rock hits," he says. "The songs on *1999* had been a significant shift in being more polished and accessible, and this was the next step in that evolution. It was definitely calculated—that word gets used in a negative way, but this was through the lens of being smart and trying to write the kind of songs that galvanized moments in a film, and vice versa."

In addition to working on the raw, snarling "Darling Nikki," with its lyric that would later incur the wrath of Tipper Gore and lead to the formation of the Parents Music Resource Center, Prince was working on a song with an even more provocative title—"Electric Intercourse." The song itself, though, is actually not the nasty rocker the name might imply but a more slinky and subtle R&B number, just electric piano and drums; it was part of the early track list for the album, built on the recording from the First Avenue benefit, but ultimately wasn't deemed essential enough to make the cut. (In a May 2014 show in Birmingham, England, Prince broke out the song for the very first time since that 1983 performance; he played it solo on the piano, though in accordance with his more conservative approach as a Jehovah's Witness, he didn't sing the word *intercourse*.)

The initial motivation for "Purple Rain" came from Prince's observation of another rock star on the road. While much has been made over the years of a rivalry between Prince and Michael Jackson, those around him say that his competitive streak reached much further than just one artist ("Michael wasn't the biggest priority to kill—it was everybody," says Melvoin, as Coleman adds with a laugh, "It was Prince against the *world*.") He was obsessively reading music and fashion magazines, tracking anyone or anything that had some heat, sensing which lessons he might absorb.

On many dates in the 1999 tour, Prince had followed Bob Seger into the arenas of middle America. One night, he asked Matt Fink why the proudly working-class Detroit rocker had such a huge appeal; Fink replied that it was Seger's big, gut-punching ballads—"We've Got Tonight," "Turn the Page"—that his fans loved, and that Prince should try writing that kind of anthem if he really wanted to conquer the pop world. (In 2004, when Prince and Seger were both inducted into the Rock and Roll Hall of Fame, Prince noted that they were "both Midwesterners" and said that Seger "had a lot of influence on me at the start of my career; he certainly influenced my writing.")

In December 1982, Prince showed the chords of a new ballad to the band during sound check at Cincinnati's Riverfront Coliseum. "I remember him coming in, and he had this idea," says Melvoin. "He made it clear: 'I need to find this thing; it needs to be *this* and it has to be *this* tempo,' and then he picked a key and we started jamming and came up with that opening chord sequence, and it just started to happen." What was happening, of course, was the genesis of "Purple Rain," even though lyrics and a title, much less any notion that it would provide the name to a movie, were still months away.

Melvoin took the chords that Prince showed the band and spread them out and added suspensions; whether the listener could follow the structure or not, the sound was something other than the obvious. "At that time, there weren't a lot of super-pop bands, other than maybe Andy Summers [of the Police], who were doing those kinds of things, doing harmonies that advanced," she says.

"He loved how Wendy was able to take it away from a country feel," says Coleman, "and then everyone in the band seemed to make it a little bit different. But when I put the high harmony on the chorus, then he was like, 'Lisa's bringing it back around again to good old American country music.'" In fact, the song retained such a classic power-ballad feel that Prince recognized its similarity to Journey's 1983 hit "Faithfully"; reportedly, he called Journey's keyboardist Jonathan Cain, who wrote the song, and played him an early version of "Purple Rain" over the phone, to make sure that the band wouldn't make a stink over the resemblance.

"The band was given the chord progression, and we ended up pretty much writing our own parts," says Fink. "I do recall during the first time jamming on that song, I played that line on the piano that he sings at the end, when he goes up into his falsetto for that big peaking line—that came from me, just by sheer accident, and he latched onto it and sang it.

"And that coda piece on 'Purple Rain,' where I play that little piano riff? I have to give Lisa a lot of credit for that, because she showed me this trick she had, where the left hand is doing one part and the right hand is doing this other thing against it, in counterpoint. It's kind of a weird rhythmic thing that she knew, and I said, 'That's really cool—show me how you do that.' So she actually taught me how to do that part."

With the music in place, Prince turned to a new friend for help with the lyrics. Recently, Stevie Nicks—the bewitching singer in his beloved Fleetwood Mac, who was currently working on a solo project—had called him, telling him that she had written a new song while humming along to "Little Red Corvette," so she was going to give him a songwriting credit and also wanted to invite him to play on the session. He showed up at the Los Angeles studio an hour later, and the song, "Stand Back," became a big hit. Nicks asked if they might write together someday, and he sent her a cassette of the ballad in progress, encouraging her to write some words.

"It was so overwhelming, that 10-minute track, that I listened to it and I just got scared," Nicks later told the *Minneapolis Star Tribune*. "I called him back and said, 'I can't do it. I wish I could. It's too much for me.' I'm so glad that I didn't, because he wrote it, and it became 'Purple Rain.'"

Once the structure was completed and the lyrics were in place sometime in the summer, those around the rehearsals recall the intense power the song seemed to have over people. Melvoin and Coleman remember a homeless woman wandering into the warehouse and listening to them play "Purple Rain" for hours; when they took a break, they found her still outside, weeping.

"Big Chick came to rehearsal one afternoon," says Alan

Leeds, "and he said, 'Buddy, you ain't gonna believe the song the boy did last night. He wrote a new song in the studio; it's gonna be the biggest hit of this album. Willie Nelson's gonna cover it, you wait and see!' It was 'Purple Rain,' and when I heard that, I was like, 'That's a hit.'" (Funk maestro George Clinton later agreed with the bodyguard's assessment. He said, "'Purple Rain' always reminded me of Jimi Hendrix singing country music—take all the effects off, and it's a country-and-western song.")

The song's title touched on an image that Prince had long been bouncing around, and that would become a defining element of his image: thirty years later, Arsenio Hall still referred to Prince's fans as "the Purple Army." One of his early demos mentioned a "purple lawn," and he had already written songs titled "Purple Music" and "Purple Shades." His father said that purple was always Prince's favorite color. The breakthrough hit of an earlier generation's African-American guitar hero, Jimi Hendrix, was titled "Purple Haze," and on "1999," Prince began his description of the impending apocalypse with the phrase "the sky was all purple"—and, of course, there was the series of signature purple trench coats that he had been wearing on album covers and in music videos.

As Touré points out in his book, in the King James translation of the Bible, immediately prior to the crucifixion, Jesus is prepared in the following ways: "And they clothed him with purple, and platted a crown of thorns and put it about his head and began to salute him." In 1984, Wendy Melvoin summarized the song title simply and plainly. "A new beginning—purple, the sky at dawn; rain, the cleansing factor."

• • •

Writing, rehearsing, and recording never stopped. But Prince saw there was so much else to be done to prepare for making a movie. Though a real script hadn't yet been written, he had a limited amount of time to get a bunch of musicians who had never acted before ready to go in front of a camera. Drawing on lessons learned from those biographies of studio moguls, rather than wait for the producers or director to take charge, he began putting a battle plan in place.

"I got a call from Fargnoli sometime in July, offering me the gig to come to Minneapolis," says Leeds. "And I said, 'Well, what's the gig? Are you going back on the road?' 'Not right away. We're going to make a movie first.' I go, 'Okay, you need me to come there because you're making a movie? First of all, I don't believe you're making a movie. Second, why do you need me to make a movie? I don't make movies.' He said, 'We got three bands: we got Prince and his guys that you tour managed, we got Morris and the Time, we got Vanity 6. They're all in the movie. Everybody's taking acting lessons, everybody's taking dance lessons, and everybody's rehearsing new music. We need an off-road road manager to coordinate all this stuff.' 'Okay, Steven—you're really making a movie? Get the fuck outta here!' "

For all of the musicians, acting classes with Don Amendolia—who had appeared on *Ryan's Hope* and *Cheers,* and would later have recurring roles on *Twin Peaks* and the soap opera *Sunset Beach*—were required three times a week. "Prince came in one day," says Melvoin, "and he was like, 'We're all gonna have acting classes, we're all gonna have dance classes,' and that's when it started getting really like, 'Okay, this is going somewhere else.' "

"I don't know where he got it, but Prince has a great work ethic, like a classical musician: discipline is everything," says Coleman. "It's not like we were even gonna be part of a big dance line or something, but we were taking classes and literally doing jazz hands."

"It was ridiculous," adds Melvoin. "But it was loosening and it was humbling and it was funny."

"The acting coach was mandatory, whereas the dancing was not," says Fink. "Prince hoped that everybody would stick around and do the dance stuff—at first he kind of required it, for about three weeks, and then people fell off. I personally stuck with it through the whole summer. I didn't go every time, but I was much more religious about it than the rest of the band. Sometimes it would just be me, the dance instructor, and a couple gals from Apollonia 6. They phased him out toward the end of the summer because people stopped going and they didn't want to spend the money. But I got in great shape; we were doing the Jane Fonda workout and then doing, like, Broadway dance moves and routines."

Fink, who had studied acting in summer school and done voice-over and radio work, was probably the most experienced "actor" of the bunch, and welcomed the additional training. (He also points out that he grew up down the block from the filmmakers Joel and Ethan Coen, and suggests with a laugh that maybe his family inspired the title of their 1991 movie *Barton Fink*.) "We did a lot of exercises and played games—for the amount of acting that each member of the band was going to be doing, it was overkill, maybe, but still a good experience."

Others among the cast were less enthusiastic about the classes. "One day, Prince was like, 'We're making a movie,'" Morris Day told *Wax Poetics* magazine. "I was like, 'Okay, fine.' So I started going to acting class and dancing class and all sorts of silly stuff. I got kicked out of acting class because I kept clowning around, and the guys said I was disrupting it for everybody. That's pretty much [how I] did the best in the movie, by cutting up."

"In acting class, they weren't working on dialogue—they were working on, like, pimp walks," says Susannah Melvoin. "The band was like, 'Why are we doing this? Can we go rehearse?'"

As for the star of the show, he participated in the classes as his frantic schedule would allow. "Prince was very, very good," Amendolia once said. "He'd flip right out of his persona and be whatever character he had to be. He's very shy, as most actors are to a degree. He took direction well, probably the best. He asked a lot of questions."

"He would come and go," says Coleman. "He was working on his dance steps all the time, anyway. But Prince really was a good coach, like, 'All right, let's show some hustle out there!'—and he also wanted to see how we were doing, and also get an idea of who's got what; where is the power coming from? They tried to make everything seem like, 'How does Lisa usually say "Good morning" when she comes in?' and then you'd just do that, trying to make it seem more natural for the nonactors."

However excessive they may have seemed, the acting classes illustrated Prince's seriousness about the movie, and were worth it if only because they revealed the natural comic timing of Morris Day and, especially, his onstage sidekick/valet Jerome Benton, which would greatly impact the direction of the *Purple Rain* script. Also, Melvoin and Coleman's roles were reversed from their initial conception. Wendy was given the more outspoken, aggressive part, and Lisa made quieter and cooler. ("I was supposed to be the mean one!" Coleman asserts with a laugh.)

Jill Jones notes that one of Prince's other girlfriends was teaching one of the dance classes, but points out that competition and rivalry for his attention was a regular aspect of the scene, and he used that to creative advantage. "Everybody knew everybody was going out with Prince at the same time," she says, "but the men also had these relationships where everyone thought they were the one who had his ear. So the roles are always constantly on a wheel, shifting, and Prince would just take his pick from the wheel. But he was so excited, like, 'Look what we're doing. We're doing something great.' I think everybody wanted everything to be permanent, but he was definitely prepared for it all to change, in a good way. He had a very Zen thing, like, 'It's *gonna* change *and* it's gonna be great.'"

"Prince could rally the team," says Leeds. "He could pull them together and convince them that they were going to win no matter who they're playing; he's that guy. So what I walked into was a situation where he had not only convinced Fargnoli and Cavallo that they're going to make a movie or else, but he had convinced even the skeptics in the groups. Nobody was ballsy enough to actually take him on and say, 'Fuck you. You're not going to do this.'"

In 1984, Matt Fink told *People* magazine that one day, Prince spoke to the band about his family life. "He mentioned something about having a tough time. Then he suddenly realized what he was doing and clammed up. That was two and a half years ago. We never heard about his personal life again." But as things moved closer to the start of filming, there was one other relationship that Prince felt the need to confront.

"He started visiting his father a lot more, driving over to his house, because his father was a relative recluse," says Jones. "He would go and visit, and I'd sit in the car—it wasn't really a long visit, but I think they started mending some fences.

"He would always have very nice things to say about his eccentric father. He'd prepare you, like, 'My dad loves you,' or 'He thinks you're great,' but John was—as a musician, I'm not saying he was superior to Prince, he just heard things that other people didn't hear. Prince was able to find a balance between the real world and the not-so-real world of how to make money in this business, whereas his father was so extreme and so complicated, and I think he had to get clear on that."

"He had a lot of reverence for his father," says Wendy Melvoin, while Coleman recalls the times that John L. Nelson would show up at the warehouse. "If his dad came to a rehearsal, we'd have to not cuss, and some of the songs we weren't even allowed to sing. We would accidentally be like, [*sings*] 'Oh, motherfucker—' and then, 'Oops!' 'Remember? We're not singing in this run-through because Dad's here.'"

"He's full of ideas," Prince later said about his father. "It'd be wonderful to put out an album on him, but he's a little bit crazier than I am."

There was still no script for the film, no budget, no shooting schedule. But there were songs, the cast was learning their craft (one way or another), and the mental and emotional preparations had begun. As far as Prince was concerned, he was making a movie—and there were expenses that were raising the stakes every day.

"Somebody was posting the money for all this," says Leeds, "because you had three bands and crews on salary, you had a professional drama coach, a professional choreographer, facilities to rent, occasional extra musicians for recordings. You had technical people to support all these activities. And, like myself, there were other people who didn't live here, and all of them were getting apartments paid for and rental cars, getting per diems on top of salaries. There was a lot of money being spent from somewhere, and we knew Prince wasn't rich—I mean, he had two hits. But there must have been enough optimism to justify finding the money somewhere."

It was all being driven from the mind of one young musician. Yet one aspect of Prince's genius was the ability to make those around him not just trust his vision but feel invested in and dedicated to the plans. "He didn't speak much, but he would sometimes rant on about 'what we're all doing is this or that'—and it was always 'what *we're* doing,' not 'what *I'm* doing,'" says Susannah Melvoin. "I know that's how guys running cults like Jim Jones sound, and it was kinda like that on a musical level. It might sound creepy and eerie, but there was a little of that. And other times, he would just say nothing. He would just come in and put on his guitar, and you knew to stand at attention and get to work, or get out of the way."

"Once his idea was put into place, even before the movie was cast, as soon as he pushed that one domino over, it was just a question of momentum," says Wendy Melvoin. "And by the time it reached its pinnacle, it was a fucking speeding train, and there was no stopping it."

FOUR

Sign Your Name on the Dotted Line

On August 1, Albert Magnoli arrived in Minneapolis and set up shop at a motel. He had a month before he had to return to Los Angeles and finish the postproduction on *Reckless*. Knowing that everyone wanted the movie, though fictional, to be firmly based in the realities of Prince's life—"We wanted it to be the Prince story without being the Prince story," is how Cavallo put it—he began meeting with and interviewing all of the Revolution, the Time, Vanity 6, and others in the community. He found that everyone was accessible and open, and he started to formulate the shape of the script and the extensive revisions he would be making to Blinn's draft.

Consider the issues going on within the Prince camp in the summer of 1983. Following a period of tension with Dez Dickerson in which he was fighting to have more input in the band's music, there's now a new guitarist in the Revolution, whom many of the other musicians resent, and who also happens to be dating the keyboard player. There's still anger just below the boiling point within the Time, who remain pissed that Prince fired two of their bandmates. Prince is making overtures to rebuild the relationship with his estranged, eccentric father, which presumably makes him more willing to talk about, or at least think about, his family conflicts. He is also dating, to one degree or another, Jill Jones, Susan Moonsie (one of the Vanity 6 singers), and several others, and is about to begin pursuing Susannah Melvoin, a woman who will further complicate his love life. It didn't require much digging for Magnoli to find his basic narrative themes: "The conflicts in the movie were real," he said, "and became the core and genesis of the relationships [people saw on-screen]."

It took eight or ten days to meet everybody and to gather his ideas. For the rest of August, when he wasn't going to hear the bands rehearse, he was camped out in his room. "I was writing longhand," he says. "I would write from seven to seven, with a ruler and pencil, on paper. Then a secretary would come in and take those pages and type everything up from that day in script form."

With an actual director in their midst—even one who was just out of film school and had never made a feature before—the musicians could feel the scope of the project changing. "For the longest time," says Coleman, "we would talk about it like, 'We're gonna make the best cult movie, it's gonna be cool, we're just gonna put it out there and see who responds to it.' Then Al Magnoli came and actually kind of connected with

Prince, and Al was the one who was like, 'If we're gonna make a movie, why don't we make a hit movie? It seems like we've got all the parts here. Let's not just make some artsy movie, just for fun. What do we have to lose?' "

"As soon as he had the serious big guns paying attention—when Al Magnoli came on, you started seeing more of Bob Cavallo and Joe Ruffalo, not just Steve Fargnoli—when those guys started making their presence known, I was like, 'They're gonna go deep with this,' " says Wendy Melvoin.

Prince had already been talking to his friends, associates, and protégés about the roles he envisioned for them in the movie. His initial idea of making a true ensemble piece, though, was shifting as he and Magnoli refined the script, which, it was becoming clear, was ultimately going to be a vehicle for Prince first and foremost. Whatever had previously been promised or implied was now leading to some resentment from the crew.

"I think he genuinely wanted to include everybody," says Jones, "but I also think that the business side, with the managers, started to come in and influence him and say, 'Well, what more can you do with the Time?' I don't think they were persuading him, but he can't manage everybody, and *that's* what created the problems. They could've kept it a little bit more realistic for him, and not had Prince come off like he was being really selfish and stingy. I think he really wanted everybody in this film. He was really excited. And then the jealousy started. Jesse [Johnson] would be like, 'Who does he think he is?' It's just normal.

"The script was still being developed, with characters and

new people coming in—how he created Wendy on celluloid had a lot to do with those new relationships with new people. He already knew how he wanted to create this thing between himself and Morris, which did exist, but maybe that rivalry existed more [in the film]."

"Al Magnoli was pushing for even more input from the band," says Fink. "He wanted more dialogue for the group, which had been written into the original script, but later never came to fruition because Prince wanted to keep the focus more on him. You had the whole side story with Lisa and Wendy, but the rest of the group was sort of peripheral, just guys hanging out, playing, with a few lines."

A few days after Magnoli arrived, he had a chance to see the Revolution in action when the new lineup was debuted at the First Avenue benefit. Though Prince had been working the band so hard that it was meant to feel like just another day's work, it was still clear that this was an important show. "There was a bit of excitement, more than usual, in the backstage area," says Coleman.

"I remember the preparation for that show, the clothes and the style, to every T," says Jones. "This was the big night, definitely. And it was special. They really worked very, very hard."

She also maintains that it was immediately evident the kind of impact that Melvoin's presence would have on the group, that Prince displayed a new kind of energy that would be critical to the film. "You could see that it just worked," she says. "His behavior onstage lightened up a lot more—the nuances, the eye contact, the interaction between those two specifically. There was something a little more human and charming and cute, because Wendy used to dote on him all the time and tell him how cute he was, and maybe it was because there was finally a girl around who didn't want to, like, shag him. Somebody saying wonderful, feminine, nurturing things, but there's no payoff like, 'What can I get from this sexually?' I think it was a nice little bit of a break for him. It was like sanctuary to be onstage, for a change."

Susannah Melvoin came to Minneapolis to watch her twin sister's debut with the band. "They had rehearsed for such a long time that it was kind of second nature," she says. "There was almost no fear; they just had it down. It was a whole group of people who had studied to be in this very powerful band for this very powerful guy playing very powerful music. And it felt like a piece of the puzzle he was looking for, like matter was collecting and turning into a star or a planet.

"It went off without a hitch—and then afterward, like always, everyone just went back and watched the video of the show to see what they needed to fix or modify for the film. The audience went nuts, but then it was right back to work."

Wendy and Lisa recall that Susannah's visit for the First Avenue show marked the point at which Prince's romantic interest in her became evident. Their relationship would last on and off for years; by the time *Purple Rain* was finished, he had cast her as the lead vocalist in the band the Family, whose 1985 album is best remembered for including the original "Nothing Compares 2 U," which Sinéad O'Connor would make a global smash in 1990.

"We were all in love with each other anyway," says Coleman, "and then Prince met Wendy and he was like, 'Well, I can't have her because you have her, and I can't compete with that.' Then Susannah showed up and—twins! He thought, 'She's like her, only available.' "

Meanwhile, Alan Leeds was grinding away, hiring technical staff to oversee all of the rehearsing, recording, and logistics that would be required throughout the summer and fall. One of his finds was a young studio engineer named Susan Rogers, who had been working at Westlake Audio in Hollywood, where Prince bought a new console and various other equipment. She initially came to Minneapolis to help set up the gear and "sort of audition" for a job, and was hired full-time in August.

Rogers replaced the console and did some repairs on the tape machine and some other pieces of Prince's home studio. "He hired me as a maintenance technician, so I wasn't doing any recording—in fact, I didn't expect to do any at all," she says. "[That work] took me a week or so, and I could hear him upstairs playing 'Purple Rain,' playing 'Computer Blue' on the piano. Vanity 6 were there rehearsing, and occasionally some other members of the band would come over and they'd be talking and preparing upstairs. I finally got the studio up and running, and the first tape I put up was 'Darling Nikki.' I never forgot it, I never forgot that experience. I'd never heard anything like it."

When Prince wasn't working, he was listening to music. "A lot of times he would put records on in his bedroom, and sometimes he would just leave the house and put the turntable on repeat," says Rogers. "I don't know if that was to annoy me or if I'm overthinking things, but I didn't dare go in there and shut it off, so I had to be hearing that thing for hours. He played Culture Club a lot, stuff that was hip at that time." ("He was listening to a lot of different music, a lot of English influence," Jones confirms. "We'd go to sleep listening to Roxy Music or Gary Numan.")

More songs were added to the stockpile for the album over the summer. Prince wrote an aching, piano-based ballad called "The Beautiful Ones," inspired by his feelings for Susannah Melvoin. He had been courting her like a suitor in a Hollywood romance, and would send flowers to her door every day for a year. "I can't say that the song was exactly our story, but he wrote it during that time," says Susannah. "He wasn't always specifically writing about what he was going through, because he also had to be consistent with the *Purple Rain* story line, but he was drawing from things that had happened in his life.

"Our relationship was definitely very intense. I remember he called me in the middle of the night, and he picked me up and we were in the car and had this strange two-hour period where he just stopped talking. I kept asking, 'Are you okay?' He wouldn't say a word. We got to the hotel; he still wasn't speaking. I was getting really upset. This was really early—I wasn't aware that if you stood up for yourself and said anything he didn't like, you would hear it from him. And I thought our relationship was different from that, anyway. So I said, 'This is not right—call me when you know how to talk.' I got into a cab and went home. He called me about an hour later, and I said, 'That's not cool, whatever you were doing.' So we were very attached, and he spoke a lot through music. He would come and play me something, and I knew perfectly well it was about me."

The other new addition—which was debuted at the First Avenue show, though that recording was not ultimately used for the album—was a hard-charging, tough but melodic rocker called "Let's Go Crazy." The song was a declaration of intent for the new band and the new era, spotlighting the precision and intensity of the musicians while adding a strong pop sensibility—and an unforgettable spoken introduction, with the invocation "Dearly beloved, we are gathered here today to get through this thing called life," a perfect way to kick off a concert, or a movie. (He also closed the song with a full fifty-five seconds of high-speed guitar shredding, a squall which, in addition to cementing his badass reputation to rock fans, would be sampled to great effect on Public Enemy's cataclysmic 1990 single "Welcome to the Terrordome.")

"When [Prince] wrote 'Let's Go Crazy,' he came and picked me up, and it must have been three in the morning," says Jones. "You just knew that it was a really different kind of a record for him to make. He'd never composed anything with that much energy in the hooks. He found his voice, with the talk-singing, and he knew it."

Though "Crazy" was written earlier in the summer, the recording came a few months later at the warehouse. "Prince wanted to be able to record his rehearsals," says Rogers, "so I was told to make a control room right in the middle of a warehouse—which breaks every rule in the book, but I hadn't been an engineer: I knew nothing about record making. Which in hindsight was why I was perfect for Prince, because he could have me make his records his way. So we brought in the console, threw a square of carpet down on the cement floor: 'All right, that's where the control room will be.' There was no isolation or anything. We recorded 'Let's Go Crazy' live at rehearsal, and then he sent the whole band home and it was just the two of us; we were going to do overdubs together. This was my first experience recording him one-on-one.

"I'm running the tape machine and he's playing the guitar solo; he's standing right in front of me and playing, and the idea is I'm going to record it and then stop and roll back and we're done. But he made a mistake, so I rolled back to the top of the solo, and he's playing along with the solo that he's just laid down, and I'm thinking to myself, 'He's playing and I didn't hit record. Have I made a mistake? Did I miss a signal?' So I took my index finger and pressed the record button and he reached out and hit the stop button and said, 'Who cued you?' I said, 'No one.' He was patient and understanding, and he just said, 'Roll back, watch me; I'll cue you where to punch in.' I said, 'Got it,' and I lived to record another day. That started a partnership where I would read his face, and that requires the engineer to literally play the solo along with him, watching for the slightest sign. As soon as his chin would make the barest move, I'd go, 'Okay, here it comes, on the next downbeat,' and we'd go. I got to where I knew him well enough that I could anticipate—'Yeah, that's the part that he's going to want to record.' You get a beautiful, symbiotic relationship between the engineer and the artist when you work that closely together that frequently, just every damn day."

The lyrics to "Let's Go Crazy" seemed a stark contrast to the party-up track, following the pattern of the end-of-the-world celebration in "1999." This time, he sang, "All excited, but we don't know why / Maybe it's 'cause we're all gonna die." In 1998, he would tell Chris Rock in an interview for VH1 that "Crazy" was about God and the devil. "I had to change those words up, but 'de-elevator' was Satan," he said. "I had to change those words up 'cause you couldn't say 'God' on the radio. 'Let's go crazy' was God to me—stay happy, stay focused, and you can beat the de-elevator."

Along with the sentiments already being expressed in "Purple Rain" and "I Would Die 4 U," the words to "Let's Go Crazy" demonstrated that the new album was going to have an even stronger sense of impending apocalypse and the striving for final salvation than Prince's earlier records. Some have traced this strain in his writing to the faith of his upbringing. Dez Dickerson thinks it was a personal crusade for Prince, a belief in his own mission on Earth. "We are messengers of some higher understanding in the guise of punk funk. . . . He had a sense of being called, if you will, of being a special messenger of some sort."

It is also significant that the specter of nuclear destruction—through both nuclear power plants and Ronald Reagan's arms race with the Soviet Union in the latter days of the Cold War (complete with the proposed "Star Wars" strategic defense initiative)—was an omnipresent theme in the early 1980s. The Emmy-winning 1983 made-for-TV movie *The Day After,* depicting the aftermath of a nuclear attack, was the highest-rated television film in history, and such popular, widely discussed books as Jonathan Schell's *The Fate of the Earth* and Robert Scheer's *With Enough Shovels* offered terrifying warnings of looming nuclear disaster. (One of my own senior-year projects in high school was a study of the futility of America's civil defense plans in light of the military realities of the time.)

Not that Prince made his own thoughts explicit, even to those closest to him. "He didn't really discuss lyrical content with the band," Lisa Coleman wrote in an e-mail. "Only if he wanted/needed help with something, but those songs would not usually be the 'message' songs. In general conversation, I think we talked about that stuff just as most people did. It was a pop topic for sure, and all the cool bands had mystery and hidden messages written all over them!

"Prince would *never* mess around with the devil. That's for sure. He can talk God all night and day, but don't give that ol' devil a single *second* of your attention! So, the safest, and the danger-est, would have to be God. The God angle! Everyone knows something about it, so the demographic is perfect!" Coleman then offered a list of popular explorations of apocalypse through the years, including Nostradamus, Orson Welles, disaster movie director Irwin Allen, and the film *The China Syndrome*. "So there you have a culture of disaster obsession. Hit films, books, psychic hotlines, and fortune-tellers.

Guilty pleasures. Ambulance chasers. It works for the politicians, so why not the Minneapolis boy puppy, the little pony boy with sad eyes?"

Wendy Melvoin notes that "at the time, he was still kneeling and praying to God, and he really believed in signs and certain things he was trying and then waking up going, 'I know this and that!' calling us in the middle of the night going, 'I've seen it! I know it—it's appeared!' He was so much more fearless about figuring it out. Now he's studied scripture, but when he was younger, he wasn't spouting scriptures and parables. It was just an abstract thing."

"He was writing songs that were not confused, but searching," says Coleman. "He wasn't limiting himself by his religion; he was allowing it to fuel his work." When Prince finally broke his silence about the *Purple Rain* songs, he tried to put these complex matters in clear and simple terms. "I believe in God," he told MTV in 1985. "There is only one God. And I believe in an afterworld. Hopefully we'll all see it. I have been accused of a lot of things contrary to this, and I just want people to know that I'm very sincere in my beliefs. I pray every night, and I don't ask for much. I just say 'thank you' all the time."

With these new songs in place, the album was taking a more concrete shape, even as the film it would support (or was it the other way around?) was still coming into focus. "He always regarded albums as having a kernel or a core," says Rogers. "For lesser artists, you might consider two or three songs as the heart of your record, and then everything else is really just filler. But for him, five or six songs could be the seeds, the core of the record and, from how much I heard him rehearse these things, he knew that 'Beautiful Ones,' 'Purple Rain,' 'Computer Blue,' those songs were representative of the record to him."

Al Magnoli continued to work on the *Purple Rain* script when he was back in Los Angeles finalizing *Reckless* during the first two weeks of September. He returned to Minneapolis to start hiring a crew on September 15, and spent the next six weeks in preproduction. He says that he was working under the impression that the project was going to be entirely self-financed, and therefore totally independent, which to him was worth the limitations of the budget.

He was told by Cavallo, however, that now studios were expressing interest in the movie and wondering why they weren't involved. "There was still zero awareness of Prince," Magnoli says, "but studios don't like ideas that they don't have their paws on." Cavallo summoned the director to LA for a series of meetings alongside him, Fargnoli, and Ruffalo, with the goal of raising $7 million, which would enable them to roll the movie out in a significant way.

"The first guy I went to was [David] Geffen," says Cavallo. "He decides not to do it; he wants more security. He says, 'I'll make it for six instead of seven, and we can't start now; we have to start after you do another tour.' I knew what he was saying, but knowing Prince, it would be 'Fuck him.' "

"Geffen's attitude," says Magnoli, "was 'Prince will never

be a major star; I'm in business with Michael Jackson, I'm not interested.' "

The next stop was Richard Pryor's company, Indigo Productions, where they met with Pryor's partner, football Hall of Famer and activist Jim Brown. "I pretty much had a deal," says Cavallo, "and he's saying, 'Look, I'll be executive producer and you run everything by me.' I said, 'Well, I've hired a cameraman—one of my best friends is a five-time Academy Award nominee, and he tells me the guy I'm getting is quiet, will not have an ego, and will help direct the picture.' I tell Jim Brown that, and he says, 'How many times have I told you that you have to run it by me?' So I go over to say to him, 'Listen, Jim . . .' I put my hand on his back, and I knew that was a mistake—someone had to jump in between us and block him from killing me. So that was that—fuck him; I was gone."

Magnoli remembers the dynamic differently. "Jim Brown took one look at us and said, 'What is this, the Italian mafia in front of me? I wouldn't make this movie with you clowns. I'm not making a movie with a black artist and no black people.' "

In Spike Lee's 2002 documentary *Jim Brown: All American,* Brown recalled that the issue was not with him but rather with his partner. "The movie *Purple Rain* was really the first venture that I wanted," he asserted, "and I said, 'Richard, this is it, man!' I said, 'Prince is just about to break out,' but Richard didn't know who Prince was, [and] somehow we passed [on] it." Shortly after, Brown left the company, and Indigo Productions fizzled out.

"Now I have nothing," says Cavallo. "[Hollywood super-agent] Mike Ovitz, somehow, eventually gets Warner Brothers to agree that they're going to do it. I gave Mike Earth, Wind and Fire and Prince when he started his [personal appearance] department; Freddy [DeMann, Madonna's manager] gave him Madonna; and that's how he opened his doors, with those three artists. So I told him in return for that, he has to help me get this movie."

Mo Ostin also helped open doors at Warner Bros., which was obviously under the same umbrella as the label. "I went to the movie people and told them how strongly we felt about Prince, how important he was to the company overall, and that we expected significant success in a sound track they would participate in," he says. "I did my best to convince them that this was a movie they should make. I don't know that they understood the music that much. They weren't sure what it was they had, but that happens a lot in the film business."

Keeping in mind Cavallo's warning about Magnoli's tendencies to embellish, here is the director's account of their initial meeting at Warner Bros.: "All of us on a couch, facing [Warners executive vice president] Mark Canton, and off to the side are the head of production and three D-girls, development girls, all dressed in black like some kind of judge's gallery. Canton said, 'We have a couple of problems,' and he turned it over to the D-girls. The girl in the middle says, 'I hate this material; it's disgusting, it's anti-woman.' The managers were as close to a heart attack as you can imagine.

"I said, 'This film is going to be junk unless it's authentic, unless kids know that Hollywood has nothing to do with it.

I wrote the script based on the culture I'm in, what I'm seeing.' Then Canton said, 'There's another thing I wonder if you would consider. We're thinking Prince isn't enough of a star to hold this movie, and wonder if you would consider John Travolta to play this role?' "

According to Magnoli, the managers were apoplectic, while he felt vindicated, since this kind of interference was precisely why he didn't want to take studio money for this movie in the first place. He was headed back to the airport to return to Minneapolis when Cavallo called in to his office (this was, of course, in the days before cell phones) and got a message from Canton. When they spoke, Canton apologized and asked if the team would come back and pitch to Bob Daly and Terry Semel, who ran Warner Bros. Pictures at the time.

A week later, they reconvened at the Warner offices. Cavallo warned Magnoli that there was one scene, in which Prince's father kills himself, that the studio hoped he would change—they were finishing a film called *Star 80,* about the life and death of *Playboy* model Dorothy Stratten, and said that the audience reaction to the murder-suicide in that movie was very bad. Magnoli insisted that he wouldn't reconsider the scene.

"I launch into the pitch," he says. "I do my whole rant and see they're with me. I come right up to the suicide and I say, 'The bullet hits him—but it doesn't kill him. Prince has learned his lessons and resurrected himself.' Semel says, 'That was the best pitch we ever heard, and we're going to greenlight this movie right now.' " The deal that Warners proposed, though, allowed them to keep the studio's name off of *Purple Rain* until they saw the finished product and determined whether they wanted to be publicly involved.

The final decision as to whether the father would die had been debated since the first draft of the script, and would continue until days before shooting started. "I think once they resurrected the characters of the mother and father, they lost a little bit of the darkness that could have been portrayed," William Blinn, the original screenwriter, has said. (Cavallo has also said that "if it was up to Prince, a lot of people would have died.")

Now that the financing seemed to be in place and the script was nearing completion, the pieces were coming together. Against tremendous odds, production was ready to go full speed ahead. But then another crisis arose: the leading lady had quit.

Vanity, born Denise Matthews, began her career as a model, competing for the Miss Canada title and going on to do commercial work. Before meeting Prince, she had acted in several B movies, including *Terror Train* and *Tanya's Island*. Following the success of Vanity 6's "Nasty Girl," a number one hit on the dance charts, her aggressive sexuality was apparently leading to new offers, and to tension with the Prince team.

Magnoli first met Vanity upstairs at First Avenue during his early days interviewing the Minneapolis principals. "It was obvious there was a strain, that her agent was putting doubt in her," he says. "She's looking at the next door, but she's not sure she wants to go through." She told him that she had been offered the role of Mary Magdalene in Martin Scorsese's *The Last Temptation of Christ.* Magnoli told her that of course she should take it—who would turn down the chance to work with Scorsese rather than with a first-time director?—but added, "This isn't really about that, is it?"

Though it does seem that Vanity's discussions with Scorsese were real, they were also exploratory: the 1983 attempt to make *Last Temptation* proved too controversial for the studio, and it was put in turnaround in December. (When the movie finally picked up production several years later, with a different studio behind it, Barbara Hershey played the part of Mary Magdalene.) Most immediately, though, there was the reality of money; Vanity, with more film experience than the rest of the cast, wanted a better deal, which the producers would not agree to. "They wouldn't pay me enough money to go through with the crap I would have had to go through," she said, and she left not only the movie but also her spot at the front of Vanity 6.

Word went out that the movie was looking for a new female lead, in a hurry, and they received hundreds of responses. Reports have stated that as many as five hundred or seven hundred women auditioned; "I don't know if we saw five hundred," says Magnoli, "but we sure saw a bunch." There have also been rumors that Jennifer Beals was offered the part and that she turned it down to attend Yale, but the director has no memory of the *Flashdance* star ever coming up in conversation.

One New York–based actress who auditioned told *Rolling Stone* that she fled from the tryout because what was being asked of her was excessively explicit. "It was way too pornographic for me," she said. "I mean, they had stuff in the script I wouldn't even let my boyfriend do to me in my own bedroom." Magnoli remembers his mother reading that story and calling him, outraged. But he insists that there was nothing out of line in the process. "Auditions were very simple; nothing degrading," he says.

He notes that there was a scene in the draft script in which Prince catches up with Vanity's character under the bridge, after he has broken up Morris Day's attempt to seduce her; it would be a key moment in the final film, as he stops himself from hitting her, suddenly aware that he is repeating his father's destructive behavior. The scene was written utilizing more violence, verging on rape. "It was clear that this was just a note to self," Magnoli says. "There was never any discussion of actually shooting it that way. But I think this particular actress fixated on that scene."

Auditions were turning up no promising candidates, and shooting was coming closer. "We had no one, and then one day Apollonia walks in," Magnoli says. "She came from the gym, in baggy sweats, no makeup. Everybody else came in leather and spandex and eighteen-inch heels. She was the polar opposite to Vanity. Vanity was danger, overt sexuality, sin; Apollonia was sweetness and light. So I called Prince and told him we had someone. I sent her over, and about an hour and a half later, he calls me and says, 'I can work with her.' "

Patricia Kotero did have some acting experience; she had starred in the miniseries *The Mystic Warrior.* Less glamorous, she had also posed for the Elyria, Ohio–based Ridge Tool Company's Ridgid pinup calendar. "I was a starving actor and singer," she said. "I saw [the listing] in *Drama-Logue,* called my agent, and had an audition within seven days. Prince took me to First Avenue; I wore black spandex and a gold mesh thin top." The producers also had her remove her shoes to make sure that her height lined up with the leading man's. Elsewhere, she said, "I'd heard a little about Prince before I went to Minneapolis to audition for the movie role, but I didn't go there to judge anything. I'm not in awe of him, so we get along just fine."

After he signed off on giving her the part, Prince bestowed the name "Apollonia" on Kotero, taken from a minor character in *The Godfather*: "You're going to be one of those one-name girls," he told her. (Kotero has always claimed that Apollonia was her middle name; though her birth certificate just lists her as "Patricia Kotero," it is theoretically possible that it was a confirmation name or something added later.) One thing Kotero has always been insistent about is that she and Prince were never involved romantically—"We're the greatest friends in the world, and we never dated," she has said—for one thing, because she was married at the time. Her husband, Greg Patschull, was identified in *People* magazine as "an aspiring actor and martial artist . . . who runs a karate studio" ("She wanted me to stay in the background," he said), though media reports also linked her to Van Halen lead singer David Lee Roth.

"When Apollonia showed up, now *she* was the new person, and we're like, 'Hmm. Oh, really?' " says Jones. "She was sweet and cute, although we didn't get along straightaway—which was good; Prince actually wanted that. I think he had read all these stories in those books about tension [on movie sets], so he made sure he kept up the tension between us. Now she's like, 'I always loved you, Jill,' but I was such a little brat."

The truth is, most of the inner circle found the time that Prince put into the comic-book-sexy girl group, which would now cease to be called Vanity 6 and instead become Apollonia 6, a silly distraction. Working with players like the ones in the Time was one thing—even if Prince was writing their music, they had to be good enough to really sell it, and the results were musically powerful. But in some ways, it was even more demanding for him to bring the limited talents of the lingerie-clad singers up to something credible.

"The whole band found it annoying, but you had to bite your tongue and let it go," said Matt Fink. "If you voiced your opinion, it usually didn't matter to Prince—and believe me, I voiced my opinion more than once. He would just say, 'Well, somebody's got to be the boss, and I'm him; that's it.' "

"I realized he's not in the business just strictly for the music, no matter what he tells you," said Wendy Melvoin when asked about the Vanity/Apollonia side projects. "He's also in it to entertain."

FIVE

Reach Out 4 Something New

Purple Rain began filming on October 31, 1983. The script had been reconceived into what Magnoli described as an "emotional biography" of Prince. The director offered this summary of his vision for the story: "Prince is a powerful, magnetic force in the world of his peers who becomes humiliated, frightened, damaged when he sets foot in the home he shares with his parents . . . but by the end of the film, he has learned to let others into his world. He has learned to love."

The story concentrated on the Kid (played by Prince, the only central figure whose character name differed from his real name), a young man trying to claim a dominant place in the music scene centered around First Avenue while refusing to compromise his creative independence. At home, he is contending with his father, a frustrated musician who takes his aggression out violently on his wife; at one point, the Kid refers to his family situation as a "freak show." When a new girl

(Apollonia) arrives in town, looking to break into the scene, and takes notice of the Kid, it heightens his competition with Morris, leader of the more accessibly funky rival band, the Time.

Meantime, Wendy and Lisa, members of the Kid's band, the Revolution, are fed up with his refusal to listen to the music they are composing or to consider incorporating it into his set. Things come to a boil when Apollonia joins Morris's girl group, leading to the Kid's feeling of betrayal, which he expresses in some impassioned, tormented performances at the club. He returns to his home just in time to see his troubled father shoot himself. Amid the rage and confusion that follow, the Kid discovers a case full of his father's compositions and concludes that they really share more than he thought; he just needs to avoid the darkness that swallowed his father.

At that night's show, he debuts a new song, built from the music that Wendy and Lisa had given him, showing that he has learned to open himself up to the input of others and use his music for salvation rather than just releasing demons. With that, he wins over the First Avenue crowd, gains back Apollonia's heart, and reconciles with his father, who survived the suicide attempt after all.

For all of Prince's time studying European cinema and David Lynch, this narrative was no *Citizen Kane*—but fleshed out with a dozen songs from Prince, the Time, and Apollonia 6, and with a close focus on the unique visual style of the Minneapolis club scene (real or embellished), there was a chance that it could feel exciting on a screen. Magnoli's main concern was to capture the personalities and spirit of the world Prince was creating, more than to worry about an airtight plot.

The Minneapolis weather was still pleasant through October. Cavallo authorized the use of a helicopter for the first day, to shoot Prince cruising around the fall foliage on his motorcycle, with and without Apollonia on the back of the bike. "We spent the day shooting the shit out of the motorcycle," says Magnoli. "And the next day, there was eight feet of snow." Film editor Ken Robinson remembers that the ice on the streets would get so thick that holes had to be cut to make them passable.

Everyone involved in the *Purple Rain* production, when asked about the actual shooting experience, immediately begins talking about the weather. "It was, like, five hundred degrees below zero," says Coleman.

"We had to be at hair and makeup on the set at, like, six in the morning," adds Melvoin, "and it's the dead of frozen tundra winter. One of us had to go outside with our pj's on and turn the car on so it could warm up for an hour, because otherwise you couldn't get the ice off the windshield."

As the shoot went deeper into the fall and the early days of winter, the weather would clearly become a major factor—serious enough that it's easy to understand why it dominates everyone's memory thirty years later. The weather reports from the winter of 1983, however, indicate that things didn't actually get really bad until a few weeks after filming began: at its worst, in December, the temperature dropped to 29 degrees below zero, with up to twenty-one inches of snow on the ground. On November 1, though, when Magnoli claims there was "eight feet of snow," the *Old Farmer's Almanac* shows 54 degrees and a trace of precipitation.

Regardless, it was clearly a grueling shoot, and within a matter of days, the production team was being told that they were going too slowly. "In the first seven days of shooting, they were telling me we were already two weeks behind," says Magnoli. "The finance company, which is called a bond company, that the studio hired sent two guys to Minneapolis, very concerned with how we were shooting this movie. The bond guys wax eloquently about how to make movies and how we're behind schedule. They tell me a story about John Wayne directing his first motion picture, and how he was behind, so he tore ten pages out of the script and said, 'Now we're back on schedule!' "

"Lindsley Parsons is the guy who got me into the Motion Picture Academy," says Cavallo. "We became friends. He had eighty credits or something unbelievable. After one week of shooting, he flies out to Minneapolis and says, 'You're a month behind.' I still, to this day, don't understand his logic, but he was horrified. So I said, 'Okay, let's sit together and work on it.'

"He takes the script and folds over a page, and then he goes two pages over and says, 'Now you and I are gonna write a little connector, and we're gonna lose two pages here.' He goes through the whole script this way, and it all made sense to me. [Magnoli] wasn't a big enough guy to have a say—I'd threaten to throw him off a balcony or something."

"The shooting was mostly frantic," recalls Alan Leeds. "Prince was unaccustomed to not being in complete control of things, and he was in a situation where he didn't have the knowledge or the skill set to assume control over certain aspects of it, and you could see that frustrated him to no end. He had absolutely no patience for the time it took to set up lighting, to set up shots, even though he had done music videos—that process was simple enough and flexible enough that his impatience might sometimes compromise a shot, and everybody would go along with it. Now you're making a movie, where continuity is an issue, and you're not as flexible. And that drove him crazy.

"You also had drama with Magnoli, who didn't have the complete faith of the crew, because he was not an experienced director; he didn't have a lot of credentials. There were some people on the crew who were—for lack of a better way of putting it—journeymen, people who had been on a lot of film projects and knew their craft and realized that he didn't have the experience to know everything, that he was questioning himself a little too publicly sometimes. All you need is one underling who's frustrated, who thinks he should be a director, and all of a sudden he's stirring shit up."

Magnoli's authority presumably wasn't helped by Prince's ongoing script revision. "He took everything away from Magnoli; he was writing the script himself," says Susannah Melvoin. "He would be like, 'Nah, that's not what I had in mind. There are no rules here—this is my movie, so I can do it myself.' He would read something and say, 'It's not popping enough, it doesn't say what I'm saying,' and next thing he's sitting on the floor rewriting it. He'd give it to Steve [Fargnoli] to take to the office, and the next day it's changed. It was always his way or the highway, and you just facilitated it."

The biggest adjustment for everyone was marrying the cultures of music and film. Despite the recent rise of MTV, these communities were still wired for very different schedules and professional methods. "I was constantly pushing the difference between the music world and the film world," says Magnoli. "Things as simple as, we don't work past seven at night. I would tell Prince that he had to convert his whole team to that idea, transition their lives from night to day. And I saw the call to arms—they were excited, and they understood we were on film time. There were never any complaints; everyone showed up knowing their lines."

"I was always of the opinion that we never had any respect from the film people," says Leeds, whose job put him right at the flash point where the two sides connected. "That they felt we were just a bunch of lucky people—and by [the film people] I mean crew, I don't mean the artists; I don't mean Prince. They resented him because, basically, they didn't believe in the movie. These were hard-nosed ADs and camera ops, and it was just another gig, in the middle of a horrible winter. They're stuck in a Holiday Inn in Bumfuck, Minnesota, shooting some kid they haven't heard of, taking orders from a director who's never done anything, from a lighting director, LeRoy Bennett—who deserves ninety percent of the credit for why the performance scenes are so good—who wasn't a film guy, he was a rock 'n' roll guy.

"The wranglers all had to go to me, because Prince laid the rules that nobody talks to his people but me. So the ADs and so on couldn't talk to Morris or Apollonia—they all had to come through me, which also gave me an inflated sense of importance, which was bullshit. Of course it created animosity between me and the ADs, because they resented me being in the middle. Even though I'm trying to be a team player, they don't see it that way; they see me as interference. So there was all this undercurrent going on that a handful of us tried our best to keep away from Prince and from Cavallo and Fargnoli, because they had their hands full trying to find the money to keep us going. Prince had his hands full just being Prince, and we just felt that it was our job to try to keep all this off their plate."

Whatever else was happening, there was obviously one primary question remaining at the center of all the activity: Was Prince going to be able to act? Even if much of the script was written around him standing still and looking cool, *Purple Rain* was going to live or die on his performance. "In my mind I was thinking, 'Wow, what are these serious scenes going to be like with Prince acting?' Because I knew that he had never really had serious acting experience," says Fink. "He always came off to the media as being mysterious and quiet and shy, but with us in the band, we all yukked it up pretty hard; he was gregarious in that sense. But I was concerned—I know that a few times I said to Bobby, 'Do you really think he's got some acting ability here? Is he gonna pull it off?' "

Everyone involved in the production uses the same words to describe Prince during the filming process: *focused, driven, absorbed, confident*. "It felt as inexorable as the progress of a train," says Susan Rogers. "It just felt steady; a slow, steady progress. There was never any doubt in those sessions, not on the movie set, not in the recording studio, not when we were doing the album or when we were doing the incidental music, not when we were doing postproduction. He would've been a great general in the army; he has this extraordinary self-confidence, coupled with extraordinary self-discipline and tempered by a really clear self-critical eye. I think he knew himself and what he was capable of. And I think making that movie, on some level, he knew he was dealing his trump cards . . . and this was the window of opportunity where he could reveal this enigma, and that maybe that window wouldn't come around again—which, indeed, I don't think it ever did."

In addition to acting and continuing to tweak the script, Prince was (as always) constantly writing and recording music—throughout the fall, he was running sessions with the Time, Jill Jones, and Sheena Easton, among others. "He was the Nutty Professor," says Susannah Melvoin. "He would call you at four A.M. and say, 'I'm cutting hits, what are you doing?' 'I'm sleeping.' 'Wrong answer'—and he'd hang up. You knew to get to the studio. It sounds a little cultish, but you did it. And, of course, I loved the music. Nobody was doing anything like that, and it moved us to believe in it. We got to do great things."

Prince took the same approach to watching the film's dailies that he did to studying video of his concerts every night on tour. "Every time Prince saw himself on-screen, anything he saw that he felt was less than he wanted, he would never do it again," says editor Ken Robinson. "There was never anything that repeated itself as an issue. He would look at it, see it, and correct it for the next time. He learned as he went along, and you could see his performance improving by leaps and bounds, which is very unusual."

He was also spending as much time as possible at Magnoli's side, trying to soak up as much information about directing as he could. "He stood behind Magnoli all the time to learn," says Jill Jones. "He was always curious, wanted to know what was going on with the lights; he loved the DP. I think he looked up to Apollonia a lot because she had more experience than him on that front, and I don't think he tried to boss his way into things that he wasn't familiar with, because he's the kind of guy who only talks about the things he knows about."

For the part of the Kid's father, the team cast the most experienced actor on the set. Clarence Williams III was best known as supercool Linc on the youth-oriented cop show *The Mod Squad,* which ran from 1968 to 1973. Since then he had gone on to work steadily onstage and in film. Though it didn't assume the bulk of the screen time, the relationship between father and son really was the emotional core of *Purple Rain,* and it was a smart call to place someone in this role who would help elevate Prince's game.

"The minute Clarence Williams came onto the set," says Magnoli, "it created a kind of professionalism that the nonactors, the musicians, hadn't seen before. Immediately, people were on set to watch Clarence work."

"When Prince saw Clarence Williams's work, he was just gobsmacked completely," says Jones. "He said, 'He's amazing. He's so powerful.' He was just excited. And when he would see those performances, I think it made him think how great this project was going; it only affirmed his dream."

The scene in which the Kid walks in on his father playing the piano—a melody actually written by John L. Nelson, which would be incorporated into the middle section of "Computer Blue"—and father tells son to never get married is often singled out as a dramatic highlight in the film. Magnoli says that the exchange came directly from Prince's own life, a conversation he had with his dad that had always stayed with him.

Probably the most challenging work for Prince the actor was the scene in which he returned to the house as his father shot himself, and then reacting after the ambulance takes his parents away—trashing the basement, seeing visions of his own death, and finally realizing that the papers he is ripping apart are a lifetime's worth of his father's musical compositions (this after his father said that he didn't need to write his own music down and "that's the big difference between you and me").

"When he did the scene where he tears up the basement at

home," says Rogers, "I had to come to the movie set to deliver some tapes. Just as I stepped in the door, the red light came on because they were going to shoot that scene, so I ducked in behind the façade so I'd be out of sight. He shot that scene, and as soon as it was done, he came around the corner and I was standing right there; I didn't realize that this partition that I had ducked behind was actually the back wall of that basement. He came around and looked at me, and I saw his face and I was smart enough to not say a word, just share that look with him. I would guess that what Prince was experiencing was a greater vulnerability than what he ever had to show on a music album. As a person who is by nature private, this may have been a moment of real cognitive dissonance, which can be revealing. Maybe what I saw and understood was how odd it is to turn a life into art, but how a true artist is compelled to do so."

"For the big scene where he destroys his room, Prince really did show up emotionally to that moment," says Wendy Melvoin. "I think it freaked him out to witness Clarence and this other character fighting the way they did, screaming, and him having to not be the big rock star who would just avoid those situations at all costs. But as an actor you make yourself vulnerable, and I think it really flipped him out, because that guy would never have shed or shown a tear, and the way that moment is shot for him is beautiful; it's a really great, true, vulnerable moment for him."

Magnoli claims that the only time he saw Prince get rattled during the entire shoot was the shot in which he sees a shadow of himself hanging from the basement rafter. "That was just freaky to him; he took that to heart," he says. "It was a turgid, charged moment for that basement scene—very concentrated, a lot of violence and soul-searching, all really intense." There was actually an additional monologue for the Kid's mother (Olga Karlatos) during this section of the movie, but it wasn't used; the emotion they were seeking had already been found.

On the opposite end of the spectrum, there were the sex scenes. Touré writes that "there's a pornish aesthetic to the entire film. It's like a porno set in the world of a nightclub. . . . Few films give us two black men of such outsized sexuality and vanity, always looking like they're about to get someone in bed." And it's true that sex infuses *Purple Rain* throughout—from Apollonia's outfits to Morris Day's leer, the suggestion of sex, the mood, is more memorable than the few examples of more explicit action.

The coy dialogue and gauzy camerawork in the scene of the Kid and Apollonia making love in his basement bedroom is more cringe-inducing than genuinely erotic, though to teens in 1984, it certainly offered the requisite titillation. The scene was shot three different ways, for three possible MPAA ratings; they went with the most daring, the "R-rated version."

"Some of the kissing scenes were like, 'That's not real.' You don't kiss people like this—it's ridiculous," says Melvoin. "You could tell there was so much showbiz to the kissing sequence and the lovemaking sequence, it was like Harlequin romances or *Red Shoe Diaries*."

To be completely fair to Kotero, though, it's sometimes clear in the final film how much of a scramble the production really was: Look closely at the scene in which Jerome Benton and Morris Day are walking around the block, discussing the problems with the girls' group; when Day mentions "that Apollonia babe we saw last night," it's apparent that the phrase was clumsily overdubbed, and that his moving lips don't match the words coming out.

If you ask someone to name a scene in *Purple Rain* other than the musical numbers, chances are good that they'll say "the Lake Minnetonka scene." The Kid drives Apollonia out to the countryside on his motorcycle, stopping by the side of a lake. She asks if he's going to help her with her career, and he says no, because she hasn't passed the initiation. The first step, he says, is to "purify yourself in the waters of Lake Minnetonka." As a demonstration of her bravery and spunk, Apollonia strips down to her panties and leaps into the water—only to have him tell her, after she wades back to the shore, "That ain't Lake Minnetonka," and pull away on his bike while she stands there dripping and near-naked. When he swings back around to pick her up, she giggles and rewards his prank with a peck on the cheek.

"It started to snow that night," Kotero later recalled, "so when we did the scene, we had Al Jones, our stunt man, wearing a scuba suit. It was a sheet of ice that I ran into. One of our crew guys, an old man, said, 'I'm going to bring you some Courvoisier tomorrow!' I had a little bit to drink, and it gave me a little warmth."

Trouper that she was, she plunged into the water three times for the shoot. In a 2014 interview with the Minneapolis public radio station the Current, she claimed that after a fourth jump, things got more dramatic. "They put me in a little tent," she said, "and they said, 'Okay, that's it, cut, we're wrapped . . . [A] nurse was in there, and she started to check my temperature. All I remember is that everything started to fade to black, and she said, 'She's going into hypothermia—we have to call the ambulance.' And I just thought to myself, Oh no, God, I don't want to die now! I want to finish this movie. And I could hear, just in the distance, her voice—she was panicking, and I just started to fade out.

"And I thought, Okay, I don't know what's going on here. I'm a fighter, I'm strong, I can do this. And then Prince came in, because I remember feeling his warmth; he held me, and he says, 'Please don't die. Please don't die, Apollonia.' And his voice kind of cracked . . . And I just remember, once I was able to talk, I just said, 'No, I'm not going anywhere! I have to shoot more, we've got to get more in the can, man! I'm not going anywhere, we've got to shoot some more!' And he kind of chuckled. . . . He saved me, with his warmth and his love and compassion."

When it came time to shoot the dialogue, the decision was made not to have Kotero undress in the Minnesota wild a second time. The rest of the scene was shot, mostly in close-up, by the side of a lake in Los Angeles, and what we see in the movie is a cross-cut, with Prince speaking in Minnesota and Kotero answering from LA (complete with some inconsistencies in her makeup and hair, which goes from dry to wet and back in various shots).

The cavalier treatment of Apollonia in that scene was one of the examples that many would point to as part of *Purple Rain*'s atmosphere of casual misogyny, along with the depiction of the Kid's mother as a victim of abuse and, of course, the lingerie-based female wardrobe. The most obvious representation of this issue, and the most difficult scene to watch today, comes when an angry woman pops up on the sidewalk, hollering at Morris about standing her up for a date. Morris and Jerome exchange a glance, and the sidekick grabs the woman and slam dunks her into a Dumpster. (When the movie was screened for Questlove's NYU class in 2014, gasps and cries of "Oh my God!" were audible during this sequence.)

Magnoli, who says that the studio challenged him repeatedly on this scene, defends the script based on his interviews with all of the cast members. "I really did hear them say that they threw a girl in a garbage bin once," he says. "If you're going to make a film about a culture, you have to honor that culture and show what it is. For me to add any kind of enlightenment to the facts would have been absurd." As to more general criticisms about the movie's gender politics, he says, "I don't believe the women are weak at all—Wendy and Lisa are empowered, Apollonia learns how to fight back. They're tough girls."

"I don't have too much of a problem with the representation of the women," says Jill Jones. "I think they're just caricatures—I really think that Jean Harlow played a big part for the Apollonia character after Vanity left. She became lighter and more humorous and not so slithery, snaky, vampy, and I could see that from the old movies that he watched. When Prince and Al were writing, they were just looking at the lay of the land, what everyone was going through. Some of the jokes are totally male-chauvinistic jokes that the guys had. But I didn't feel that much sexual objectification. It was kind of nice to see a young girl a little bit tougher than the *Flashdance* girl, a little more independent. The mother getting hit? It existed—and if I think about it, they weren't doing many films about domestic violence back then.

"I do think Prince has a Madonna-whore complex," she continues. "For most guys in that vein, in that era, it's kind of what they are: he's got good girls and he's got bad girls. I was a good girl—good, crying, weak. There was no filter. So the girl in the garbage can, those were just inside jokes—they thought it would be funny, Chaplinesque or something, in really bad taste. It was just dumb."

Lisa Coleman offers a similar, tempered response. "It's immaturity," she says. "This was a film written by a boy, and they were bully boys. They had, like, a bad sense of humor, laughing at people falling down on the street, that kind of stuff. So throwing the girl in the trash can, that's really funny to them. I just thought that was immature and stupid. I wasn't insulted by it as a feminist, because I didn't really relate to that culturally, anyway. It was just dumb, it was ignorant. If anything, Prince hired women all the time and worked, obviously, really closely with women."

Wendy Melvoin, though, believes that the women in *Purple Rain* are indicative of a more troubling part of Prince's personality. "He's mean when it comes to what he is in a relationship to a woman," she says. "He may seem like he glorifies and exalts them and puts them on a pedestal, but it couldn't be further from the truth. He is so debilitated by the idea of true intimacy that he needs to be in complete control. And it has been consistent with every female long-term relationship he's ever had."

Prince himself waved off the issue in 1985 when MTV asked him about accusations that the movie was misogynist. "I didn't write *Purple Rain,*" he said, conveniently handing over responsibility for words he assembled and approved. "Someone else did. And it was a story, a fictional story, and should be perceived that way. Violence is something that happens in everyday life, and we were only telling a story. I wish it was looked at that way, because I don't think anything we did was unnecessary. Sometimes, for the sake of humor, we may've gone overboard. And if that was the case, then I'm sorry, but it was not the intention."

If the female figures in the scene were meant to be seen as (relatively) fictional, the more complicated relationship depicted on-screen was between Prince and his band. The central narrative hinge is the Kid's unwillingness to truly be part of a creative group, to be open to input from the others. Only when he allows himself to listen to Wendy and Lisa's music with a generous mind can he experience the love that culminates in the performance of "Purple Rain," which he introduces as "a song the girls in the band wrote."

Though publicly Wendy and Lisa were always adamant that *Purple Rain* was not meant to be an accurate portrayal of the band's inner workings, Prince's history shows that he has been more and less eager to collaborate with the others at different times. "He didn't really like it if I presented a finished song to him," says Fink. "Any time that he gleaned an idea off of me was during jam sessions. He didn't want to hear everything with lyrics done and melody written and produced in the studio; he preferred spontaneity during rehearsal, because he had his own vision of lyric and melody." Though the band members all seem to look back at rehearsal during this era as a joyous time, there's no way that working with such an ambitious, brilliant, and independent leader couldn't have been difficult, and Magnoli did a good job of tapping into those tensions and amplifying them for dramatic effect.

"The scene where Lisa and I are in the dressing room alone, and he walks in and says something to us and we're all fucking quiet and weird with him?" says Wendy Melvoin. "I remember there being a bit of truth in that."

"That part was all real, none of that was made up," says Susannah Melvoin. "He could only do what he knew. He knew there was tension and how talented Wendy and Lisa were, how highly evolved they were as people, and that demanded that he be more evolved, too. In the movie, when Wendy stops and says, 'This is bullshit'—in that moment, it becomes a film, an internal dialogue that you gather is highly charged. It even takes Prince off-guard in that scene. Everyone in the world who sees it knows that was real."

Despite their crash course in acting, the band members were also nervous about how they were doing. Though in the end, only Wendy Melvoin's role would be really substantial (and Mark Brown would be the only one without a single line of dialogue), they were all trying something new, very visibly and with little safety net.

"The band always stayed pretty close and always checked in with each other—like, 'Are you okay? How is this working for you?' " says Coleman. "There was a camaraderie for sure, and because we felt a little out of our element—a *lot* out of our element, I guess—we were always like, 'Is this horrible?' 'Do I look ridiculous?' We shored each other up."

For the members of the Revolution, Prince's skull-cracking band rehearsals had helped prepare them for the discipline and tedium of a movie set. "It was job, job, job," says Susannah Melvoin, "as if everybody had nine thousand films behind them. A lot of sitting in trailers waiting, nothing glamorous. Just putting one foot in front of the other, day-to-day. We all knew it was a huge moment in music history, but we didn't feel entitled. We just felt honored to be part of it."

The band wasn't around for most of the critical dramatic moments in the shoot, but if they couldn't really see the whole thing coming together, they were still getting a sense of which elements were working. "I was never privy to the major, important scenes in the film, other than the dressing room scene where we were all in there and he's doing his shtick," says Fink. "I thought he knocked that out of the park, so I'm thinking to myself, 'Okay, he's probably going to pull this off.'

"In some of the acting, I could see a certain amount of inexperience," he continues, "but it still worked great and it was authentic because they were being themselves. There's one scene toward the end where Morris says something mean, something about, 'How's the family?' and then they show him reacting to that, regretting it and feeling sad. He did a great job of emoting that on-camera."

One thing that was evident was that Morris Day and Jerome Benton, separately and together, really were natural screen comedians. Certainly, their parts were written very broadly, verging on stereotype at times, but their ease and interplay injected a loose humor that pulls *Purple Rain* back from the edge of pretentiousness. Their banter and timing was so effortless, in fact, that the scene in which they try to set a password for Apollonia's arrival at First Avenue—a direct rip-off of Abbott and Costello's immortal "Who's on first?" bit—was shot live, in one master take, on the last day of filming. Ken Robinson claims that part of the reason the Morris and Jerome subplot was condensed was because their chemistry was distracting from the focus on Prince.

Off-camera, though, Day was feeling angry and creating problems. Lingering frustration over leadership of the Time was apparently being exacerbated by drug use. "The politics of the Time, those issues of control and whose band it was, never entered the filmmaking discussion," says Magnoli. "But one day we were watching dailies, and Prince said, 'I think Morris might be using something.'" Day showed up late to the set, and reportedly he and Prince came to blows. ("I had to break it up," claimed Time drummer Jellybean Johnson.) In one scene, Benton comes to the Kid's dressing room and tosses him tickets to that night's Apollonia 6 performance; the scene was supposed to be Day's, but no one could find him that morning.

"Morris was a real pain in the ass," says Leeds. "He was going through a lot of issues and was very difficult—chronically late to the set, uncooperative, and it was a significant enough role that it wasn't a minor irritation; it was an annoyance. There were days when they had to frantically change the shoot schedule because he didn't show up. And it was like, 'Okay, we got how many hours left in the day? What can we shoot that we have on hand to shoot?' That's complicated, it's not like making a record, where you can just pull a guitar out and play a different song. Lighting, wardrobe—everything's different."

In 2012, Day would still express ambivalence about the movie. "I got paid forty grand for being in *Purple Rain*," he said. "I wrote all my own lines, so again, my creative input was overlooked, but you know, it was a great experience. It was an innocent effort, because we had no idea that it was going to go where it went, or take our careers."

Among the other actors, Magnoli acknowledged only the challenges posed by Apollonia: "She was a new actress, and we did what we did with her." Prince's stand-in, Byron Hechter, was actually fired from the production after he told a local weekly that Kotero "can't act to save her life." Ultimately, up to a third of her scenes would be reshot later, in Los Angeles, to try to improve her performance. (Still, she would later be singled out by the Golden Raspberry Award Foundation, which annually "honors" the worst movies of the year, with a "Razzie" nomination for Worst New Star.) Another rough spot was Billy Sparks, a Detroit promoter who had been cast as the manager of First Avenue. For his speech in which he explains to the Kid that with the creation of Apollonia 6, there are now one too many acts vying for stage time, he was sufficiently nervous that it was the one time the director had to clear the set to give an actor more space and privacy. Representing his hometown with a Tigers baseball cap in the final scene, Sparks added some urban credibility to the cast, though his work on-screen feels stiff and is among the movie's least convincing performances.

There were a number of scenes that either appeared in the shooting script but never actually got filmed or which were shot but ultimately cut from *Purple Rain*. Jill Jones's character, a waitress at First Avenue, was initially much more important; she had a scene with Prince at the piano, he gave her a puppy and she had a song of her own, "Wednesday," which made it as far as the first test pressings of the sound track. (The only evidence that survived was the shot of her in the band dressing room prior to the climactic "Purple Rain" performance, where she is seen clutching the puppy.) Magnoli mentions a scene with Morris, Jerome, and Apollonia running through a neighborhood in the dark, and another of the Time showing up at the Kid's studio and "roughing him up—putting him on the ground and stepping on his head."

Magnoli confirms the long-running rumor that there was another sex scene between Prince and Apollonia, shot in a barn and involving a shower of almost literal "purple rain." Though he's been cagey about this in the past and says that it was never included in any cut of the film, shots from this scene actually appear in the *Purple Rain* trailer and in the "When Doves Cry" music video. "That scene was shot in the first week," says Ken Robinson. "We looked at dailies, and she was playing it a little bigger than she was supposed to, and you could see the awkwardness, the uncomfortableness on his face. When we saw that, the scene was immediately gone."

Various subplots were tried and dropped, with the idea that no one could be sure beforehand which stories and which actors would deliver. "There was one scene that I was going to do that was supposed to be sort of a funny, almost Harpo Marx comedic moment," says Fink. "I'm waiting, I kept going up to the people and saying, 'Oh, are they gonna get that scene in today?' I'm waiting all day at First Avenue in hair and makeup, with nothing happening. I go up to Al Magnoli: 'Hey, Al, you think we're gonna do that fun scene that I'm in at some point?' I was being a little selfish, I will admit. My ego was a little bruised when that one ended up on the floor. It never even got shot. We experimented with it, we did try a little improv on it with Jill Jones, and then they just thought, 'Ah, this is kind of too irrelevant, let's just skip it.' So that was the end of that."

"I've always been a little perplexed with Prince with the things he's given me," says Jones. "Like, 'Wednesday' was about suicide, so I was a psycho girl. He loved that scene, and it was hard when he had to tell me they cut it, because I was really bitter. I don't think I had a project that was ready to go, so it wasn't really mandatory. But when I'm crying at the end of the movie, I remember being so bitchy and going, 'Now, what the hell am I standing out here crying for? I have no freaking idea.' The Time had some other stuff [cut], too, and that became a problem, having to tell your friends when we've all committed to this. There were expectations for everybody, because Prince talked everybody up so much about it. So when you don't have all of those things coming, it makes for a 'the hell with this' kind of feeling, like, 'You lied to me.' But that was the business part of it."

Jones notes that Prince's representations of his friends and associates proved accurate in ways that even they could not see at the time. "What's so weird about the film is that his impressions of us, that he embellished, all manifested in our relationships with him," she says. "Even if they weren't real at the beginning, by the time it ended, we were all those people. It's like he wrote what he wanted [us] to be, and then you became that."

Howard Bloom was summoned to Minneapolis to start assembling publicity material; once he got there, however, he was never actually allowed to observe any of the action. Instead, Prince had him sit with Kotero, Jones, and the other new members of the team who had future projects in the works. "I went out to spend a week on the set, and I didn't get to see the film; he just fed me these protégés, one after another," says Bloom. "But I wrote ninety pages on the film while I was there. I really didn't know what the nature of the film was going to be, but we all knew what he was up to—this was going to be a personal expression of a radically different kind from what's normally found in film."

In 1985, legendary Detroit DJ the Electrifying Mojo asked Prince about the difference between making a movie and making an album. "There is no difference," he said. "There have been people who have tried to tell me contrary to that, but . . . I strive for perfection, and sometimes I'm a little bullheaded in my ways. Hopefully people understand that there's just a lot on my mind, and I try to stay focused on one particular thing. And I try not to hurt nobody in the process."

Displaying the unified and singular vision that was such an asset for *Purple Rain* and would prove to be the undoing of his future film projects, he continued. "A movie is a little bit more complex, but to me it's just a larger version of an album. There are scenes and there are songs, and they all go together to make this painting. I'm the painter. Y'all is the paintees."

SIX

Don't Break Up the Connection

Standing onstage at First Avenue, it sure feels like a small room. It's a little hard to believe that this is where a myth was forged—though isn't that how it usually works? The venue's capacity is approximately 1,500, but because it's wide rather than deep, and because the balcony accounts for a good chunk of that number, it practically feels like you could stage dive and bounce off the back wall.

The stage itself is pretty big proportionally, but looking around from the lead singer's front-and-center spot and blocking out the Revolution setup, with two keyboards and drums taking up much of the footprint, it's almost impossible to imagine Prince executing the explosive choreography displayed in *Purple Rain*. Also, with multiple 1980s-sized cameras occupying much of the floor space, it's evident how claustrophobic the club must have felt for the movie's performance shoots.

Still: this is the spot! The center of the stage, where he

rolled on his back during the climax of "The Beautiful Ones" and turned somersaults and dropped into splits on "Baby I'm a Star." Right here, where he stood for both the public appearances that earned him his stripes and for the seven songs that are the reason *Purple Rain* will never die. It takes every bit of self-control not to throw dignity to the wind and intone "Dearly beloved . . ." from this vantage point.

You can no longer visit the original Cavern Club, where the Beatles honed their craft (the one in Liverpool today is actually down the street from the old club). CBGB, birthplace of New York City punk, was sold and now houses a John Varvatos clothing boutique. Manchester, England's Hacienda club, the Holy of Holies for UK dance music, couldn't make it to the twenty-first century. San Francisco's first Fillmore moved, while New York's Fillmore East closed outright. But First Avenue has never stopped going—in fact, presumably aided by the years of tourist traffic generated by *Purple Rain*, it has expanded over the years, adding a restaurant and an upstairs rental party space called the Record Room. The inside of the club has been renovated occasionally and the balconies extended, but otherwise things remain more or less as they were in 1983.

On this January afternoon in 2014, the club is setting up for another benefit show, this time for the Minneapolis public radio station the Current. Outside, it's an authentic Minnesota winter; earlier, the temperature hit a low of –17 degrees. The area around First Avenue has certainly transformed in three decades. The Target Center arena, home of the NBA's Minnesota

Timberwolves, opened in 1990 and now looms across the street. There's a Hard Rock Cafe down the block. The club's outside walls are covered with painted stars containing the names of acts that have played the room; a quick glance turns up such names as U2, Radiohead, and the Beastie Boys. A star on one of the inside balcony walls commemorates the first show in the former Greyhound station: Joe Cocker, in April 1970.

"First Avenue gave people a chance to be creative in a town that doesn't have many venues," Bobby Z has said, also pointing out that in the '80s, while Prince was the main attraction in the club's big room, the tiny second stage, known as 7th Street Entry, was ground zero for an alternative rock movement headed by the Replacements; simultaneously, there were "two major kinds of music forged in the same room."

So there was never any question as to where the performance scenes in *Purple Rain* would be filmed. First Avenue was not only comfortable and familiar turf, it also exemplified the musically adventurous, multicolored, mixed-gender scene in Minneapolis that Prince wanted to celebrate. (As Kotero put it on-screen, "It was multiracial; you had the Latin woman making out with the black guy, the Jewish guys, the lesbians—it was just a beautiful mix of cultures.") The filmmakers had decided that all of the music would be shot after the dramatic scenes were finished, so that the musicians had their characters, with their particular experiences and motivations, in mind for the performances.

As the time came to move operations to First Avenue, though, there were two big issues: first, once again, there was the weather. Maybe Magnoli was exaggerating the conditions of the first part of shooting, but by the first week of December, temperatures were down to the single digits, and there was over a foot of snow on the ground. "We put together a side team of Teamsters, and they were given equipment to melt the snow," says the director. "After the truck that provided our electricity froze overnight and had to be thawed out, the batteries of the trucks were removed each night. There were snowplows in caravan to drive ahead of us so that we could get to the set in the morning. People had to figure out how to enable us to do our jobs."

"When we were shooting at First Avenue," says Lisa Coleman, "there were trucks outside with these big cables that would have to go in and out the door, so the door is cracked open. They'd block off a little area with a sheet, and we're changing clothes and freezing, totally freezing, but then you'd go and shoot a scene, and it was hot and sweaty on the stage. Then you'd go back there and you're covered in ice. It was insane."

More problematic, though, was the actual shoot schedule, and the rapidly approaching deadline to finish the film. "In the production schedule, we had a month to do all of Prince's music, all the Time music, and the girls' music," says Cavallo. "But by then we were three weeks behind, and the studio could take the picture away from the director. They can do that—we'll be out, and they'll finish it. Meantime, Albert would love to shoot the license plate on the motorcycle all day." He remembers Magnoli spending hours on one shot of Prince coming down a fire escape, a setup inspired by something Brian De Palma did in *Scarface*.

Magnoli wanted as many takes of each song as he could get; Prince initially proposed that he would do one take per song. The compromise ultimately reached was three performances of each song. With four cameras set up in the club, each to be reset between every take, the director would have twelve angles to work with for each number.

"Each song needed its own visual interpretation," says Magnoli. "There was an enormous amount of smoke, and each time the whole thing needed to be restructured." Other than the final three songs—"Purple Rain," "I Would Die 4 U," and "Baby I'm a Star," which ran in the film as a sequential part of one "show"—each song also had its own costumes and lighting; it would have felt false if they all seemed to come from the same night's work. Magnoli's visual approach to the concert footage, masterfully executed by lighting director LeRoy Bennett and director of photography Donald E. Thorin, was heavily influenced by director Bob Fosse, especially his work on *Cabaret*. "He made live performance emotional, erotic, sensual," Magnoli said.

Not that it was easy for the band to muster the energy required for these scenes, which would obviously form the real core, and greatest appeal, of the film. "The performance stuff came toward the end of filming," says Fink. "Those were long days. You're on call from extremely early in the morning, getting into hair and makeup, and then you're just there. You're onstage when they're ready to go, and then it's, 'Take a break, we've got to change angles, lighting, blah blah blah.' To be in that situation where you've got all these people around you moving stuff, sets, making, doing, pounding, cameramen, how do you remain unself-conscious when you've got these people standing in front of you, watching you do the scene, and stay in character?"

But this was when Prince's dedication to rehearsal and preparation would pay off the most. Being able to match live shots from multiple takes meant that his lip-synching skills needed to be impeccable, even while dancing, soloing, and interacting with the band and the actors in the audience. And he nailed it, every time. "It was like he was a miracle man," says Cavallo. "When he lip-synched, it was always perfect. He hit the same spot every time."

"He was a stickler with all of that," says Wendy Melvoin. "'Don't fuck up your parts.' 'Don't fuck up your choreography'—to the nth degree. That was not fun. Because he really kind of liked to humiliate you in order for you to do better; it was one of his tactics. Instead of encouraging, like, 'You can do it! Come on, girl!' he'd be like, 'You look white and dorky, and what are you doing up here?' And you'd be shamed into doing it right. So there was a lot of pressure." (Prince also, consciously or unconsciously—though presumably consciously—reached back to the August benefit concert when he wandered over to Wendy during the "Purple Rain" solo and gave her a peck on the cheek, just as he had done in her first show.)

For the filming of the title song, Prince sent word that he wanted Apollonia in the audience, and she was summoned to

First Avenue, though she was officially off that day. "I had my pajamas on, I didn't have any makeup on," she said. "I brushed my teeth and put on a big coat, and I was on top, where the light system is, and the board. So if you look at the movie, a couple of times he glances up, his eyes go up, and he's singing to me."

In addition to the bands onstage, the First Avenue audience was also crucial to the feel of *Purple Rain*'s performance sequences. The club was dressed up with additional neon and lights, and with the cameras in place, the capacity was cut down by about one-third, to a crowd of nine hundred. The call for extras went out to the Minneapolis hipsterati, and the city's most cutting-edge fashion and makeup filled the room. Magnoli kept the color palette limited and dramatic, and made a great decision to keep the club activity present in the stage shots—you can see hands waving, cigarettes being lit, trays of drinks going by. Rather than feel like a staged shoot, these scenes retain the feel and excitement of watching a band play live in front of a real audience. Many of the shots look slightly up at the stage, from the vantage point of an audience member, rather than the more traditionally "perfect" angles above the performers' heads.

"The performance scenes in *Purple Rain* not only were singular for the movie's success, but were at that time the gold standard for how film handled rock 'n' roll," says Alan Leeds. "How many rock 'n' roll movies were ruined because they just couldn't pull off the immediacy and the urgency of a concert? It just didn't translate."

The bands came prepared, the venue looked right, and the filmmakers had bet on a good strategy. And as a result, a shoot that had been budgeted to take four weeks—capturing seven songs by Prince and the Revolution, two performances by the Time, and Dez Dickerson's new band's "Modernaire"—was done in less than ten days. "We went in three weeks behind," says Cavallo, "and came out of it on schedule."

There would still be seven days of shooting in Los Angeles—bringing the total number of shoot days to forty-two, and the final budget to $7.2 million—to fill in and clean up certain shots that the increasingly difficult Minneapolis weather wouldn't allow: the Kid driving his motorcycle through city traffic, Morris and Jerome walking down the sidewalk, and, of course, the rest of the "Lake Minnetonka" dialogue. (This did lead to some continuity issues, if you look closely: a palm tree, not native to Minneapolis, is visible at the end of the "When Doves Cry" montage.)

But in the larger sense, when the First Avenue scenes were completed right before Christmas, Prince had finished filming his first motion picture. Not that it slowed down his recording pace: on December 30, a few days after shooting ended, he cut two songs that his fans would later count among the most beloved of his non-album B-sides, "She's Always in My Hair" and "Erotic City." (The latter song had a purer dance-floor beat than anything that would end up on the album; it was inspired, he said, by attending a Parliament-Funkadelic concert in Los Angeles.)

"The last day we shot was a short day for us," says Wendy

Melvoin, "and then the two of us got on a plane to come back to LA. With the wind chill in Minneapolis, it was minus seventy-four, and when we got off the plane, it was seventy-four degrees here."

"I left Minneapolis on December twenty-fifth or twenty-sixth," says Magnoli, "and the plane lifted up, and it was the first time I had seen the sun since October thirty-first. We were working in this dark, dank world, and when the plane broke through the clouds, I just went, 'Wow, the sun hasn't shined in a long time.' "

In the February 2, 1984, issue of *Rolling Stone,* an item in the Random Notes section was headlined "Prince Wraps His First Film." The brief story reported that "director Al Magnolie [*sic*] is currently readying it for springtime release," and that "the film's plot revolves around a love triangle, with Prince and Morris Day of the Time vying for the affection of one Apollonia. . . . Some who've seen the dailies say that while Prince acquits himself well, Day and valet-sidekick Jerome Johnson [*sic*] yank the movie out from under the pint-sized potentate."

Perhaps not the most carefully fact-checked paragraph the magazine could have run, but it began the drumbeat that would get louder as the year progressed. To be fair, there were at least two other stories that *Rolling Stone* was tracking much more intensely than the plans for Prince's movie: Bruce Springsteen's long-delayed new album, and the constantly shifting plans for the Jacksons' tour, which would effectively be Michael Jackson's Thriller tour. All three events would reach fever pitch and compete for the hearts and minds of the pop audience by summer 1984.

Before everything had been fully assembled, it was time to screen a rough cut of *Purple Rain* for the Warner Bros. executives. "I was horrified," says Cavallo. "I knew that the movie wouldn't play without drastic editing to some of the bad, over-the-top bullshit, and some of the scenes, like the 'When Doves Cry' video and a bunch of the comedy stuff, weren't finished yet. It ran at, like, a hundred forty minutes. I'm just sliding down in my chair because of the embarrassing scenes that would never have been in the movie, scenes that they should never have seen.

"When it's over, Terry Semel stands up, and he's talking to Bob Daly and Mo Ostin, and he says, 'So, Mo, you wanna bring me another one of your fucking music guys to do a movie on?' Because he's gotten burned on *One Trick Pony,* he lost a lot of money on it. I walked over to Mike Ovitz, I go, 'Mike, I don't think they're gonna give us the money,' and he goes, loud enough that they can hear, 'If they're not gonna give you the money, if they don't want to do this, we'll take this over to Paramount and this is gonna be a smash. I see it.' The next day I get a call: we got the money."

Prince sat out all of these studio meetings; that's what his business team was there to handle. Besides, there was more music to make. Most urgently, there were still a few holes in the sound track that had to be filled. Deciding that they needed a lighthearted song to reinforce the budding romance between the Kid and Apollonia, Prince took back a tune that was originally intended for the Apollonia 6 album and recorded "Take Me with U" on January 24 as a duet for him and Kotero, to match the footage in which they're riding his motorcycle through the fall foliage.

Susan Rogers recalls the challenge of recording Apollonia's vocals. She warmed up with the Beatles' singsongy "When I'm Sixty-Four," and required the kind of patience and support that usually wasn't associated with Prince. "That took a bit of time, but she got it," she said. "He coaxed her into being more assertive. He has an incredible talent for recognizing strengths and weaknesses. He has marvelous natural leadership, is very good at knowing just how to push you to get the best out of you—and he knew when to stop, in most cases." In the end, the skeptical engineer was won over by Kotero's performance. "She had this campy quality to her voice that was perfect," Rogers says. "She sounded like an actress pretending to sing."

The breezy feel of "Take Me with U," with its playful asides ("You're sheer perfection." "Thank you!"), added a lighter mood that helped round out the *Purple Rain* album. Lisa Coleman did the string arrangement, and a new arrival, who had shared vocals on the "Erotic City" recording a few weeks earlier, handled the drums: Sheila E., the percussion-virtuoso daughter of Santana band member Pete Escovedo, who would become perhaps the most successful of all Prince's protégées.

"When I met Sheila for the first time, she came from the airport right to the warehouse where we were rehearsing," says Rogers. "She was wearing Converse All-Stars and jeans, and she had a football jersey on. That was the first and only time I ever saw her in tennis shoes and jeans." Sheila was given the full Prince makeover, glammed up to almost cartoonish proportions, reconceived as a sex goddess. "She was transformed—the hair, the makeup, the clothes, everything," Rogers says. "Just like with each band member—'Here's your identity, and your identity, and your identity.' "

The album's title song was finalized from the live First Avenue recording. The intro and guitar solo were shortened, the piano part was beefed up, the third verse (an awkward four lines in which he expresses his lack of interest in his lover's money) was cut. Additional vocal harmonies were added. A touch of echo tweaked Prince's voice in some spots, and understated yet dramatic strings gave "Purple Rain" an even more triumphant, anthemic feel.

But there was still one final piece missing, and though it came at the last minute, it would prove to be the most important addition of all.

Nearing the end of the editing phase, Magnoli decided to cut in a montage, a moment that would convey the Kid struggling with all the forces swirling around in his head. "I needed a song," says the director. "I told Prince that it was about his father, his mother, loss, redemption, salvation—all the themes we were dealing with in the film. The next morning, he called and said, 'Okay, I got two songs.' "

On March 1, after attending the Grammy awards ceremony in Los Angeles, Prince went into Sunset Sound studio and recorded one of these new compositions, a song that may have been inspired by his relationship with Vanity/Apollonia 6 member Susan Moonsie: "When Doves Cry." The lyrics sometimes seemed to touch on material from the movie ("Maybe I'm just like my father, too bold"), but more striking was the grinding, almost industrial sound, full of lust and frustration and unlike anything he, or anyone else, had ever done before. Rendering the track unique and challenging, Prince stripped the bass part out of the song, which made it subtly disorienting, unsettling.

"We cut ['Doves'], and when he was playing with it before he did the vocals, he took the bass out," recalled Peggy McCreary (nicknamed and credited as "Peggy Mac"), who engineered the sessions. "He said, 'There's nobody that's going to have the guts to do this.' And he was smiling from ear to ear. He felt this was the best, and he knew he had a hit song . . . so he decided to do something really daring."

"Prince was renting a big old white Cadillac that he was driving around LA," says Matt Fink. "He invited Bobby and me out to the studio and said, 'Hey, let's go for a drive; I want to play you this new song for the movie.' We get in the car and we're driving around and he pops the cassette in, and it's the song 'When Doves Cry'—we're hearing it for the first time. The song ends, and I say, 'There's no bass on that thing. It's just all kick drum—is it done?' And he goes, 'Yeah, it's done.' I go, 'But there's no bass on it, how come there's no bass on that thing?' And he goes, 'Because that's just how it is—that's how it's gonna be.' And I go, 'Really? You really like the fact that there's no bass on that?' I was questioning him on it, because I wasn't ready for this; it was, like, not in my worldview. He said, 'No, this one is gonna be just like you're hearing it.'

"I was skeptical, and I thought, 'Oh God, are people gonna get this? Does it sound too empty? What is the deal with this?' I couldn't get to it yet—I couldn't wrap my brain around it—but when I look back on it now, it's pure genius, because it was so different. It would have been one thing if the melody or the lyric wasn't working or it wasn't touching people the right way, but the reality is, it was the greatest hit off the album. I didn't believe in it at first, I didn't like it. I had difficulty being critical of him, and very rarely was I. In all the time I was in the band, that was the first time I questioned something he did creatively—the greatest song on the record, and I'm having an issue with it because there's no bass on it."

Though the mix may have been extreme, especially for a song destined to be a single, it was also an extension of an approach Prince had been toying with. In his 1989 autobiography, Miles Davis recalled an exchange between the two musicians, who worked together toward the end of the great trumpeter's life. "One day I asked Prince, 'Where's the bass line in that composition?' He said, 'Miles, I don't write one, and if you ever hear one, I'm gonna fire the bass player, because a bass line gets in the way.' "

"I heard the version of 'Doves Cry' with a bass line," Questlove has said. "It wouldn't have grabbed me. Without bass it had a desperate, cold feeling to it. It made you concentrate on his voice. The narration of the song is dealing with 'Why am I the way I am?' and it's important that you let the words paint the scenario, and with the bass line you could get lost. It was distracting. With the bass line, the song was cool. Without it, it was astounding."

Susannah Melvoin remembers the day that Prince delivered "When Doves Cry" to the full team. "Everybody had been sitting around the production warehouse for hours waiting for him," she says. "He came in wide-eyed, like he'd been up for four days straight. He pulled his limo into the warehouse and played it as loud as possible. He was in a state, he loved it so much—he was in a hurricane of excitement. And in that moment, everybody knew this was going to be history. He had wrapped up what the movie was about, and it set everything in motion. He found his grail, the apex that was going to release this thing. And that same day we all heard this song was the day they shot the video."

As he wrote more and more music, Prince bumped all the songs by other artists that had been in play for the sound track—songs by the Time, Dickerson, and Apollonia 6 all moved over to their own albums. Jones's "Wednesday" had made it as far as the album's first pressing, but was dropped when her scenes were cut. "The Beautiful Ones" had replaced "Electric Intercourse," and another Prince song titled "G-Spot" was also cut, later to appear on Jones's album.

Back in the days when vinyl LPs (and cassettes) were the means of music distribution, there was also the issue of how long an album could actually run, how much music a side could hold. Though Prince had extended "Let's Go Crazy" to allow Magnoli to work with it for the movie's opening scene, the full version (with a wild, dissonant piano solo) was saved for the 12″ single and a shorter edit was used on the album. "Father's Song," an instrumental with a writing credit for John L. Nelson, had been its own track at one point, but on March 23, Prince assembled a new configuration of the album with a short version of it woven into "Computer Blue," which would also be cut down for time, with the "hallway speech" finally gone for good.

The final version of the *Purple Rain* album was airtight—nine songs, just shy of forty-four minutes, all performed by Prince, with and without the Revolution. It had evolved from a true companion sound track to a perfectly balanced album that could stand alone, separate from the movie. There wasn't a wasted second in these grooves—the music offered variety and range, from the rocked-up blast of "Let's Go Crazy" to the yearning intensity of "The Beautiful Ones" (which, electronic musician Moby once pointed out, "goes from being all synthesized to a [live] band—it's almost four songs in one"), from the party jam "Baby I'm a Star" to the angry screams of "Darling Nikki." Prince was deliberately and consciously presenting himself as a badass guitar player who was the front man of a band, a construct that fit the worldview of rock fans. The sonics of something like "When Doves Cry" were entirely unprecedented, impossible to mistake for the work of any other artist, but the more extended, more experimental tracks that had been an element of most previous Prince records were left aside this time around.

A few more crucial decisions: Prince slightly altered the sequence of songs from the order in which they ran in the film, moving "Purple Rain" into the final slot on the album, the last thing that listeners would hear. If the song offered a dramatic climax in the film, setting up the final triumphant performances after he has won over the First Avenue audience, on the album it was left to echo as a final emotional peak. After "Darling Nikki" concluded the LP's first side, he added a brief, backward recitation; when the record was spun under the needle in the wrong direction, he could easily be heard saying "Hello, how are you? I'm fine, 'cause I know that the Lord is coming soon. Coming, coming soon." (Not since the days of the Beatles had fans spent so much time manually rotating a record in reverse; the message came as a particular surprise following the album's most sexually explicit track.)

"Sequencing for the record was a big deal," says Susan Rogers, "doing those segues and backward pieces and cutting all those in. That was a very important part of the process back when the album was the work of art that the consumer was purchasing, not singles. On those earlier records, you hear that unrestrained, unfiltered rawness on some of the tracks, whereas *Purple Rain* was very carefully arranged. It's a masterpiece."

While Prince was completing the album, Magnoli and his team were trying to finalize the edit of the film. Cavallo claims that he went into full, cliché producer mode and made his instructions very clear. "I said, 'Picture me as a big, heavy Jewish guy with a cigar,' " he says. " 'Here's how the movie should go: song, tits and ass, joke, story. Song, tits and ass, joke, story. If you have to skip a joke, you don't have enough, it's okay.' Or maybe I said, 'Song, story, tits and ass, joke'—whatever, you know. I wanted to be as vile as I could, because this wasn't a great work of art; it was all about Prince. And in some ways it was brilliant." Cavallo understood the film's best chance of success was to keep the focus fully on Prince and make him indisputably a star, rather than try to create a cult-style art piece that wouldn't have mass appeal.

Magnoli realized quickly that the key to the movie would be to make the performance scenes and the dramatic scenes work together, to make them all feel like part of the same project. "We were essentially making a backstage musical," he says. "It was important to find a way to truly integrate the performances so that the music would flow from the words, not just be a commercial break from the dialogue. We were able to mirror music and reality through cutting to audience reactions. That's when I started to really see the wallop in it.

"Prince would come in, and he was kind of overwhelmed by it, how three takes could be brought together in one. He would notice, 'My shirt is unbuttoned in this shot and then buttoned in the next,' or 'My spin there is not as strong as I did it in the third take.' Just a couple of things like that."

The director also says that there was a brief debate with Cavallo about the opening of the movie. "He said Prince didn't want to open with music. It's a common mistake in rock movies; musicians want to establish credibility by showing acting chops. But I said no, we have to constantly honor the fans. If we do that, as soon as the movie starts, we will also be accumulating crossover fans. If you don't know who Prince is, you will by the end of those seven minutes."

Yet another challenge arose when Magnoli discovered that the negative for the crucial scenes of the Kid and his parents fighting in the basement had been lost. For five shots, they had to use the work print, and this footage is visibly darker than the rest of the film. But the time had come to deliver a final edit.

"I got a call from [Cavallo]," says publicist Howard Bloom, "and he said 'I've been editing this thing for weeks, and I just cannot make it into a film. It isn't working, and we're showing it to Warners at eleven o'clock tomorrow morning and I want you to be there.' So I flew out in the morning, arrived at Warner Brothers, and went into the biggest screening room I had ever seen. I sat way in the back, ten rows behind any other human being, to see how I would respond emotionally, without being inhibited."

He says that his "conscious self" had no real idea what the movie was actually about, but that "the second self, the self below the floorboards" was knocked out by the visceral power of *Purple Rain*. When the screening ended, the execs and advisors all filed into a conference room.

"They started getting opinions, and they were funereal, timid, guarding their speech. But everything they were saying was, 'This film is dead,'" says Bloom. "When my turn came, I got up and gave the Moses-parting-the-Red-Sea speech. I said, 'This is one of the most important movies in the history of film, and if you fuck this movie over, you are committing a sin.' I gave them a history of movies like *The Wizard of Oz*, which had been done off-set and everybody was convinced it was going to be a failure.

"Then I got to the real point—up until 1964, if you were a singer, there were a bunch of people in Tin Pan Alley who wrote your songs; you had a manager who determined your image; you were an artificial creation. And then the Beatles came along and did something revolutionary. They took control of their own music. That seems normal now, but it was shocking back then. No artist in the history of the film business had ever done what the Beatles did with music, and that's what Prince has done. And I said, 'If you kill this film, you are desecrating a piece of entertainment history.' And the tone of the meeting changed. I think it was extremely important to Bob to hear this speech, because they were saying they were going to give it a chance and roll it out in six theaters in Arizona, but he then went out and got this thing to open in hundreds of theaters."

Magnoli remembers a meeting with the Warner Bros. business affairs and marketing people. "They said, 'Our analysis tells us that this movie will play for one weekend, and the audience will consist of fourteen-year-old black girls in the inner city.'" Cavallo claims that—without even challenging this premise, or making any assumptions about a crossover audience—by this point he knew it was going to work. "I told them that I thought we were gonna do $40 million. Bob and Terry were laughing at me. I said, 'I'm just gonna do the numbers: you put an ad saying "Warner Brothers presents Prince in his first motion picture, *Purple Rain*," in every city that has a black community, everybody has to go see that fucking movie. When was the last time there was 'some studio presents some black artist in his first motion picture'? I mean, it's a big fucking deal. Plus the fact, we're gonna have hits, and we're gonna do a radio campaign long before. We want to give the movie to the major station in each city, to throw a screening at midnight and all that shit.' So I added my numbers up and said, 'We got a good $40 million.' "

While the Prince team tried to keep clearing the marketing hurdles, the movie's technical challenges continued when it came time to do the final mix of the music. "The way Prince produces," Magnoli explains, "he has a bunch of tracks, never takes any notes—like I would build a montage, step by step. But to mix the movie, the mixers needed all of the tracks that made up every song to place them properly in the Dolby system. We put up one song, and Prince just sat there saying, 'How are you going to find the song in that?'

"It was a crucial moment, exciting but scary. After a day, we decided that we would leave the music alone, take the songs as they were, and bring in a music mixer to work side by side with the film mixer. We would take the music and harmonize—run the music on two or three tracks, add all the ingredients to those, offset out of sync to create a bigger sound. It created a wall-of-sound harmonic of the original track, so now we could add the crowd sounds, supporting and helping this idea that it happened in real time, in a real club. It wasn't perfect, it was a little ragged, but it sells the idea, making it sound even more live and present."

At least one positive note came from the studio screenings. "When the studio saw the final cut," says Magnoli, "they said, 'Are you running credits over "Baby I'm a Star?" Let that play out, and then run credits after that.' I didn't anticipate they would want more, but that's what they asked for. I said, 'That song is only three and a half minutes long, but Prince could add more music.' So they allowed me to shoot more to elongate the song properly. They gave me one more shoot in LA."

"We had to simulate First Avenue, and it's not quite working," says Rogers. "The cameras have to be in really close, we've got a few audience members there, but it was kind of nasty. They were shooting the fog onto the stage, but this stage was smaller than what the First Avenue stage would be, so the fog machines were closer to the dance floor, and they're leaving this oily residue in the place where people are dancing. Prince was slipping, and he said, 'We've got to fix this,' but the movie people were just standing around. So I ran out to the parking lot and went to a planter, and I grabbed up handfuls of dirt and I came running in and, without asking, scattered dirt all over the floor and got on my hands and knees and rubbed it around, and it absorbed the oil.

"Alan Leeds told me afterward that Prince was very happy with that, so I learned that that's what he wanted from us. He wanted us to think for ourselves. He wanted us to see his world through his eyes and do what needed to be done. Having some empathy with him went a long way. I think those of us who lasted, who stayed with him, had that mind-set."

SEVEN

Something That You'll Never Comprehend

Warner Bros. may have been convinced to release *Purple Rain*, but they still didn't really know what it was (and they still had not determined whether they were going to put their name on it or not). The next order of business was to see how a real audience responded. The studio set up a screening in Culver City, California, an area that could produce a multiracial crowd.

They showed the movie in a big theater, with a capacity of six hundred or so. The young audience went wild watching the film. Afterward, following the usual protocol, they filled out cards that offered their scores on different aspects of the movie. What came back were, according to Cavallo, the best numbers Warners could remember ever seeing. "The numbers were so high from that first screening that Terry Semel got really abusive with me," says the producer. "He said, 'You can't do that. What do you think this is, some fucking radio station—you go bring your fans and fuck up the numbers?

They're meaningless!' I said, 'We did nothing of the kind, I wouldn't even know how to do it . . .' Well, that's not *quite* true. 'Well, they've got to stop this. You've wasted our time.' But when I was in the audience with that group, they went insane, and I thought, 'This has to be a sample of something.' "

The studio decided they needed to do a second screening as a reality check, away from LA, and to not even let Cavallo know where it would be so that they could be sure he wasn't stacking the audience. "They said, 'You're gonna get on a plane, and we're not gonna tell you where we're gonna do the screening; we'll tell you when we're in the air.' So we go to a Denver suburb, and a guy comes running to the limousine that I'm in with Terry and Bob, and he says, 'I don't know what we're going to do—there's so many people that there's going to be a riot. We have to give them permission to do multiple shows.' I said, 'Oh, yeah, I did that. I got them packed in.' Anyway, those numbers were fantastic, too. Kids were fighting to get into the second showing, even though they had already seen it once."

There was one final screening, this time in San Diego. Yet again, the numbers came back huge. "There were a bunch of Warner suits in the lobby," says Magnoli. "They go, 'Okay, three times in a row, reviews are through the roof. Al, we were wrong. We're gonna go from opening this in two hundred theaters to as many as we can to open this movie properly, probably more like nine hundred.' "

Howard Bloom used the San Diego screening as his chance to start working the media on *Purple Rain*. "Cavallo called me and said, 'We're having a screening in San Diego, and the press is not supposed to know about this'—okay, so that means I'm going to get the press down there, because Warner still doesn't believe in its film. If I can sneak a couple of key people in, it gives them an ego stake in the film; they're in on something. We picked a few of the lead critics—Mikal Gilmore [*Los Angeles Herald Examiner*], David Ansen [*Newsweek*], Robert Hilburn [*Los Angeles Times*]—and let them know we would try to sneak them into the theater if they got down to San Diego at the right time of day. And they all became huge advocates for the movie later."

During the screening process, Magnoli also won his fight for the controversial Dumpster scene. He agreed to try removing it for the second showing and then putting it back in for the third. Maybe it was a sign of the times, but the bit got a strong enough laugh from the audience that Mark Canton agreed it should stay in the final cut.

As the time came to start setting up the schedule for *Purple Rain*'s release, there were tricky decisions to be made about coordinating all of the various parts. Mo Ostin wanted the album to come out well in advance of the movie so that it was at less risk if the film turned out to be a flop. This meant releasing a single months ahead of the movie reaching theaters. Which was, of course, not without risk of its own; if the single died or the album underperformed out of the gate or disappointed in any way, the buzz around the movie could be crushed. So there was, to put it mildly, a lot riding on the single that would give a first taste of the entire project.

According to Cavallo, while he and the team had decided

that "When Doves Cry" was the obvious first single, the urban department at Warner Bros. wanted to go with the less experimental "Let's Go Crazy." Their selection put doubts in his mind. "I said, 'Could I be wrong?' You never know, and sometimes Prince's stuff did sound a little weird. So I'm going out to dinner with Clive Calder [who would later become the richest man in the music business when he sold his Zomba/Jive label, home of Britney Spears and 'N Sync, to Sony for $2.7 billion in 2002]. I pick him up at a hotel and say, 'I'm gonna play you two songs. You tell me which one you think should go.' I play 'Let's Go Crazy' first, and he likes it, and I put the next one in. The intro goes into the first verse and the start of the chorus, and Clive goes, 'What is this, a joke?' And I go, 'You don't like it?' And he said, 'No, it's fantastic.' "

"When Doves Cry" was released on May 16. The end of my senior year of high school was approaching, and I stayed up late the night before, cassette recorder at the ready, glued to Cincinnati's R&B radio station, WBLZ, waiting for them to premiere Prince's new single at midnight. Finally it came on, and the moment was unforgettable. I'd seen Prince onstage and knew what he could do as a guitar player, but the explosive dissonance of the song's introduction was devastating.

What *was* this song? It was funky, but it sure played like a rock song. What was he talking about—"animals strike curious poses"? What? The sound was mechanical, on the verge of annoying, hypnotic. By the time it built to the keyboard coda, ascending up and up at high speed and then cutting short, I was knocked out. I couldn't stop listening, over and over and over.

I certainly wasn't alone. "When Doves Cry" reached number one on the pop charts in six weeks—Prince's first single to hit the top spot—and then stayed there for five more. It would become the bestselling single of 1984.

"It was very rare that a first single off an album was that ridiculous," says comedian and hardcore Prince fan Chris Rock. "Usually it was just a taste of the album, and the best single was the second or third one. On *Thriller*, the first single was 'The Girl Is Mine.' Back when there was a real strategy to singles—no one started like that.

"And the lyric was not corny at all. It makes all the sense in the world, and it makes no sense. You can't write a song like that now—music today has no metaphors, it's all literal. Now they would make you say 'when love dies' or something. 'What is this about *doves*?' "

(Sometime around the year 2000, while I was working as the editor in chief of *Spin* magazine, I was booked for the premiere episode of a VH1 show called *The List*. The premise was that four panelists would give their top three picks for a certain category, debate them, and then the audience would vote for the winner. On this day, Melissa Etheridge, French Stewart from the sitcom *Third Rock from the Sun*, actress Kathy Najimy, and I were to determine "The Best Song of All Time." My nominations were Chuck Berry's "Johnny B. Goode," Bob Dylan's "Like a Rolling Stone," and "When Doves Cry." I don't recall many of the others, aside from Etheridge submitting

Peter Gabriel's "In Your Eyes" and several folks bringing up Beatles songs. When all was said and done, as far as that Los Angeles audience was concerned, "When Doves Cry" was the greatest song ever.)

The B-side of the single was a melodic non-album cut called "17 Days"; the full title, written out on the sleeve, was "17 Days (The Rain Will Come Down, Then U Will Have 2 Choose. If U Believe, Look 2 the Dawn and U Shall Never Lose)," which might imply a song with a religious theme, though the lyrics actually described another favorite scenario for Prince—being left lonely and forlorn by a woman. The track had initially been intended for the Vanity-turned-Apollonia 6 album, but it was rerecorded with Coleman and Melvoin's backing vocals. (That album had a hard go of it—among the other songs that were taken away from the group was "Manic Monday," which made it to number two on the charts for the Bangles in 1986.) Most significantly, while "When Doves Cry" was credited just to Prince as per usual, "17 Days" was listed as a recording by Prince and the Revolution. Other than the tease on the *1999* cover, this was the first time that a Prince release was billed as a band, rather than a solo project (as the whole album would eventually be).

The "Doves" video played constantly on MTV, though it didn't really set up the movie; there were some unexplained shots from *Purple Rain* cut into the clip, but the focus was on scenes of Prince crawling out of a bathtub (not a hair from his complicated updo out of place) and of the Revolution, stylish in paisley and ruffles, posing in an empty white room. A still from the video shoot would be included as a poster in the *Purple Rain* LP, the first thing to be hung on my dorm room wall a few months later. In small print on the back of the "Doves" 45 it said, "From the forthcoming Warner Bros. album and motion picture *Purple Rain*," but there was still very little information circulating about the movie.

In late June 1984, *Rolling Stone* ran another Random Note (not yet even a full news story) with the headline "Prince Film Due Out in July." The item noted that the movie was planned for release "right when the Olympics are in full swing," and that "those who've seen the newly completed movie are primarily raving about its concert sequences."

Albert Magnoli got another boost in confidence when he went to the movie theater one day and the first *Purple Rain* trailer popped up on the screen. "I hadn't seen it before," he says, "and I saw that they duplicated the style of our editing in the trailer. This completely white crowd just went nuts, and I thought, 'Whoa.' It was so electrifying. The trailer was doing its job, and there wasn't any hype besides that—the audience was able to say, 'This is ours, not theirs.' There was no actor on TV telling you to go to the movie, no interviews, no baloney."

Indeed, what had also become evident was that there was still at least one more way in which Prince was going to violate the rules of opening a movie, especially a major studio production: he really was not going to do any interviews. Meaning, not one. He did not speak to the press at all following the release of *1999* in 1983 right up until the release of the *Around the World in a Day* album in the spring of 1985, sitting out the entire cycle of the *Purple Rain* album, movie, and tour.

"We did not need to have Prince do interviews anymore," says publicist Bloom. "We humans have very little memory, and it's not until you repeat something fifteen times that it rises to level of consciousness. So I worked on a Pavlovian philosophy almost, getting Prince's name repeated as frequently as possible. Doing publicity of this kind, you're like Sisyphus, rolling that big round stone up the mountain. Except when you're building a Prince, if you're moving that stone by repeating his name over and over again in every context possible, when you get to the peak, gravity takes over and the thing keeps moving with a momentum of its own. We had passed that peak. Prince had his own momentum by the time that movie came out.

"Liz Smith [a syndicated gossip columnist] had always been kind of an adversary of mine, but I managed to put together item after item that was perfect for her, and she became my greatest ally. With a gossip column, you can get somebody's name out every single week. So by the time you went to see the movie, his name had been trickling around you for a long time."

On the record company side, Bob Merlis claims that there was no great pressure to force Prince in front of the media. Radio promotion was more important to his marketing than press, and his previous interviews had been odd and unpredictable enough that maybe it was better to retain his mystery than risk messing it up.

Still, today it's almost impossible to imagine a movie studio, reluctant to put out a film in the first place, agreeing to terms in which their star would do zero promotion. "Those were simpler times," says Alan Leeds. "It was easier to manage a cohesive campaign without him than it would be today with social media and everything. But he was good at something that you could only get away with once. If anybody else tried what he did, it would be like, 'You're trying to be like Prince.' But he really did sell not just the industry but the world on the concept of his mystique, and the value of it and the legitimacy of it was based around this reclusiveness. He worked it brilliantly, for an awfully long time, to his advantage."

"I don't know if it was preplanning or if it was just coincidence," says Susan Rogers, "but this is where being an enigma paid off, because he became more and more of an enigma from *Dirty Mind* onward, and if you're an enigma who's selling a lot of records and making millions, and you say, 'I want to make a movie about my life,' someone is going to say, 'Now this I've got to see!'

"There was Prince and there was Michael Jackson and Madonna and Bruce Springsteen, and Prince was the only one who was so extremely enigmatic. Michael Jackson we *thought* we knew, Madonna we could sort of figure out, Bruce Springsteen had no artifice, so I can see how being an enigma would play to your advantage. But you only get one shot at that; there's only so much you can reveal, and then after it's revealed, there's your story."

The *Purple Rain* album, credited on the cover to Prince and the Revolution, was released on June 25, 1984, just as "When

Doves Cry" reached number one. Until the last minute, the members of the Revolution didn't even know how or if they would be acknowledged; Bobby Z said that it was only when he saw the test pressing of the album cover that he realized how prominently the band was going to be billed. "That's when I really had the chills about it," he said.

On the eve of the next step of his multimedia attack, Prince later admitted that he was anxious about reactions to the album in the press. "Apollonia and I slept under a hotel table waiting for the reviews [of the album]," he claimed. "We were so excited we couldn't sleep. When we saw them, they were all good."

For much of the rock press, though, the album's release was overshadowed by the fact that Bruce Springsteen's long-delayed *Born in the USA* album had come out a few weeks earlier. In its summer double issue, *Rolling Stone* gave Springsteen the featured lead spot in the reviews section, with *Purple Rain* coming second. And where *USA* received the magazine's coveted five-star rating, Prince was given a more modest four stars.

Kurt Loder's review leaned too heavily on comparisons to Jimi Hendrix and Sly Stone, seeming to bend over backward to create a familiar context for a rock audience that might be encountering Prince for the first time. Loder (still several years away from leaving *Rolling Stone* to become the voice of mature journalism at MTV) wrote that Prince's "extremism is endearing in an era of play-it-safe record production and formulaic hit mongering." He speculated that *Purple Rain* "may not yield another smash like last year's 'Little Red Corvette,'" but concluded that "anyone partial to great creators should own this record."

In the *New York Times,* the brilliant music writer Robert Palmer gave the album a well-informed, even prescient, rave. (In a sign of the times—so different from the instant response expected, even required, today—his review ran almost a full month after the album was released, just ahead of the movie's opening.) *Purple Rain,* he wrote, is "musically and emotionally tougher and considerably more personal than his last album, *1999,* released two years ago, or any of his earlier discs. Prince's personality shines through more brightly than ever, but it's something of a new Prince we're seeing." He noted that, especially in combination with the film, this music represented a new openness from the mysterious artist: "[It] begins to clear the air, to bring Prince and his world into sharper focus. The film and certain lyrics on the album suggest that Prince never talked much about himself or his background before because he found the subject too painful. . . . Prince has chosen to reveal himself to us in a more meaningful manner than the sexually explicit verbal striptease of his best-known earlier songs."

Palmer also commented on the impact of Prince working with a band rather than as a solo musician, which made the music "sound more alive and more sensual." Concluding his review with the inevitable comparisons to the other—and at that point, bigger—music stories of the season, Palmer wrote that "long after this summer's hits are forgotten and the Jacksons and Springsteen albums are packed away, *Purple Rain* will still be remembered, and played, as an enduring rock classic."

In its final form, *Purple Rain* had truly become a masterpiece. There isn't an ounce of fat on it. ("There's not a bad [song] on *Purple Rain*," says Chris Rock. "*Thriller*, that's allegedly the best album of all time, and that has at least two bad songs on it. There's no 'Baby Be Mine' on *Purple Rain*.") Every one of the nine songs could have worked as a single on its own, yet the cumulative effect was even more impressive. Prince's sound was entirely unique and irresistibly accessible. He struck a perfect balance between rock and R&B, with nothing forced or pandering. He was as daring as the throat-shredding screams on "Darling Nikki" or the new wave chill of "Computer Blue," as purely pop as the bouncy "Take Me with U."

From the rockabilly kick of "Let's Go Crazy" to the gospel lift of "Purple Rain," the album felt like it encompassed all of American pop music history to that point. Even before one saw the movie, the songs felt cohesive, a complete emotional experience. And whether the rock 'n' roll kids who were dazzled by Prince's guitar pyrotechnics realized it or not, as Touré put it, "the album takes us through the structure of a religious event by opening with the preaching of the word and ending with the audience being forgiven and baptized." Every possibility that Prince's career had previously presented was fully realized in the forty-five minutes of *Purple Rain*.

"The album *Purple Rain* is as enigmatic as Prince himself," Adam Levine of Maroon 5 (and TV's *The Voice*) told NPR.

"It's Hendrix, it's James Brown, it's outer space, it's church, it's sex, it's heavy metal. But at the end of the day, it's just Prince at his absolute best. . . . What makes it so special is that no one had ever really heard anything quite like it. It's such a fearless record. The music is just completely limitless and unself-conscious about what it is."

Tour manager Alan Leeds recalls that he felt like the lone voice expressing any disappointment in the album. "I was lamenting the fact that the music wasn't black enough," he says. "I knew 'Doves Cry' was a hit, knew 'Purple Rain' was a hit, but I was very unsure about the rest of the record. I was a little concerned that he was turning his back on his base audience and would catch some flak. Maybe because I was brought into the business by James Brown, I had this dogma in me that you never turn your back on your base; it's okay to express yourself limitlessly and be the complete artist you should be—I'm not suggesting restriction or limits—but don't turn your back on your own folks.

"But I also realized that I was the only one in the camp who was the least bit concerned about that. Nobody else was. Perhaps that's because the management team was all white. Their experience with black music was people like Earth, Wind and Fire, who had equal crossover aspirations and potential. Fargnoli had worked for Sly. So they didn't think like that—thankfully, because if there had been too much thought like that, it wouldn't have been good. And as it turned out, Prince was right, because he took his black fans with him to a place they hadn't been before."

When *Purple Rain* came out, the leading black music critics expressed no such concerns. As Greg Tate put it in *The Village Voice*, "No album since Funkadelic's *Let's Take It to the Stage* has so amorously bedded down black and white pop. . . . It's the record Prince has been wanting to make all along, since the music sounds like the kind of mulatto variation he probably was piecing together and performing in Minnesota before he got his deal."

The public response was immediate. *Purple Rain* sold 1.5 million copies in its first week on sale (the last week of June), and another million in the following four weeks before the movie even opened. It matched the total sales of *1999* in a matter of weeks. On July 18, with "When Doves Cry" still the biggest song in the country, "Let's Go Crazy" was released as the second single, with "Erotic City" as the B-side. It was perhaps Prince's greatest ever one-two punch of rock and funk, with both songs taking over radio stations (despite the fearless sexuality of "Erotic City"—was he saying we could "fuck" or "funk" until the dawn? It was a chance many, but not all, broadcasters were willing to take) regardless of format. The "Crazy" music video was also a preview of the movie's opening scene, complete with the Revolution in full flight and Prince's finest guitar gunslinging—the best possible trailer, in round-the-clock rotation on MTV. Though *Born in the USA* had held the number one spot on the album charts for four weeks, in the first week of August, just days after the film's premiere, *Purple Rain* took its slot as the biggest seller in the nation.

Everything had been teed up. There was only one thing left to do: open the movie and see what would happen.

The world premiere of *Purple Rain* took place a month after the album's release, on July 26 at Hollywood's ultimate movie palace, Mann's Chinese Theatre. Throngs of screaming kids lined the sidewalks. The arrivals of the band members were covered by MTV. Prince pulled up in a purple Rolls-Royce, wearing his signature purple trench coat. He carried a single flower that he'd picked before he stepped into the car, and he spoke to no one as he strode the red carpet into the theater.

The array of celebrities in attendance seems like an impossibly perfect cross section of '80s stardom: Eddie Murphy, Pee-wee Herman, Talking Heads, "Weird Al" Yankovic, the members of Kiss. "I remember John Mellencamp and all these other artists came and paid homage to him," says Bob Merlis. "That made me think, 'This guy is really a thing—they have nothing to gain from being here.' "

The after-party at the Palace was also covered live as an MTV special. VJ Mark Goodman interviewed a number of the attendees, with varying degrees of success. Wendy Melvoin explained that the movie centered on "the struggle to let [Prince] know that we do care about the music," while Lisa Coleman said that *Purple Rain* "starts out pretty negative, goes through a lot of things, but the film takes you to a better, happier place." Little Richard, brandishing a Bible that he hoped to give to Prince, asserted of the star, "He's me in this generation!"

"I'm a Prince groupie," said Eddie Murphy. "The man is a genius." A very serious Lionel Richie expressed his respect for Prince's accomplishment: "He didn't try to go after *Gone with the Wind,* he just did his thing. . . . He made a motion picture out of his album, and I think that's a very important step." No surprise, Weird Al got off the best line of the night—"We all knew Prince was a great actor, but who knew he could sing?"

For the members of the Revolution, the night of the premiere was a sign of things to come. "We drove up to the theater, the quintessential Hollywood premiere, and there's massive crowds and screaming and yelling and it was a big thing," says Fink. "Then going into the packed theater and seeing the reaction of the audience, hearing the people around you as it's playing—then I knew we were onto something for sure. I thought, 'Okay, this is it. This is going to be a big tour coming up in the fall, and people are going to be singing the praises of the movie and all that.' "

"Having been through the cycle of 'write, record, tour; write, record, tour,' there was a lot of momentum, and it seemed to always work and connect and take us to the next level," says Coleman. "So this was like, 'Wow, where is *this* gonna go?' We were really playing it to the hilt, dressed to the nines, spending tons of money on makeup people and day rooms at the Beverly Hills Hotel. The day of the premiere it was very much like that, talking about how to get out of the limousine and everything. It was really like finishing school. We had to present ourselves like we were worthy of being big stars. Back then, the fashion was weird and crazy, but it was fun to be weirder and crazier. 'Oh, yeah, you have big hair? Look at my hair!' It's insane when I look at it now. We destroyed the ozone layer."

Conspicuously, Prince and Morris Day did not speak at the party, where there were performances by a breakdance trio and by Sheila E. Prince and the Revolution took the stage for three songs—"17 Days," "Irresistible Bitch" (the B-side to the final single from *1999*, "Let's Pretend We're Married"), and "When Doves Cry," with a bass part added for Mark Brown to play.

The guest who may have inspired the most curiosity at the after-party was Prince's mother, Mattie Baker (she married Hayward Baker after divorcing John Nelson). She expressed no surprise about his skyrocketing success.

"When he was three, he said he'd be a star," she said. "Back then he would play pots and pans, anything he could make music with." It was the beginning of a slight lifting of the veil around Prince's actual family. His sister, Tyka, was quoted as saying, "It was cute, I guess, in a funny kind of way, that people thought that what happened in *Purple Rain* happened to our family . . . but of course, people wanted to know about the gun, all the bad stuff."

Asked at the party how much of the film was based on Prince's real life, Baker replied "You'll have to ask him that."

It was out of their hands now. Nothing to do but wait for the reviews. "When the movie was about to come out," says Rogers, "I remember him saying to us at rehearsal that he had had a dream the night before that Siskel and Ebert were reviewing *Purple Rain* and he said, 'The fat guy was just tearing me up.' [*laughs*] But in actual fact, when they did review it, Roger Ebert loved it, just loved it."

On their PBS series *At the Movies,* both Gene Siskel and Roger Ebert were indeed wildly enthusiastic about *Purple Rain.* Ebert called the film "one of the best combinations I've seen of music and drama," and proclaimed it "the best rock film since Pink Floyd's *The Wall.*" He paid special (almost alarming) attention to Kotero: "I'm only a human being," he said. "Can I be human for a second? I thought she was electrifying. I thought their scenes together were the most erotic love scenes that I've seen in a movie in a long time."

"I think this film ought to be studied for the way it uses music dramatically," added Siskel. "This film is very sophisticated in the way it has music videos . . . move the story along, adding new information." He compared the movie to *Saturday Night Fever,* calling it "very, very well directed" and also singling out Morris Day as "an excellent actor." At the end of 1984, both critics put *Purple Rain* on their Top Ten list for the year—Ebert at number ten and Siskel at number five.

In the *New York Times,* Vincent Canby was less generous, calling *Purple Rain* "probably the flashiest album cover ever to be released as a movie." He compared Prince to "a poster of Liza Minnelli on which someone has lightly smudged a mustache," to "Kermit the Frog on a Harley-Davidson" with "all the pent-up rage of a caged mouse." Canby described the range of Prince's musical influences and, revealing the confusion that Prince still seemed eager to perpetuate, claimed that "Prince's background is also mixed." Calling the female characters "suckers for the men who knock them around with brutal regularity," Canby concluded that "the offstage stuff is utter nonsense" and that the musical sequences were "the only things that count."

Pauline Kael of *The New Yorker,* probably the most influential movie critic in the country, seemed bemused by Prince's image and performance. "He knows how he wants to appear—like Dionysus crossed with a convent girl on her first bender. And his instinct is right . . . his impudent pranks make the audience laugh and his musical numbers keep giving the picture a lift. It's pretty terrible (there are no real scenes—just flashy, fractured rock-video moments), but those willing to accept Prince as a sexual messiah aren't likely to mind." Kael wrote that "it's not difficult to see the attraction that the picture has for adolescents: Prince's songs are a cry for the free expression of sexual energy, and his suffering is a supercharged version of what made James Dean the idol of young moviegoers." She also singled out Morris Day as "a full-fledged young comedian . . . who suggests a Richard Pryor without the genius and the complications."

Greg Tate was one of few black writers given a major platform to weigh in on *Purple Rain.* "The movie rises above, rather than drowns in, its own pretensions," he wrote in *The Village Voice.* "Take the scene in which Prince finds his father at the piano, which evokes something tragic about the frightful gaps in communication that can go for years between black father and son. . . . [The movie] is certainly truer to the humanity and milieu of its black principals, looney-tunish as they may seem, than I've come to expect outside of independent black cinema." (Black film historian Donald Bogle characterized Prince's performance a bit differently, writing that it evoked the stereotype of the "tragic mulatto" while also stumbling into self-parodying vanity: "Never has any black star been so adored and so worshipped in a film. . . . He pouts, broods, flirts, and struts like a 1950s screen siren; he's a coquette turned daredevil.")

The rock press—presumably a more receptive audience, but also probably more important to potential ticket buyers—was over the moon. In *Rolling Stone,* Kurt Loder (back on the case) said *Purple Rain* "may be the smartest, most spiritually ambitious rock & roll movie ever made. Not since the Beatles burst off the screen in *A Hard Day's Night* twenty years ago has the sense of a new generation's arrival on the pop scene been so vividly and excitingly conveyed." Calling the movie "a creative coup for its charismatic star," Loder wrote that the concert sequences rivaled those in *Woodstock* and *The Last Waltz,* high praise indeed from the magazine initially created as a voice for the '60s rock explosion.

Interestingly, Loder argued that the most distinctive element of *Purple Rain* was a strong sense of morality in the offstage story. "The characters . . . spend most of their time working—rarely has the work ethic been made to seem so cool," he wrote. He mentioned the "nonsalacious sexiness" and added that "the simple equality with which the characters interact is quietly inspiring," ultimately concluding that "in its simple positivism alone, *Purple Rain* marks a radical break with the rock-movie past." In the *Los Angeles Herald Examiner,* Mikal Gilmore—one of Bloom's media plants at the San Diego advance screening—compared *Purple Rain* to *Citizen Kane* and simply called it "the best rock film ever made."

From a distance of thirty years, all of these reviews, good and bad, speak some part of the truth. The performance sequences in *Purple Rain* have lost none of their impact. Magnoli's finest decision, without question, was the opening sequence; the blistering "Let's Go Crazy" is almost immediately followed by the Time funking its way through "Jungle Love." We don't leave the stage of First Avenue for more than eleven minutes, other than via the quick cuts that introduce the other characters. It's breathless, exciting, the music is magnificent—at this point, it almost doesn't matter what happens in the rest of the movie.

Considering, too, that *Purple Rain* ends with four consecutive songs, totaling more than twenty minutes of screen time, we're left with not much more than an hour of actual narrative in between, and even that is consistently broken up by musical interludes; in some very savvy editing, only once in the film does more than ten minutes pass before cutting to a song (and that stretch has the sex scene in the middle). Once you've made it to the one-hour mark in *Purple Rain,* the reward is seven musical performances in the final forty-five minutes.

It's impressive how much work the music does to propel the story and flesh out the characters (and interesting to think back and realize that since the album was out a month before the movie, we had already absorbed and memorized the songs before we understood their function in the film). "Each song works really well within that moment of the movie," says Matt Fink, "and [Prince] was able to hone in on that and make it work. It's a testament to his genius—it's like building a musical, like Rodgers and Hammerstein." And even Prince's performances of the more experimental songs, while supposedly alienating to the club audience ("Your music makes sense to no one but yourself," says Billy Sparks), are never less than riveting.

The acting and scripted dialogue, tenuous even at the time, don't stand up quite so well. Though Prince mostly holds up his end during the most dramatic scenes, especially the father/son moments with Clarence Williams, he's best at striking a pose and letting the camera appreciate his coolness—which is no small thing, since without his powerful presence at its center, the movie would collapse. Wendy Melvoin's delivery has some spark, but it's hard to find much in the Apollonia story line besides pure camp; it's presumably the "romantic" component of *Purple Rain* that would later inspire *Vanity Fair* to call it "perhaps the best badly acted film ever."

It's also evident that this is a movie that was made just before the notion of "political correctness" would take root as a concern. From Apollonia's attire to the infamous Dumpster moment to Fink's line about Melvoin's PMS, the presentation of women is generally pretty appalling (though, to be fair, the Wendy and Lisa characters do help balance out this mean-spirited chauvinism). Most complicated is Morris Day's role; on the one hand, his natural comic timing and interplay with Jerome Benton still sparkle, but his pop-eyed, cackingly libidinous character does come dangerously close to offensive stereotype. ("I'm capable of better," he once said. "Black people don't necessarily act like this"—though one can't help recall that he also claimed to have written most of his own lines.)

"It was a time before you had porno on your phone," says Chris Rock, "so to see Apollonia playing with herself, naked by the lake, that was reason enough to go see the movie four times. It was almost like a black exploitation movie, kind of a precursor to gangsta rap—guys dumping a girl into a Dumpster headfirst, Prince smacks the shit out of Apollonia, his father tells him never to get married. It would be hard to make that movie today. It's closer to *Taxi Driver* than to, like, a Justin Bieber movie or the kind of movies they make with musicians now."

My recollection from 1984 is that we knew some of *Purple Rain* was silly; some of the most awkward lines were the ones we would quote back and forth to each other. But the concert sequences were proof positive that Prince was the most gifted musician working, and his style, his image, the way he carried himself offstage—the side of him that even his biggest fans had never experienced—did not disappoint us. The truth-versus-fiction aspect of the story line only got more interesting the deeper we dug: was making his mother white a way to show that this wasn't to be taken as a documentary, a play for more crossover interest, or both? Wendy and Lisa took pains to make clear that they did not feel stifled creatively, as they were shown in the movie, but were they just stand-ins for Prince's conflicts over control with the Time and Vanity and others in his orbit?

"Ambiguity, mystery, fiction or real, or what, that was exactly what it was, even for those of us on the inside," says Susannah Melvoin.

Maybe the critics mattered, maybe they didn't. Most crucially, word on the street was that the movie was good—that it was better than it had to be—and the reaction at the box office was immediate. Despite the studio's skepticism, *Purple Rain* took in $7.8 million its opening weekend, essentially earning back its entire cost and replacing *Ghostbusters* as the top-grossing film in the country. Mo Ostin's strategy of releasing single, album, and movie in May, June, and July, respectively, played out perfectly, and *Purple Rain* made Prince the first artist in history to have the same project simultaneously number one on the singles, albums, and movie charts in the United States.

"The huge impact of *Purple Rain* was somewhat unexpected, except by Prince," says Leeds. "He didn't seem surprised by reports of audiences reacting to the movie like it was a concert." The tour manager accompanied the singer when he snuck into a Los Angeles movie theater the day after the premiere. "I thought he had been spotted a few minutes into the film," Leeds says, "until I realized the kids were shrieking at the screen."

Albert Magnoli ran into Prince that same day, while the singer was cruising around Westwood in a white limousine. "He saw me, and we just drove around and said 'What the hell? This is wild.' "

Warner Bros. Records publicist Bob Merlis remembers looking at the *Hollywood Reporter* that Monday, seeing the opening weekend box office numbers, and thinking, "We aren't hyping ourselves—it is real!" The publicist credits Cavallo, Bloom, and the rest of Prince's brain trust with that big initial burst by "making it important to people who didn't think he was important before," and also points out that the good reviews and strong word of mouth indicated that the film might stick around for a while. "It wasn't like today's movies, where the first weekend is everything and then it disappears; it really was a more organic process."

Merlis notes that in 1984, MTV had not fully saturated the culture, and watching music performances, with such strong visual presence, was still a novelty. Wendy Melvoin recalls that she had precisely that reaction when the movie opened. "I remember thinking to myself, 'The album's been out, so *Purple Rain* is actually the video for this record—how genius! It's not MTV; it's a *movie*, boom!'"

"What really puts [the album] over the top is how the music is performed in the film," said Adam Levine. "It's as exciting and eclectic as the music itself. People never would have fully understood what it was unless you could see it unfold in front of you visually."

"It was the first truly long-form music video," says Leeds, "at a time in his career where you had an interest level from an audience that either already knew something about him and wanted more, or had never seen him perform—had heard '1999' and 'Little Red Corvette' on the radio, but had never seen him perform, and just witnessed this dynamo come to life on the silver screen. So it was the perfect storm of an amazing performer amazingly captured on film at, amazingly, the right time and the right place. There was certainly a lot of planning that went into it, but there was a lot of luck, too. There's the old saying, 'You're only new once,' and for a huge audience, discovering the depth of his performance ability was new to a great many people at that time. The timing couldn't have been planned better."

Tori Amos recalls the first time she saw *Purple Rain,* on a date in Rockville, Maryland. "I was with somebody who did not get it, and that was that—if you don't get this, I have nothing to say to you. Next!

"It completely changed how I saw live performance," she continues. "His energy, how he was able to put his hands on this force field, it was almost like a new language. I had never seen anything—except possibly Led Zeppelin, and maybe Mick Jagger—where the front person had such a power and they were completely present with it, almost staring you down. It was like he reached off the screen, grabbed you by the throat, and shook you awake.

"It was a complete awakening in my suburban existence. This wasn't a storybook Prince—at least not a storybook that you were allowed to have in your library as a minister's daughter! He was not like any prince in a Disney story."

Darius Rucker, the lead singer of Hootie and the Blowfish who went on to became a country music star, also vividly remembers the first time he saw the movie—on a first date with a girl named Stacy Miller in his home town of Charleston, South Carolina. "For us living in the black community, here was this kid from Minneapolis, and they were letting him make a movie!" he says. "For us, it was like 'Wow, this is really happening!' And then the movie succeeded, which made it even better."

Rucker, who guesses that he saw *Purple Rain* eight times that summer, claims that the movie had a very direct impact on his own future. "Up until I saw *Purple Rain,* I wanted to be a solo artist, but after I saw it, all I wanted to do was be in a band. It really changed what I wanted in my career—to be part of something rather than going all by myself."

After the media saw that *Purple Rain* was a genuine phenomenon, the next wave of media coverage kicked in. *Rolling Stone* put Prince back on the cover of its August 30 issue—still without any access to the star himself. Kurt Loder, keeping on the *Purple Rain* beat, observed that the movie's "director had never been in charge of a feature before. The cast . . . had, with only two exceptions, no acting experience. The tight budget ($7 million) and rushed shooting schedule (seven weeks) did not augur well for stellar production values." Perhaps more notably, though, by the next issue the leading rock magazine was now dedicating significant space to the rest of the acts in Prince's orbit. The following issue featured a news story about Sheila E. and a review of her *Glamorous Life* album, as well as a longer interview with Morris Day—who confirmed that his relationship with Prince had grown strained and that the Time had not survived the movie's release.

"In the past, there's been a secrecy. In the future, I'm going to talk," he told writer Michael Goldberg in that *Rolling Stone* interview. "There's a lot of negative things I could say. But I don't want to see these things in print. I still consider the guy my friend." Day indicated that the attention his performance had received, and his own relocation to Los Angeles to pursue his acting ambitions, had created tensions with Prince. (Presumably—hopefully?—attempting to stay in character, he also spoke to the issue of misogyny in *Purple Rain* by saying that "you just kind of have to keep [women] in place. If that means tossing them in the Dumpster, then that's what you've got to do.")

The more mainstream press seemed unsure what to make of Prince, which served, as such a reaction always does, as the strongest endorsement for the real fans. *Time* magazine called him "a suitably odd [star] for these askew times." The official Soviet newspaper *Pravda,* of all places, offered a perceptive commentary, noting "with thorough disapproval that a large, demoralized section of American youth was beguiled by an icon who seemed to imply that a holocaust—nuclear or otherwise—was inevitable and desirable."

Prince's overt, daring sexuality, which was a novelty or curiosity earlier in his career, also inevitably became a primary focus as he entered the mainstream spotlight. *People* magazine spoke to Dan Peters, a minister at the interdenominational Zion Christian Center in North St. Paul, Minnesota, who called Prince "the filthiest rock 'n' roller ever to prance across the stage." Peters had been leading an anti-rock crusade for several years, urging people to destroy "offending" albums.

Not only was Peters unconvinced by the backward message at the end of "Darling Nikki," but he singled it out as objectionable. "Kids come up to us and say, 'See, that shows he is a Christian,'" he protested. "And I say, 'As far as we can tell from listening to the lyrics, his Lord is a penis.' " This reaction to *Purple Rain* would, of course, find its most significant manifestation the following year, when Tipper Gore overheard her daughter listening to "Darling Nikki," noticed the line "I met her in a hotel lobby / Masturbating with a magazine," and set in motion the project that would reach the floor of the United States Senate as the Parents Music Resource Center and lead to warning stickers being placed on albums deemed to contain explicit lyrics.

Whether you considered it a source of outrage or not, Prince's sexuality was unlike anything pop music had ever witnessed. As shocking as Elvis Presley, Mick Jagger, and other rock gods had been when they first appeared, he had raised the stakes to a new level. "His songs were propelled by how incredibly palpable his sexuality was," marvels Wendy Melvoin. "He was wearing, for all intents and purposes, women's clothing and makeup—not dissimilar to Bowie or Little Richard—not being a homosexual, still having a certain amount of badass factor in him, singing in falsetto and wearing black underwear and high heels. It's remarkable to me that twenty million people gravitated to that and were like, 'Not only do I love that music, but he's fuckable to me.' "

"Prince gets over with everyone because he fulfills everyone's illusions," wrote Miles Davis in his autobiography. "He's got that raunchy thing, almost like a pimp and a bitch all wrapped up in one image, that transvestite thing. But when he's singing that funky X-rated shit that he does about sex and women, he's doing it in a high-pitched voice, in almost a girl's voice. If I said 'Fuck you' to somebody, they would be ready to call the police. But if

Prince says it in that girl-like voice that he uses, then everyone says it's cute."

As extreme as the carnality was in *Purple Rain*, though—aside from the sex play with Apollonia, which was entirely straight, the movie had him humping the speakers during "Nikki" or sweaty and shirtless with a bandanna over his eyes, S&M style, playing "Computer Blue," which also saw Wendy Melvoin kneeling in front of him and simulating a blow job during the guitar solo—even this was at once more toned down and more stylized than his earlier image. The elaborate ruffles and cascade of curls may have hinted at some kind of androgyny, but they were a long way from taking the stage in a trench coat and bikini briefs. "Nikki" made reference to masturbation, but it was far more acceptable than songs titled "Jack U Off" or "Head."

Prince's recasting of his sound and image into the role of the guitar-slinging rock god also allowed him much more latitude to mix and match gender signifiers. It's hard to think of another rock star, or almost any prominent straight male, who would dare to offer himself up as a character with the vulnerability and femininity of the Kid. In the first few scenes, we see him putting on makeup, checking his hair in the mirror, returning to the home where he lives with his parents, and getting knocked down by his father—not exactly Rambo. Yet simultaneously, we watch him playing the shit out of his guitar and parting the crowd in front of the club with his custom motorcycle, always conveying a sense of aggressive masculinity.

"When he played the guitar and when he soloed, there wasn't a chick in there—that was straight-up dude," says Melvoin. "He perpetuated that even if he sat in on people's sets; he would try and kick Bruce Springsteen's ass or Sting's ass or whoever. So when he held a guitar, he knew, 'I could be wearing pink lipstick right now; I'm still one hundred percent guy.' "

In September, the next shot in the promotional assault was fired with the release of "Purple Rain" as a single. It would climb to number two on the singles chart, kept out of the top spot by "Wake Me Up Before You Go-Go" by George Michael's candy-coated duo Wham! If "Let's Go Crazy"/"Erotic City" was Prince's most muscular A-side/B-side combination ever, this 45 was by far his most Divine-with-a-capital-D; the B-side, titled "God," was a quiet meditation whose lyrics were evocative of a Bible passage. An instrumental version of the song was heard in the movie score during, of all things, the sex scene—and was released as a 12″ single in the UK titled "God (Love Theme from *Purple Rain*)"—but on August 20, Prince rerecorded the song in Minneapolis, this time with vocals. "God made you, God made me / He made us all equally," he sang, before instructing us to "wake up, children / Dance the dance electric."

The momentum carried through the fall. The movie was on its way toward taking in nearly $70 million ("The ticket prices were, what, $2.50, in those days?" notes Bob Cavallo. "So that would make it $300 million today.") In October, *Rolling Stone* reported that the *Purple Rain* sound track was outselling its competition by as much as four to one. Norman Hunter of the

160-store Record Bar chain said that "with Prince, we're getting an extra 10,000 sales a week. *Purple Rain* right now is our biggest selling record of all time outside of the Christmas season."

"I don't think there's anyone who has had as massive a cultural impact—hip-hop as a genre has, but I don't think you can isolate a specific artist," says Leeds. "Prince influenced how people dressed, who they hung out with, how guys were willing to express their masculinity, or not. I think that's what separates it from the pack, because you started seeing fashion in general for young males change, for young females change—arguably people who didn't even like the record, but the ruffles on their sleeves changed. The impact was amazingly dramatic. I don't think we had seen anything, other than maybe the Beatles on *Ed Sullivan,* so rapidly capture and change the culture."

The album clamped down on that number one position, remaining there for almost a full six months before passing the torch back to *Born in the USA* in mid-January 1985. Springsteen continued to offer formidable competition for the top of the rock 'n' roll mountain. But by the end of 1984, even *Rolling Stone* had proclaimed a winner, naming *Purple Rain* the Record of the Year in its year-end issue. The magazine called the album "essential listening" and dubbed its maker "a true original"—in a recap that ran just above the capsule on *Born in the USA,* reversing the order in which the original reviews had appeared.

As Greg Tate had written, "With *Purple Rain* (the movie and the album), he's established himself as the most cunning black producer since Berry Gordy in plotting a course of conquest over American pop apartheid."

EIGHT

Dig If U Will

One crucial aspect of the *Purple Rain* phenomenon that must be taken into account is its exact timing. The year 1984—and, even more precisely, the summer of that year—marked a fascinating, unprecedented moment in our culture. It's always impossible to reconstruct history with any real sense of accuracy, but as great as the music and performances in *Purple Rain* would have been at any time, it seems reasonable to conclude that the film would not have had the same impact had it been released even a year, maybe even a few months, earlier or later.

Especially for those of us in the class of '84, the year had always loomed large, and somewhat ominously, because of the dystopian warnings in George Orwell's visionary novel: the distant future invoked by his words in *Nineteen Eighty-Four* came speeding at us through our school years. Winston Smith's battles with Big Brother may not have come to pass in full, but as Ronald Reagan's first term came to a close and it became clear that his victory over Walter Mondale would be a history-making rout, many young people certainly experienced a strong sense of alienation and despair.

With serious debate around the "Star Wars" strategic defense initiative and an official in the Department of Defense claiming with a straight face that with enough shovels we could dig our way to safety in the event of nuclear attack, the apocalyptic visions that Prince was expressing felt very close at hand. "It was the worst of times," wrote novelist Rick Moody in an essay about the year 1984. "Atomic jitters were everywhere." With such political folly as the invasion of Granada and the exposure of the Iran-Contra machinations dominating the news but having little actual public impact, the government seemed ridiculous, out of control—while the popularity of Reagan, with his Hollywood-honed paternal cowboy image, only kept soaring.

The codification of modern conservative values meant big things for business. Corporations were expanding; money was defining the culture. This extended to the popular arts, where blockbusters became crucial commodities. It was a time of extravagance—big hair, bright colors, grand ambition.

"Have you heard that in the United States, when a conservative government is in power, the standard of beauty for women is large breasts, and that when a liberal government is in power, it's small breasts?" says Susan Rogers, who is currently a professor at Boston's Berklee College of Music. "In class, I talk to my students about how, as an artist, you need to be able to read your culture and know what's coming. In the height of the Reagan excesses and that movie *Wall Street* and 'greed is good' and all that, you would pay money to see an artist onstage whose hair was done, whose makeup was done, and who wore clothes and shoes that were worth more than your whole life. Then by the nineties, it was Bill Clinton and it was grunge and the rawer rap, the gangster stuff. It was inevitable that the glam thing was going to collapse, along with Wall Street and everything else with it."

Nothing exemplified the era more than MTV, which had transformed the rules and the scale of pop success. The network, which had launched in 1981, had effectively become the equivalent of a national radio station—a video in heavy rotation meant a hit single. In the channel's earliest days this was exciting, because the simple fact that MTV had to fill up all of its hours of programming before there was a surplus of videos to play meant that some weird stuff got exposure, and a band like Talking Heads could reach an audience that radio formats never would have granted them. But as the power of music video became evident, the clips became mandatory for even the biggest acts, and the higher production values started to push out the smaller bands.

Not all rock stars were quick to embrace music videos. Some found the idea crass or felt that it compromised their music, taking away the listeners' ability to create their own images and associations for a song. Bruce Springsteen initially said that he wouldn't make videos; he grudgingly allowed an abstract black-and-white clip—in which he did not appear—for

"Atlantic City," from his stark, somber *Nebraska* album. By the time of *Born in the USA*, of course, this attitude had changed, which marked a crucial shift in Springsteen's entire career.

Prince, however, had no such qualms about music video. "Instead of thinking, 'Ugh, MTV ruined music,' he was like, 'MTV!'" says Coleman. "He was always very visually oriented."

"Prince was stoked about MTV," adds Wendy Melvoin. "He loved the idea of videos and doing performance stuff for them."

"I'll never forget the time I went in and he was playing a new song," says Alan Leeds. "The volume was jacked so loud, he's trying to say something and you don't even hear a word, you're just nodding, pretending you hear him. Finally I realize he's describing a video treatment for the song. And I'm like, 'You just wrote the song this morning! You've already got the video?' And he says, 'Alan, you don't understand. Today, people don't hear music; they see it. It all comes together to me.' It was an aha moment for me, being old-school and thinking video was just an add-on, and recognizing that he literally created those things simultaneously was very profound to me."

The impact of MTV extended well beyond the music business. It shook up all forms of visual media, including advertising, graphic design, and film. "The movies took their cue from the music," wrote Aaron Aradillas in an essay about *Purple Rain* for *Indiewire*, "as Hollywood entered into a symbiotic relationship with MTV, both as a new form of storytelling but, more importantly, as a powerful marketing tool to reach the coveted youth audience." He mentions the role of music and the MTV-influenced high-speed editing in such 1984 movies as *Footloose* (the sound track from which was the biggest-selling album of the first half of the year), *Against All Odds*, and *Repo Man*. The sound track and scores of projects like *Streets of Fire* and *Body Double* moved pop music further to the center of the movie experience; Ray Parker Jr.'s *Ghostbusters* theme would be the song that knocked "When Doves Cry" out of its number one position. Talking Heads' concert film *Stop Making Sense* was an art-house blockbuster, and both Paul McCartney (*Give My Regards to Broad Street*) and Rick Springfield (*Hard to Hold*) even released their own (failed) star vehicles that year.

The real power of MTV, though, and the escalation to a true sky's-the-limit potential for music hinged primarily on the accomplishments of one man, who cast a shadow over everything that happened in pop in 1984: Michael Jackson.

The cyclone known as *Thriller* came out in late 1982 and sold impressively from the beginning, but it really went into overdrive a full year later. Jackson's unforgettable appearance on the *Motown 25: Yesterday, Today, Forever* television special, when he introduced the moonwalk—a dance move that would have the biggest impact on the world since Elvis shook his hips—aired in the spring of 1983. It was followed in December by his most ambitious creation to date, the fourteen-minute "short film" for *Thriller*'s title track, which is still generally recognized as the most important music video of all time.

"Thriller" solidified what the clips for "Billie Jean" and "Beat It" had already put into motion: Jackson was the most creative, most popular force that MTV had to deal with, and the network's initial resistance to playing black artists (because they felt that the channel had to maintain a "rock 'n' roll" format) simply was not viable. As *Thriller* continued its march to more than 25 million albums sold, and the racial and stylistic walls for programming on MTV fell, the playlists of pop radio nationwide began to transform.

"Pop fans, now accustomed to seeing black artists and white artists on the same video channel, came to expect the same mix of music on pop radio," wrote Steve Greenberg in "Michael Jackson's 'Thriller' at 30: How One Album Changed the World," a 2012 report for *Billboard* magazine. "It was impossible to keep the various fragments of the audience isolated from one another any longer. Mass-appeal Top 40 radio itself made a big comeback due to this seismic shift. Beginning in early 1983 in Philadelphia and rapidly spreading through the country, one or more FM stations in every city switched to Top 40, and many rose to the top of the ratings playing the mix of music made popular by MTV—young rock and urban hits."

The representation of black music on the pop charts quickly skyrocketed. "If 1982 was the genre's low point in terms of pop success," said Greenberg, "by 1985 more than one-third of all the hits on the *Billboard* Hot 100 were of urban radio origin." *Thriller* had, virtually single-handedly, changed the racial composition of pop radio and reopened doors that had been closed to black artists in the post-disco days.

The relationship between Prince and Michael Jackson has been the source of much speculation, with frequent references to a competition between the two. Those within Prince's inner circle offer conflicting ideas about how much attention he was paying to Jackson. Alan Leeds recalls that well before *Purple Rain,* Prince saw Jackson as a professional target. "Even on the Controversy tour, I was already picking up on the fact that there was a feeling of rivalry in the Prince camp, that Prince was out to get [Jackson]," he says. The month that the *Purple Rain* album was released, while Prince was still conceptualizing his own tour, he chartered a jet and took Leeds and lighting director LeRoy Bennett to see the Jacksons' mega-hyped Victory tour at a stop in Dallas. "It was about 'I want to see their show before we finish mounting ours.' We very much wanted to see it, just to know what we were following professionally—but with the attitude that 'this is our competition,' like, 'he's the Yankees, but we're the Red Sox.'"

Howard Bloom, who worked with both Prince and Jackson, remembers it differently, maintaining that he had no sense that Prince was scoping out Jackson. "I actually experienced it the other way around," he says. "There was somebody in Michael's camp who was telling him that I was a spy for Prince, and that I was there to make sure that Michael didn't outshine Prince. Fortunately, he didn't buy it. But Prince's job was to be

Prince—he was sui generis; there was no competition, and it wasn't that we were looking for competition and there wasn't any. It was that, in his world, everything dropped out of sight except for Prince and the audience." (According to bodyguard Bill Whitfield, Jackson still felt a rivalry until his final days, possibly scheduling the fifty dates at London's O2 Arena that he would not live to see so that he could break Prince's record twenty-one shows in the venue: "Mr. Jackson was always competitive about being compared to Prince," he said.)

"Everybody was playing *Thriller* on tour, but he wouldn't talk about it and he wouldn't be playing it," says Jill Jones. "If he did, he kept it on the down-low, and in those days, we weren't politically correct; Prince would laugh about somebody's record in a second. He was very competitive with Michael Jackson, but would he really admit it? No. He had to be the *different* black guy."

According to journalist Ronin Ro's 2011 book *Prince: Inside the Music and the Masks,* Michael Jackson attended one of the Warner Bros. screenings of *Purple Rain,* leaving ten minutes before the end. "The music's okay, I guess," he reportedly said to one of his entourage. "But I don't like Prince. He looks mean, and I don't like the way he treats women. He reminds me of some of my relatives. And not only that—the guy can't act at all. He's really not very good."

When Prince and Jackson met in September of 1984 to discuss the possibility of collaborating, according to Jackson's lawyer John Branca, Prince freaked Jackson out by presenting him with a voodoo amulet. ("I never want to talk to that guy again," Jackson said to Branca.) Prince would resist Jackson's overtures to record the song "Bad" as a duet. "The first line of that song is 'Your butt is mine,'" he explained. "Who's gonna sing that to whom? Right there, we got a problem." Years later, in the documentary *This Is It,* which chronicled Jackson's 2009 rehearsals for the series of concerts at London's O2 Arena that he did not live to perform, Jackson joked that if he didn't follow through on ideas that he dreamed up at night, God might give them to Prince.

In 1984, between record sales, the Victory tour, endorsements (including his record-breaking Pepsi deal), and numerous other business deals, Michael Jackson earned $91 million. In that same year—the most important, if not necessarily the most lucrative—of his career, Prince (who turned down an endorsement deal from Coca-Cola, which they offered after Jackson signed with the competition) took in $17 million. But Prince achieved something that Jackson dreamed of his entire life yet never accomplished: he became a movie star.

Prince and Michael Jackson weren't the only black figures who were changing lanes, breaking rules, and making history in 1984. The year marked a genuine revolution in terms of the visibility and impact of African Americans across popular culture. As Nelson George points out in 2010's *Thriller: The Musical Life of Michael Jackson,* "Michael was a harbinger." Among the highlights of 1984, some of which seemed significant at the time, others only in retrospect: on January 4, Oprah Winfrey made her debut as a cohost of *A.M. Chicago*; in February, Run-D.M.C.'s self-titled debut hit record stores, becoming the first rap album to go gold; on June 19, the Chicago Bulls made Michael Jordan their number one choice in the NBA draft; on September 20, *The Cosby Show* debuted on NBC; in November, L. L. Cool J's "I Need a Beat," catalogue number DJ001, was the first official release on Russell Simmons and Rick Rubin's new Def Jam label; and on December 5, *Beverly Hills Cop* opened, elevating Eddie Murphy from star to genuine superstar level.

Concurrently, Jesse Jackson was running for president, claiming the "Rainbow Coalition" as his constituency; widely dismissed when he announced his candidacy, Jackson won five primaries and caucuses before his own missteps (the infamous interview in which he referred to New York City as "Hymietown") and lack of support from the Democratic party machine caught up with his campaign. Yet he left a significant impact on the national debate, as well as the voter rolls, and thus helped play a part in the election of multiple black candidates at the state and national levels over the coming years.

One remarkable aspect of these monumental figures is that while they all had their eyes on the mass market, they were also proudly and strongly black-identified. Writing in *The Village Voice* about the parallel phenomena of Prince, Murphy, and young jazz virtuoso Wynton Marsalis, Greg Tate stated that "right now black America's got more crossover acts happening than it's had since the '60s, and the funny thing is that they're all taking Babylon by storm in an era noticeably absent of agitation from the streets . . . unlike their forefathers, they've managed to make it to the mainstream without compromising their edge."

Tate acknowledged the role that Michael Jackson played in this explosion of black culture for a general audience, but concluded that with *Purple Rain,* Prince had taken things even further. "Although Michael may have kicked the door in," he wrote, "Prince done stormed the whole castle and come back handing the brothers and sisters the keys to the rock and roll kingdom."

With MTV as a unified promotional front, *Thriller* illustrating the new and unprecedented heights that music could reach, and radio open to a more integrated version of pop, everything was in place for a remarkable moment. And 1984 did not fail to deliver. In 2012, Chris Molanphy wrote on NPR's website, "Widely agreed to be the greatest year for pop a generation ago, 1984 offered amazing variety on vinyl and represented a cultural peak for Top 40 radio." And in 2014, *Rolling Stone* called it "pop's greatest year," offering a list of the one hundred best songs of 1984 that was topped by "When Doves Cry" and featured no less than five Prince compositions (three *Purple Rain* singles, plus Chaka Khan's "I Feel for You" and Sheila E.'s "The Glamorous Life") in their Top Ten.

Van Halen set the tone for the year. Perhaps the most popular hard rock group in America, they had proudly boasted of using no synthesizers on their previous albums. They titled their sixth record *1984,* added a synth part as the most prominent sound on the single "Jump," and watched the song turn into the biggest hit of their career. What's overwhelming about the year's releases set end-to-end are the number of true blockbusters, how many albums would have been the phenomenon of the year at any other time: Cyndi Lauper's *She's So Unusual,* Tina Turner's *Private Dancer,* ZZ Top's *Eliminator.* John Cougar Mellencamp's *Uh-Huh* marked the start of his transition from snotty young rocker to more mature singer-songwriter, especially when "Pink Houses" took off. It was the year that U2 cracked pop radio with their first Top 40 U.S. hit, "Pride (in the Name of Love)," and that Bon Jovi broke through with "Runaway."

"Everything seemed to be getting bigger," says Bob Merlis. "For the first time, the Warner Brothers record division eclipsed the film division for revenue—the company's biggest revenue source was now music. We knew it was bigger than it had ever been; it felt like something historic was happening. It was an era of great possibility, a lot of it realized by things like *Purple Rain*—well, as if there *were* other things like this; it really was the one."

Several events demonstrated that there was a passing of generations under way. In April, Marvin Gaye was murdered by his father, an incomprehensible tragedy that seemed almost biblical. Coming so soon after John Lennon's death, it was a bracing reminder that the utopian dreams of the 1960s were long gone. In fact, the gestures and images of rock 'n' roll's greatest era (solidifying into the playlists of the classic-rock radio format at the time) had become so laughably clichéd that they fueled the definitive rock parody, the "mockumentary" *This Is Spinal Tap,* which was also released in 1984.

There was a new strain of underground rock emerging: sounds from the sloppy punk funk of the Red Hot Chili Peppers to the literate moping of the Smiths debuted during the year, as the nascent "college rock" of the time continued its journey toward the "alternative rock" explosion of the early '90s. And, of course, there was plenty of junk—some enjoyable, some not—that was also hugely popular in 1984, songs (often propelled by videos more compelling than the music) that were just as omnipresent but didn't have the same enduring appeal: it was also the year when Yes' "Owner of a Lonely Heart," Billy Idol's "Rebel Yell," Huey Lewis and the News' "The Heart of Rock & Roll," Deniece Williams's "Let's Hear It for the Boy," and Duran Duran's "The Reflex" were in constant rotation. If that doesn't add up to a list of classics, it's certainly indicative of an impressive range of styles happening concurrently.

"Two things, I'd argue, produce good years for pop music: variety and shared pleasure," wrote NPR's Molanphy, celebrating the "monoculture" of music in 1984. "For us in the pop world, it means the idea of a shared cultural experience—the Beatles-and-Motown AM radio of the mid-'60s or Michael Jackson's cross-cultural peak in 1983–84—and for years, many of us have been mourning its passing."

That sense of music that everyone was aware of, that everyone had an opinion about and a relationship to, peaked during the summer with the battle for supremacy between *Born in the USA* and *Purple Rain*. In both cases, these albums represented an artist embracing his full potential as a pop stylist, striving to find a version of his music that would retain his essence yet connect with the greatest number of people possible. Bruce Springsteen utilized cleaner, more modern production on his new songs, put the musical hooks in the foreground (as in the '60s pop records he loved), and worked out obsessively to resculpt his body. He dove full-on into the music videos he had scorned, frolicking with the young, unknown Courteney Cox at the end of the clip for "Dancing in the Dark" and allowing producer Arthur Baker to remix the song for a 12-inch dance single.

Yet Springsteen didn't abandon the fundamental themes of his writing—the struggles, economic and emotional, of the American working class; the attempt to maintain faith in justice and moral principles in the face of constant betrayal; the need for friendship and camaraderie during trying times. Despite the scathing protest of the often-misunderstood title song (famously quoted by President Reagan in a clumsy attempt to connect with young voters) and the despairing mood of songs like "Downbound Train" and "My Hometown," the album spun off seven hit singles on its way to selling more than 15 million copies.

"I was very conscious of being an American musician and addressing the issues of the day," Springsteen told me in 2006, looking back at his decision to pose in front of an American flag on the *Born in the USA* cover. "There was a sense that the flag was up for grabs, that you had the right to stake out your claim to its meaning and to the kind of country you wanted your kids to grow up in. I wanted to write music that was charting the ever-changing distance between American ideals and American truths, to explore what was happening in the middle, to be a creative voice in that discussion."

Prince and Springsteen expressed admiration for each other's work. The Boss had come to check out a show on the

1999 tour in the spring of 1983, and the members of the Revolution recall that if Prince was quiet on the subject of Michael Jackson, he made clear that he respected Springsteen as a live performer.

The ascendance of *Purple Rain* and *Born in the USA* was a moment of pop music at its best. There was the usual tribal affiliation of fans claiming one artist or the other, but no one attains sales of more than 10 million without crossing a lot of boundaries. Whatever the eventual limitations of the grandiosity of the '80s, the universal connection that these two projects offered, testaments to blowing up without selling out, was an inspiration.

It was "[a] summer, then, of two albums by two titans with two different views of American experience," wrote Rick Moody, "each of them very moving, each of them struggling for a response to all the trouble back in Washington."

The summer of 1984 ended with an event that represented and encapsulated pop's new world order: on September 14, MTV's first Video Music Awards were held at New York's Radio City Music Hall. Herbie Hancock's "Rockit" and "Every Breath You Take" by the Police were the most-nominated clips, while the Cars' "You Might Think" won the prize for Video of the Year (the Prince and Springsteen albums came out too late for any of their videos to be eligible). David Bowie and Rod Stewart were among the performers, while a hodgepodge of artists from Diana Ross to Iggy Pop, the Go-Gos to Carly Simon, made appearances.

But really, there was only one thing most viewers remembered from that night, and it marked the true arrival of the final figure in the Mount Rushmore of '80s pop. For this was the night that Madonna sang her new single, "Like a Virgin," while writhing on the ground in a wedding dress and flashing her undergarments. Her first album had been a success, starting on the dance/R&B side (her clear target, as her first single was released without a photograph on the sleeve in an attempt to ease the way onto black radio) and eventually reaching the Top Ten on the pop chart. But it was with the Nile Rodgers–produced *Like a Virgin* that Madonna would join Michael Jackson, Prince, and Bruce Springsteen as another defining act of the era.

"I remember in 1983, while we were making the *Purple Rain* movie, Prince said, 'When a woman comes along and does what I do, she will rule the world,'" says Susan Rogers. "And it wasn't long before Madonna did exactly what he did, and ruled the world."

Springsteen and I spoke about the fact that *Rolling Stone* had put him on the cover of an issue celebrating the music of the 1980s, and he invoked this same Fab Foursome. "It easily could have been Michael Jackson or Prince or Madonna," he says. "They were all massively influential. But using me, well, I suppose that's what I was aiming at. I was very aware that the people I was referencing were people who were not afraid to take on some history as part of their song and dance. I worked through [the eighties] to find my link in the chain of artists who were willing to do that—whether it was Woody Guthrie or Bob Dylan or Elvis or James Brown, Curtis Mayfield,

Marvin Gaye. That was the kind of impact I was interested in having."

In 1984, the kind of impact those pivotal figures represented, that feeling of universal connection with music, reached a peak. Even in the 1960s, at the pinnacle of creativity for the Beatles, Bob Dylan, and the Rolling Stones, it wasn't the same common currency; there was still widespread resistance to rock in the average adult community. But it can be argued that 1984 represented the moment when pop music's audience got too big, and the center could not hold. When there were multiple albums selling 10, 15, 20 million copies at the same time, it was inevitable that things would start to fragment and that the various subgenres of pop would grow big enough to sustain economies of their own.

Maybe there have been bigger years than 1984 in terms of pure sales; as formats and pricing change over time, it's almost impossible to make definitive comparisons. Certainly, the teen-pop boom at the turn of the twenty-first century saw Britney Spears and 'N Sync and the Backstreet Boys move millions of units, but those acts did not span a cross section of listeners, radio formats, and generations the way that the '80s megastars did. The audience for music—and, I suppose, culture in general—began to grow narrower but deeper, and we've never since experienced the universal effect, the monoculture, of 1984. Prince achieved his goal of "White, black, Puerto Rican / Everybody just a-freakin'," writ larger than he ever could have dreamed.

There was one other factor, too, that was altering the

playing field even as Prince and his contemporaries were changing the world in 1984. Spurred by the surprising success of the *Run-D.M.C.* album, in June the Fresh Fest tour—the first national showcase for New York rappers and break-dancers—set off on a twenty-seven-city tour. Hip-hop had been steadily hammering away at the pop charts for five years, since the Sugarhill Gang's "Rapper's Delight" in 1979, and the new street dancing had already been co-opted into some lightweight but fun "breaksploitation" movies like *Breakin'* and *Beat Street* (though after being featured as part of the opening ceremonies at the 1984 Olympics in Los Angeles, it would soon be perceived as an overexposed novelty and pushed back into the clubs). But with evidence that rap, with its new sense of strong black masculinity, was popular enough to sell actual albums and concert tickets, the record industry—though still befuddled by the music itself—began making a move to develop the genre into a real business.

In another few years, those seeds would explode into the multiplatinum sales of Run-D.M.C.'s "Walk This Way" remake with Aerosmith and the *Raising Hell* album, followed by the Beastie Boys' number one *Licensed to Ill* album. By then, the solidarity of 1984 had crumbled—superficially, along hip-hop's racial divide, though if you looked more closely, really between a young generation who accepted a new, boldly aggressive musical and cultural movement and an older audience who did not comprehend it. The rise of hip-hop would throw Prince off his game, too, as he first railed against the new movement and then tried to catch up with lame, unconvincing attempts to integrate rap into his own music.

Finally, and in some ways most important of all, technology was undergoing a transformation in 1984. Though it wasn't immediately apparent, it was also over the course of this year that the next two revolutions in music distribution were initiated. The first commercial compact disc players had been put on the market in the U.S. in 1983, but it was the next year that the first portable players were sold, and that the first CD players were installed in cars. As the format became more convenient and offered better sound than cassettes and albums both, it soared in popularity, and by 1988, CDs would be outselling vinyl LPs. This was a bonanza for the music industry; as consumers rushed to replace all of their old albums with CDs, it was as though billions of dollars of found money was raining down on the labels.

Meanwhile, during the Super Bowl on January 22, 1984, Apple Computer ran perhaps the most famous advertisement in television history. Directed by Ridley Scott (*Blade Runner, Alien*), it aired nationally only this one time. In the sixty-second spot, a blond woman in athletic wear runs into a gray, dystopian setting—clearly invoking the milieu of Orwell's novel—in which bald human drones are listening to their leader address them on a giant TV. The woman, chased by storm trooper types, triumphantly heaves a sledgehammer through the screen. A voice-over delivered the text that flashed on televisions around the world:

"On January 24, Apple Computer will introduce Macintosh. And you'll see why 1984 won't be like *1984*."

Buying the spot during the most expensive broadcast of the year nearly destroyed Apple, but the company sold 72,000 computers in the next three months, over 50 percent more than their most optimistic projections. As has been well documented, it was a bumpy ride for Apple over the next two decades, but eventually, while the record companies had grown lazy assuming that the profits of the CD boom would continue forever, they came up with the iTunes model that would define the next generation of the industry. One key element of that model would be continually increased personalization; the construction of playlists would largely supplant the communality of radio.

In the social media universe that accompanied this digital revolution in music, it's increasingly difficult to imagine anything that would be able to reach across boundaries of age, race, and gender the way that the recording giants of 1984 did. Of course there will always be songs that capture a wide imagination; in 2011, Adele's *21* album proved that it was still possible for a piece of music to have a long-term and far-ranging impact, and something like Disney's *Frozen* sound track showed that the marriage of music and film could extend the lives, and the reach, of both.

But from the way it took advantage of MTV's rising power and novelty to its perfect anticipation and mirroring of a shift in the culture's racial attitudes, more than any other project, *Purple Rain* as both an album and a film represented the culmination of an unprecedented moment in pop history. Crossing barriers of color, gender, musical style, and media, it perfectly embodies the remarkable cultural convergences of 1984.

"It brought all the races together, it really did," says Jill Jones. "It wasn't a black movie, it wasn't a white movie, and I think that may be why it had its tipping point. He was speaking that language already—he just caught hold of a shooting star.

"It wasn't even so much about color in the eighties, it was everybody trying to stretch their hair in that same freaking direction. It didn't matter if someone was black, white, green—they had that *hair*."

NINE

Let Me Guide U

Now that Prince had the biggest album and movie in the country, promotional requests kept pouring into his camp. He stuck to his guns about maintaining absolute silence, though, and decided that Lisa Coleman and Wendy Melvoin would become the spokespeople for him and the band.

"The way he put it to me," says Melvoin, "which I think was just him working me, was 'I can't speak well, I don't speak well. And you speak well, you're eloquent. And I need some-one smart to represent something that I can't do well.' And I was like, 'Okay, all right. What can I say, and what can't I say?' He would always say, 'Just tell the truth'—ooh, that's fucking snake oil right there, man. That was not true. That was not true at all."

Management arranged practice interviews for the two musicians, without informing them that the sessions were re-hearsals. "I remember in one hotel, they had called a few journalists who wanted interviews," says Coleman. "I don't know what they bargained with these people, but they came in and asked us questions. And I remember Steve Fargnoli interrupting and saying, 'Well, this is something that they're not gonna talk about right now,' or he'd kind of [whisper], 'Tell them this.' There were a couple of moments where he intervened and made sure that we were gonna follow the company line."

Most of the reporting was pretty innocuous, anyway, because the next big news was the announcement of the Purple Rain tour. Unfortunately, it would not be possible to re-create the full excitement of the movie's music on the road, because while Apollonia 6 appeared as guests during Prince's set, the Time—whose onstage power had pushed Prince so hard on the two previous tours and who had garnered such a strong response in *Purple Rain*—had broken up. Rumors had been rampant even before the movie opened; in his review of the *Ice Cream Castle* album, which included "Jungle Love" and "The Bird," *Rolling Stone*'s Christopher Connelly asked whether the band was "Prince's AAA farm team, his comic relief, or his competition," and noted that "word from the Twin Cities has Morris going solo any day now."

After playing at the movie premiere party, the band was no more; on the tour, they would be replaced by the woman *Rolling Stone* was calling Prince's "main squeeze," Sheila E. When Prince finally broke his media silence in 1985, he expressed only regret about the disintegration of the Time. "They were, to be perfectly honest, the only band that I was afraid of," he said. "And they were turning into, like . . . Godzilla, and certain things happened and different waves flowed, different winds blew, and everybody fell apart. But I still love all those guys . . . and I hope they get back together, 'cuz I want some competition, ya know?"

Elsewhere, he expressed even deeper admiration for the group that still stands as the finest of his numerous alter egos. "Jesse and Morris and Jerome and Jimmy and Terry had the makings of one of the greatest R&B bands in history," he told MTV. "I could be a little pretentious in saying that, but it's truly the way I feel. There's no one who could wreck a house like they could. I was a bit troubled by their demise, but . . . it's important that one's happy first and foremost." Soon it would be reported that Morris Day had signed a "hefty seven-figure, three-picture" deal with Twentieth Century Fox.

While guitarist Jesse Johnson also struck out on his own, signing a solo deal with A&M Records and bringing two Time alumni (keyboard player Mark Cardenas and bassist Jerry Hubbard) with him, Prince immediately got to work creating (yet another) new band out of the ashes. He invited Jellybean Johnson, Jerome Benton, and "St. Paul" Peterson to form the basis of a new band, which he named the Family. The other members of the new group were already familiar within the camp—Susannah Melvoin as the lead vocalist alongside Peterson, and Alan Leeds's brother Eric adding saxophone and flute.

The Purple Rain tour was announced in September, with an opening set for November 4 at Detroit's Joe Louis Arena; when the first four shows sold out in four hours (at ticket prices ranging from $12.50 to $17.50, well below the $30 seats on the Jacksons' 1984 Victory tour that had inspired such outrage), another three dates were added.

The first matter of business was for Prince and the Revolution to try out the new show on a small stage, without all of the elaborate arena staging that would follow. They attempted to set up a surprise show in Detroit, but had to cancel when word leaked that Prince would be playing. Eventually, on September 23, the band performed at Bogart's in Cincinnati, a club with a capacity about the same as First Avenue's. The show was promoted with radio spots announcing a "Purple Rain Ball," featuring a new band called Red, Hot, and Blue. At about eleven o'clock, the Revolution took the stage and played a ninety-minute set, ending the night with an encore that re-created the "I Would Die 4 U," "Baby I'm a Star," and "Purple Rain" sequence that closed the album.

(At this point, you might recall that Cincinnati is my own hometown, and that in September of 1984, just a few weeks before this show, I had departed the city to start college. I leave it to you to imagine how I reacted to the news that Prince had played a rehearsal date for the most highly anticipated tour in the world—quite possibly while I was watching *Purple Rain* yet another time with my new friends—at a club I had often gone to during the previous few years.)

Meantime, work was proceeding on the plans for the real, large-scale shows. The stage set cost around $300,000, and the touring party would ultimately grow to 125 people, with thirteen trucks carrying all of the gear, including thirty wardrobe cases. There were problems with the initial stage design. "It was so big, Prince didn't like it," says Fink. "He said, 'This isn't intimate enough. It's too large for the band.' Everybody was spread out from each other too much, so he had them rein it in."

The set featured a claw-foot bathtub—long a favorite Prince motif, as seen prominently in the "When Doves Cry" video—that rose from the stage on a hydraulic lift. Fink remembers a near disaster during one of the final dress rehearsals. "The very first time he tried it, he goes up behind Bobby Z, and he's up on this giant platform. He lays back in the tub and it's got kind of a slanted back, and the tub is not secured to the lift—it's a fiberglass, lightweight tub—and all of a sudden it starts to teeter, and then it went over completely, with him in it, to the floor. It's a long drop, twenty-five or thirty feet, and of course, we all gasped and he just lay there, motionless. We all thought, 'Oh my God, we hope he's not severely injured,' and we don't know what to do. Everybody rushed over and checked him out, and fortunately, nothing had broken, but he was bruised pretty badly. Heads rolled for the stage people [who clearly hadn't thought], 'Gee, do you think this might go over?'—there was no foresight on that one."

Bob Cavallo remembers the incident as one of the few times that Prince revealed any jitters about everything that was happening during the *Purple Rain* explosion. "The only way I could tell when he was nervous is if he would get furious, get over-the-top about something going wrong," he says. "It was two or three days before the tour, we were set up at a big soundstage and we're running through all of the gags we have, and the bathtub doesn't work right, and I know what that meant—that meant, 'This isn't ready. I'm gonna be embarrassed.' He walks from the stage, over to where the costume designers and everybody are in a big row. Me and Steve [Fargnoli] are sitting there. He walks down, jumps up on the table, takes out an imaginary dick, and pisses on [everybody]. He looks at us, and I said, 'Don't do it. Don't even fucking think about it.' He backed off and he gets off the bench and he said, 'You don't know what you're doing.' I said, 'You ever see a fucking Earth, Wind and Fire show? I understand the reason you called me in the first place is that Mo Ostin said, "Bob Cavallo is the reason those shows are the way they are."' So he walks away."

As the tour rolled into Detroit, which had been one of the first markets to really support Prince, it was becoming clear that the band was about to experience something they had never really imagined. "Even after the movie was released and stuff was happening," says Coleman, "I don't know what it felt like—we were just in it. But I remember that first gig in Detroit. It felt different. Even just the hotel, it was huge . . ."

"And we were on the hundredth floor and covered in fog, remember that?" Wendy Melvoin continues. "We were *freaked*. You could look out the window and see the arena that we were gonna be playing in, and they had the purple lights going, and it was like a massive party."

"That's when we first got assigned bodyguards," says Coleman. "Prince was being shuttled around, and he would travel separately, which was kind of a bummer. They'd drive the limo right up to the plane, things like that."

In a lengthy review in *Rolling Stone* of the opening night in Detroit, Chris Connelly offered a wildly mixed set of reactions. He described the crowd as "neither a predominantly black audience nor a typical white rock & roll one," and then, in the next sentence, mentioned the "predominantly white crowd." He observed that the evening's five costume changes "seemed to slow the show's momentum and stifle Prince's natural spontaneity," and seemed a bit mystified by some of Prince's stage banter during a three-song mini-set played solo on the electric piano. " 'Do you know the difference between life and death? God,' said the singer. 'Do you want to spend the night? Do you want to take a bath?' " By the final encore of "Purple Rain," Connelly said, "many in the audience filed out."

In *Billboard,* Nelson George echoed this hesitation about the performance. "Prince has led us to expect him to reach for greatness and this show, for all his appeal, simply doesn't do it," he wrote. (George suspects that this review was the reason Prince later wrote the violent revenge track "Bob George," which is widely assumed to be directed at him, on 1994's *The Black Album.*) Bob Merlis, on the other hand, recalls that in Detroit "it was electrifying to have that thing come to life in a big arena. . . . Prince really delivered, significantly, onstage."

The Detroit dates marked the beginning of Prince's charity efforts throughout the Purple Rain tour. A number of tickets were sold to benefit Chicago teacher Marva Collins's inner-city training program, as would be done at many of the tour stops. At the end of the month, the band also performed for 2,500 deaf and handicapped students at Gallaudet College in Washington, D.C., one of four shows they would perform for special-needs children during the tour.

Ticket sales continued booming: in the same issue of *Rolling Stone* that ran the Detroit live review, the two top spots in the "Top Ten Concert Grosses" chart went to Prince's stops in Landover, Maryland, and Philadelphia. On November 28, "I Would Die 4 U" was released as a single, and would climb to number eight on the pop charts. The B-side, "Another Lonely Christmas," was an almost absurdly over-the-top ballad, with Prince "drink[ing] banana daiquiris till I'm blind" while lamenting the death of a girlfriend on Christmas Day (cause of death: "Your father said it was pneumonia / Your mother said it was stress").

The Purple Rain tour would go on to play ninety-eight shows in thirty-two cities. "The nature of the tour was ridiculously ambitious," says Alan Leeds. "The focus that was put on it was something that really none of us—including Cavallo and Fargnoli, and me with James Brown, let alone any of the performers—had really experienced. This idea that we're in this capsule and we come to town and just take over for a week, streets are closed and there's security at the hotel elevator, I'd never rolled like that. This is shit that you read about—it's Beatles, it's Rolling Stones, and that's pretty much it."

Thirty years later, the sense from everyone within the *Purple Rain* bubble is that it really was a blur. "There are certain things I remember, specific cities that were highlights to me," says Matt Fink. "The Syracuse show that we shot for the live performance video—I remember that one just because it was important. The venue was too big to do a show; playing the Superdome or the Orange Bowl was the same thing. Any of those large football dome stadiums are just not fun to play in, because the echo slap-back coming at you is insane. You're trying to hear yourself and it's confusing. And then the audience, like ninety thousand people, is roaring at you during all of that, it's very disorienting. So those really stick out for me, just for the sheer size and the experience and the scale."

As well rehearsed and (some said overly) planned as the show was, not every night went off without a hitch. In Birmingham, Alabama, the curtain mechanism stalled in the opening "reveal" of the band, the hydraulic lift failed to get Prince up to the stage, and his guitar didn't "climax" at the end of "Baby I'm a Star." On top of all that, the touring party then had to sprint to beat an ice storm out of town. Leeds remembers Prince coming to him after the show and saying, "What can you tell me so that I know none of this is going to happen again?"

Mostly, though, the concerts were triumphant. "It was the greatest show on earth," says Susannah Melvoin. "It was the greatest band, it was perfectly sequenced. The lighting director, LeRoy Bennett, was practically another band member. It was all just dialed in so perfectly. Every single night, I couldn't wait to see it."

As the tour rolled from town to town, Prince never let up on all of his other recording projects. "On the Purple Rain tour, we went into studios a lot because we were making Sheila's record," says Susan Rogers. "So I would scout recording studios and book them in advance, and we'd go into those studios after a set—after a four-hour sound check and a three-hour set, we'd go into the studio at midnight or one A.M., record all night, and then get on the bus and drive to the next city to do a show the next day. We also did video editing; we did the video for "Take Me with U" somewhere in Texas, maybe it was Dallas. We had to spend a day off editing that video. We worked every day, that's for sure."

"Almost every off-hour, we were finding a recording studio somewhere or renting a truck to follow us around," says Leeds. "There was always something else going on besides the shows, for better or worse."

The emotional high point of the tour came during a five-show hometown stand at the St. Paul Civic Center over the holidays. The governor of Minnesota, Rudy Perpich, designated the days of Christmas week as official "Prince Days" for the state. Prince's mother and father attended shows on different nights; when his mother arrived, she found a note he had left on her seat that read "This one's 4 U." (On December 26, he couldn't resist playing "Another Lonely Christmas" for the one and only time onstage.) At the final show, a visibly moved Prince said, "This has been the best Christmas I ever had." He expressed his thanks to the unlikely city that he had brought into the international spotlight, closing the night by saying, "We belong to you forever."

There was another reason that Prince was so emotional during his holiday season in Minneapolis. Unbeknownst even to most of those around him, while *Purple Rain* was still the biggest record in the country, that week he also finished his next album. Four of the songs, in fact, had been recorded before *Purple Rain* was even released.

But it was a demo that Wendy and Lisa brought him that had been recorded by their respective brothers, David Coleman and Jonathan Melvoin, that provided the linchpin for the next project. A shimmery, winding track with flutes and strings reminiscent of the Beatles circa *Magical Mystery Tour,* it had a sound and feel that Prince loved, and he began to build the album around the psychedelic overtones of the song that would ultimately give the album its title, "Around the World in a Day."

Wendy and Lisa were closely involved in most of the album, and would remain the closest thing to true collaborators Prince would allow during this period. "We started making the album all that summer," says Melvoin, "and that's when it started getting super-creative."

Yet despite the vision of a communal utopia he offered in the song "Paisley Park"—which would soon become familiar as the name of the recording compound he built in rural Chanhassen, Minnesota, and of his new label imprint—the rest of the band was kept in the dark about the new album. "The thing about *Around the World in a Day* is I wasn't totally aware that he had been tracking that album," says Matt Fink. "I was not involved in it, and maybe a little disappointed that he, again, went within himself only—although he did have Lisa and Wendy involved. But I just wish I had been a part of that one more. I was okay with it, but at the same time, you always want to be in there if you can."

Despite the advantages gained from the Revolution's prominence on *Purple Rain*, Prince reverted to a solo focus on *Around the World*: six of the album's nine tracks were essentially solo recordings by Prince, with some vocal contributions from Melvoin and Coleman. The three full-band performances—"Pop Life," "America," and "The Ladder"—were recorded in February, July, and December respectively, so it's easy to imagine that the Revolution weren't even aware that an album was actually taking shape. ("The Ladder" and the title track both had a co-writing credit for John L. Nelson—obviously not bothered by his fictional portrayal in *Purple Rain*, he was playing an even more active role in his son's life during this period.)

"*Around the World in a Day* was really fast," says Susan Rogers. "We mixed a lot of it over Christmas in Minneapolis. We were on tour in a mobile truck, and on Christmas Eve and Christmas Day I was in that truck, parked in the driveway of his house, working on 'Tamborine' and 'The Ladder' for that record." At 4 A.M. on Christmas morning 1984, the follow-up to *Purple Rain* was completed.

Asked later by Detroit DJ the Electrifying Mojo about his mood while recording *Around the World*, Prince said that he had "an f-you attitude, meaning that I was making something for myself and my fans, and the people who supported me through the years—I wanted to give them something, and it was like my mental letter. And those people are the ones who wrote me back, telling me that they felt what I was feeling."

But even if his focus had turned to the new music, he still had to go directly from Minneapolis to Dallas, the next stop on the Purple Rain tour. To those close to him, Prince was starting to display signs of his usual restlessness. "He was bored," says Melvoin. "He gave it everything onstage, and he was always in that. But he was gone, he was uninterested, and he had moved on."

"I think he kind of took things for granted for a minute there," says Coleman "and he'd never done that before."

"Creatively, he was over it," says Alan Leeds. "I'm sure it was fun playing the music for a while, but this is a guy who never stopped rehearsing, so they were all tired of playing the songs long before the tour started—they'd been playing them every day in rehearsals for a year, and the crew had been hearing them every day for a year.

"Also, there was a decision made to basically replicate the movie as much as possible. For the sake of the audience, that's what you had to do; it's what you were selling. A no-brainer. But what it also meant was a very constricting set, because the show was so theatrical, it left no room for spontaneity—in wardrobe, in choreography, or in the music. All the theatrical aspects of it made for a great production, but essentially it was a Broadway play with no give or take, with the exception of the encores, where he could stretch out. We paid a lot of overtime in a lot of buildings, because the only time of the night when he had any fun was the encores, which could go on for hours."

One stunning example of the high points was the second night in Atlanta; Questlove showed some bootleg footage from this performance to his NYU class. Prince is in a buoyant mood, stopping and starting the Revolution like they were one of James Brown's finest bands. He turns somersaults, brings out Jerome Benton to dance the Bird with him, and repeatedly teases a final exit during the encore, driving the audience further and further into a frenzy. "Chalk one up for the Kid!" he crows. "Now who gonna mess with us?" He may have been getting tired of the routine, but he could still whip himself and his musicians into something near perfection.

In the *Los Angeles Times,* though, Robert Hilburn—the respected critic who had conducted the final interview with Prince before Prince's self-imposed media silence—skewered the show for its more staged aspects. "Prince became a near-parody of himself, pandering to the audience's fascination with his sexy persona," he wrote, expressing his concern that "Prince's lame sexual posturing on the Purple Rain tour meant he was becoming the Bo Derek of rock."

Nor was any of the touring party prepared for the security issues and general madness that would explode in each city they hit. "Your privacy level goes away," says Fink, "and you can't get out of the hotel or you're in a restaurant surrounded by people—they find out you're there. We were in a mall in Atlanta, and Bruce Springsteen was hanging out that day in the mall, too, at the same time. He was incognito; he looked like a bum. We ran into him: 'Hey, Bruce, how you doing, man?' And then we went into a restaurant and somebody knew it was us and spread the word, and the next thing you know, there was a crowd outside blocking the door to get out of the restaurant. So that freaked me out."

"Prince always acted as if 'this is really going to blow up,' but I don't think even he thought about what that meant, how did that translate into day-to-day existence," says Leeds. "The old-school in me only saw that within the parameters of the traditional music business—'Okay, he's gonna have a huge album, it's gonna cross over, and we're gonna play arenas.' But not this, not closing motels and city streets.

"We're in D.C., staying at the Watergate, and Prince, as his habit was, had his hair styled—we'd find a salon that he could then rent out for the day, chase all the employees out, pay them off, and put newspaper in the windows and privatize it for an hour so he'd have the facilities. But somehow the word leaked—maybe the proprietor leaked it, because he's no fool—and I'm sitting in the hotel with Gwen, my wife, who was my assistant on the tour, and somebody called and said, 'You got the TV on? Well, turn on channel whatever,' and it's like every local station in D.C. had their trucks in front of the salon and Wisconsin Avenue was closed down. The police had closed the street, because the people had come out of every building and clogged the streets and the sidewalks! So, no, nobody anticipated that, nobody really thought that that's what it was going to mean."

As the new year of 1985 dawned, Prince also had to add a new round of performances and appearances to his schedule, since *Purple Rain* was nominated for a battery of awards. The album would win two Grammys—for Best Rock Performance by a Duo or Group and Best Album or Original Score Written for a Motion Picture or a Television Special—and, more incredibly, an Oscar for Best Original Song Score. (Apollonia Kotero later recalled that one night, after watching the *Purple Rain* dailies, she told Prince, " 'You know you're going to get an Oscar for this movie—not for the acting, but for the music.' He . . . slid off his chair, joking around, and said, 'You think so?' ")

Each of these shows offered a new opportunity for Prince to make an international impression, which he took full advantage of. At the Grammys, his onstage entourage included a little person. At the Brit Awards, hulking bodyguard Big Chick joined him onstage. Prince wore a pink feather boa, and his entire acceptance speech was "All thanks to God. Good night." When his name was announced at the Academy Awards, he grabbed Melvoin and Coleman, bringing them to the podium and handing off his trophy for Melvoin to hold.

"Of course, with Prince every TV appearance had to have something amazing or weird or shocking to stick out, so that's what we would start focusing on at sound checks," says Coleman. "We'd work out how to play 'Baby I'm a Star' or whatever on the next awards show. He put his energy into that—and I think he was having a great time. He had everything at his fingertips, and he started really planting a lot of seeds and he was riding high. He was pretty confident about everything—almost too cocky, in a lot of ways, and he kind of burst the bubble a little bit. Like, 'I can do anything,' 'Muthafuckas will buy anything.'

"He had these personalities, and he could just get mean. There was a part of Prince that we called Steve, and that was the guy that you could bum around with."

"That's the guy you spent the night with, and ate grapes and went to the grocery store with, and he was adorable," says Wendy Melvoin.

"He'd buy ice cream cones and wore sneakers," says Coleman, "but the next minute, he'd be like 'Hey, muthafuckas—' "

"He'd be fucking George Jefferson. And you'd be like, '*Oh, God.*' "

"I knew at that point that it was the beginning of the end," says Susannah Melvoin. "He had found the thing that was going to throw him into the stratosphere of stardom, but also that he couldn't stop. He became more moody, more superstitious, more compelled to keep his image solid and not break the mold, and that became confining. It's hard to live on a day-to-day basis that way. He had to live and breathe this character, and it was like, 'Who the fuck is that guy?' Sometimes it could be really scary."

Things came to a head on January 28, following the American Music Awards in Los Angeles, at which Prince was nominated for ten awards (Sheila E. had two nominations, and the Time picked up one, as well). A few days earlier, "Take Me with U" had been released as a single, the final single from *Purple Rain*; it was also the only one with another track from the album, an edit of "Baby I'm a Star," as the B-side, and the only one to fall short of the Top Ten, peaking at number 25.

The night of the AMAs that year was a historic moment in the music business, when dozens of the world's top recording artists, rather than going to parties or back on their tour buses after the ceremony, headed to Hollywood's A&M studios to record the song "We Are the World" to benefit African relief efforts. Written by Michael Jackson and Lionel Richie, produced by Quincy Jones, and featuring the voices of such legends as Stevie Wonder, Bob Dylan, Ray Charles, and Bruce Springsteen, the song would become the fastest-selling single in U.S. history and serve as the climactic moment of the Live Aid concert in Philadelphia in July.

Prince had, of course, been approached to participate, but he passed and proposed a different kind of contribution to the project. "I was with Prince one day at his home studio, just the two of us," says Rogers, "and he got a call from Quincy Jones asking him to come be part of 'We Are the World.' I only hear Prince's side of the conversation—I was in the control room waiting—but he declined it. It was a long conversation, and Prince said, 'Can I play guitar on it?' And they said no, and he ultimately said, 'Okay, well, can I send Sheila?' And he sent Sheila. Then he said, 'If there's going to be an album, can I do a song for the album?' And evidently they said yes."

At the awards show, it was a whirlwind of logistics and scheduling; everyone was buzzing about what was planned for later in the evening. "They kept us so cloistered that a lot of information never would get to us," says Coleman, "so I don't remember even knowing about 'We Are the World' until that day, when everybody was talking about it backstage. Like, 'We'll see you tonight, right?' And I was like, 'What are they talking about?' "

"Prince was pissed," says Wendy Melvoin. "He was like, 'I don't want to see any of you there, you're not allowed to go there.'"

Until the last minute, Prince's managers were still trying to persuade him to show up for the session. "At the American Music Awards, he keeps telling me the only thing he'll do is play guitar," says Cavallo. "So I call Quincy, and he says, 'I don't need him to fucking play guitar!' and he got angry. I said, 'All right, I don't know, he's not feeling well'—I start this whole campaign that he's getting the flu. I say to Prince backstage, 'I'm gonna say you're sick—if you go out tonight and you're seen, I can see the headlines: "Prince Parties While Rock Royalty Saves Millions" or whatever the fuck they want to write. They suspect you anyway. You've got to stay home, ride it out, and be sick.' 'Okay,' he says. They go directly from the American Music Awards to some fucking club on Sunset. On their way out, his bodyguard—idiot guy—smacks somebody, the press picks it up, and that was it."

After Prince, who won three trophies and delivered a blistering performance of "Purple Rain," left the awards ceremony, he and his entourage sped back to the Westwood Marquis hotel—at least for a while.

"We implore him, no matter what happens at the awards, we cannot go out in the streets and celebrate if you're not going to go to A&M and show up for this," says Leeds. "Fargnoli and I were like, 'Dude, the eyes are on you, okay? You just cleaned up. The two biggest things on the planet tonight are this recording session and you, and everybody is going to want to know why that's not one thing. So take your awards and keep your ass in the hotel. You cannot run the clubs the way you usually do, with two bodyguards, chasing girls. Not tonight, not while this is going on.'

"So that was good until about two in the morning. I think Bobby and his wife, Vicki, and me and Gwen were the last ones to leave his room. We stayed with him on purpose—but it was a big night, and he was on cloud nine. We left him around two, two-thirty in the morning, and at maybe four o'clock, four-thirty, the phone rings and it's Chick. 'Hey, buddy, better get back up!' 'What?' 'Well, we were at [the popular club] Carlos and Charlie's, and Big Larry, the bodyguard, he's in jail, the sheriff's got him.' I've had scandals on tour where musicians got busted and shit happens, but I've never read anything that was on page A1. It was just plain weird."

The UPI wire service story led with the contrast between Prince's problems that night and the good vibes of the "We Are the World" session: "Quick-fisted bodyguards provided a violent counterpoint to a night of international camaraderie." Ken Kragen, one of the USA for Africa organizers, was quoted as saying that "the effort would have been much more marketable with Prince's participation." The *Los Angeles Times* later offered a pithy summary of public opinion, writing that Prince's actions "led many to think of him as an arrogant jerk."

It was left to others to try to pick up the pieces. "I was doing all these interviews at that time, and everybody wanted to know why he wasn't there [for the recording session]," says Wendy Melvoin. "I wasn't allowed to say the real reason—which he would've gotten his fucking ass kicked hard for. . . . I had to say, 'We were in a mobile truck somewhere, he couldn't make it, duh-de-duh.' I knew there's no way I can say, 'Because he thinks he's a badass and he wanted to look cool, and he felt like the song for "We Are the World" was horrible and he didn't want to be around "all those muthafuckas."'

"It was horrible. He had us go to Carlos and Charlie's and have a fucking party. I remember it perfectly, thinking, 'This is so wrong. This is so wrong.' We were embarrassed. Everybody in the band was horrified. And that's where it felt like, there's something shifting here, where he's getting nasty. The entitlement—it was almost like a kid with too much candy."

"I think he was just too self-involved," says Coleman. "Even though he was reading all the magazines, he wasn't reading *Time* magazine; he was reading music magazines and fashion magazines. So his view of the world, politics, or anything—he just didn't know. He wasn't in tune with that. That wasn't his cause. He just became his own cause; the message went away."

As bad a decision as it may have been to blow off the "We Are the World" recording, it is worth remembering that Prince was in the middle of a tour that included an ongoing charity component that raised $250,000 for Marva Collins's work in Chicago and included multiple food drives and four free concerts for special-needs children. He would write a song, "Hello," that would be released in July as the B-side to *Around the World*'s "Pop Life" and would present his side of the incident with the paparazzo.

When he spoke to MTV at the end of 1985, Prince offered

something close to humility. "We had talked to the people that were doing USA for Africa, and they said it was cool that I gave them a song for the album," he said. "It was the best thing for both of us, I think. I'm strongest in a situation where I'm surrounded by people I know. So it's better that I did the music with my friends than going down and participating there. I probably would have just clammed up with so many great people in a room. I'm an admirer of all of the people who participated in that particular outing, and I don't want there to be any hard feelings. . . . The main thing [the song 'Hello'] says is that we're against hungry children, and our record stands tall."

Five days after the AMAs, following a sold-out show at the 80,000-plus-seat Superdome in New Orleans, he recorded "4 the Tears in Your Eyes," the song he contributed to the USA for Africa album. "We had a mobile truck there, and Prince recorded the song during sound check," says Susan Rogers. "As soon as the check was done, he came back into the truck and we stayed up all night, did the overdubs, finished it, mixed it. The next day we're still there, we've been up all night, and he's got another show to play. He was hungry, and he said, 'Do you think you can find any food here?' So I left the truck and went upstairs, and there were some people who were clearing out a room; they had catered a party and they had some leftover cold cuts and bread and pickles and chips and warm soda that they were going to throw out. I asked them if I could have some of it, and they said, 'Yeah, help yourself,' so I made up a couple of plates and I brought them back, and he and I had our leftover sandwiches and our warm soda, and we finished the track.

"A bit later, I remember reading in *People* magazine that at the 'We Are the World' session, they had champagne and caviar. In the papers, they had just torn Prince up: 'How dare he? He doesn't care about starving kids.' And I thought, 'No, actually, he was the one who went hungry on their behalf, who sat up all night and was happy to eat stale bread and warm soda to make a track for your record. He's the one who didn't have caviar and champagne.' But you can't say those things. I asked him, 'Aren't you going to say anything?' And he said, 'No, if you say anything, they got you.' "

The USA for Africa album shot to number one, and "4 the Tears In Your Eyes" was well received by critics, though it didn't generate any real radio interest or move the needle for the project. And the damage was already done. Bob Cavallo looks back on the "We Are the World" fiasco as a crucial turning point in Prince's entire career. "All of the superstars there just said horrible things about him," he says. "I don't know that they said anything to the press, but I know how incensed they were.

"I believe that moment is what made people ambivalent about his greatness. When you get negative press going, you need twenty years for people to stop reflecting on it. And if guys like Springsteen or whoever are talking about how great he is, like they used to, it would add to the legend. But instead, everybody kind of backed off, like, 'What the fuck kind of idiot is he that he would go to some dance club instead of just going there and singing two lines in the song?' "

Saturday Night Live opened the February 2 episode with

a sketch about the situation. Cast member Rich Hall, playing MTV VJ Mark Goodman, introduced the bit, saying, "As you know, Prince did not appear in the big USA for Africa video because he was busy bailing out his bodyguards after they beat up some of his fans outside of a Hollywood restaurant." But now, the "sultan of screen" had organized his own video effort for world hunger. Billy Crystal, as Prince, sang:

I am also the world,
I am also the children,
I am the one who had to bail them out,
Now ain't that givin'!
It's a choice I made!
The kids will have to wait,
There's got to be another way to get on MTV.

Cast members playing Bruce Springsteen, Paul Simon, and Willie Nelson all entered the studio, trying to sing, but each time "Prince" signaled to his bodyguards—played by Mr. T and Hulk Hogan—who manhandled the other artists and tossed them out of the room.

TEN

Why Must We Play This Game?

My new best friend Keith and I were counting down the days until the tickets were going on sale. I forget if it was actively snowing or there was just snow on the ground, but it was the middle of winter, and we knew it was going to mean sleeping on the sidewalk and waiting for the doors to open at Cutler's record store in New Haven if we were going to have a shot: their allotment for seats to the six Nassau Coliseum dates in Long Island would presumably be small. (We were still a long way from the days of online sales, for better or worse, and were entirely dependent on how many actual physical tickets could be accessed in this market.)

It was my freshman year at Yale, and my across-the-hall neighbor Keith and I were inseparable at the time, and comparably obsessed with *Purple Rain,* so we made the commitment to do it. He took the overnight shift, lying out on the freezing sidewalk with a couple of other diehards. I relieved him at five or six in the morning, counting down until the store opened. And then—at nine or ten or whenever it was—someone unlocked the door and informed us that Cutler's wouldn't actually be selling the tickets. In an effort to foil scalpers, I guess, a little ticket booth spot a few blocks away, which mostly handled the local theaters, had the precious block of Prince ducats.

I grabbed Keith's sleeping bag and sprinted across campus. I think I moved up a spot or two as the line reassembled. I recall that I bought six tickets, as many as I could afford with the cash in my hand; I huddled with an upperclassman who was known for running a side business brokering tickets, and traded him four of the upper-deck seats I had for two in the middle of the arena. I guess we sold the other two at some kind of markup—that must have been the plan, though I can't recall if we had already set that up or found someone or how we handled that transaction. Anyway, we were set, with a pair of decent seats at only a slight premium.

Getting to the show was another matter. The date was March 23, 1985, which was during spring break, so we hung around campus until it was time, and then took the train into Manhattan to stay at our friend Dicky's family's apartment. The Long Island Rail Road trip to Uniondale was bonkers: almost everyone on the train was wearing purple (I borrowed someone's skinny purple tie for the occasion). The whole car was singing and dancing and was, to borrow Prince's own word, delirious with anticipation.

Almost thirty years later, it's hard to come up with too many details about the show. I remember the segment with

Prince alone at the piano most clearly, for some reason. He played "Raspberry Beret," which was still a few months from being released, and it was obvious in seconds that it would be another huge hit. He played the heartbreaking B-side "How Come U Don't Call Me Anymore," and Keith and I were ecstatic because it was a particular favorite of ours. Some doves flew around the arena during "When Doves Cry," which closed the main set, and there were mirrors and the bathtub set up onstage to re-create the video.

The most remarkable moment came at the end. The first encore was a lengthy jam on "I Would Die 4 U" / "Baby I'm a Star," with and some horn players and opening act Sheila E. joining on percussion, that seemed to go on for hours. The second encore, of course, was "Purple Rain," and it seemed like there was no way to follow that. The house lights came up and most of the audience filed out, but for whatever reason, we stayed to keep soaking in the excitement of the night.

After a long pause, with the lights still on, Prince and the band ambled back out and played a lengthy version of the not-yet-released "America," a song Prince would describe as "straightforwardly patriotic," with yet another warning of nuclear Armageddon. Keith and I scrambled over the empty rows of seats and were dancing on top of chairs maybe ten rows from the stage. There haven't been too many moments when I've ever felt happier.

Looking back on the set list from that show, we did draw—on paper, at least—a good night. The concerts had gotten longer since the thirteen songs performed in Detroit on opening night; most sets by this stage of the tour were more like eighteen or nineteen songs. With the extra time at the piano and the additional encore, we got twenty-three songs, including all nine numbers from the *Purple Rain* album.

For eighteen-year-old me, it was a joyous night, but maybe I would have seen something different if I were looking closer. At this point, almost ninety shows into the tour, Prince was growing tired and irritable. In 1998, Prince would describe his state of mind to Touré: "I was doing the seventy-fifth Purple Rain show, doing the same thing over and over—for the same kids who go to Spice Girls shows. And I just lost it. I said: 'I can't do it!' They were putting the guitar on me and it hit me in the eye and cut me, and blood started going down my shirt. And I said, 'I have to go onstage,' but I knew I had to get away from all that. I couldn't play the game."

"Things started cracking during the tour," says Wendy Melvoin. "He'd have these terrible mood swings, which he was prone to having anyway, but during that time he would get really shitty to one of us or fire one of the techs for, like, breathing on his microphone—he started getting a little bit more paranoid about that kind of stuff, and his moods started getting a little bit freaky. I think it was just because he was exhausted, and when you're that exhausted and you're in denial about how exhausted you are, there's a pathology to it. You can't be clear."

"He still was really convinced that he should be the leader," says Coleman, "but I remember we had a conversation where he said, 'You need to know when to ask for help.' I couldn't believe he was saying that—I'm like, 'Who are you? What have you done with Prince?' But it was a really smart thing for him to discover."

"He would deny saying that now," adds Melvoin.

"I lost touch with him for a good year, while he was being a big rock star, a movie star, getting any girl he wanted, getting petulant and needy," says Susannah Melvoin. "Everyone would have to go to his hotel room after each show to watch the show, every night, to critique the entire thing. It got to be more and more of 'You need to do this,' 'Do this when I'm doing that,' until no one in the room could breathe. It was not as fun as it was in the beginning."

Alan Leeds could feel the pressure getting to everyone as the Purple Rain tour rolled on. The triumphant mood of the first few shows had begun to sour. "At first, everybody was sharing the quest," he says. "Despite all these little dramas and subsidiary plot lines, I can honestly say that everybody from the crew to the band members to even the disgruntled Jesse Johnsons and Jeromes of the world, everybody shared this idea that 'we're all on this very unique ride together that is really beyond anything any of us ever imagined. Let's don't fuck it up, because this is a ticket you just can't go buy. It's hard to get to the Super Bowl, and you may not get here again, so even if you lose, enjoy it.'

"By the same token, as the tour went on, like any tour, you're away at camp; you're not in the real world. It becomes such an insulated environment, particularly when a tour is so security conscious. Everywhere we were going, there were hundreds of people trying to get at him and media trying to get at the rest of us because he doesn't talk, which meant they were yelling at everybody else that they would ordinarily ignore. So everything became a challenge to the media to find an angle to somehow get a story. You'd go to—pick a town, Charlotte, North Carolina—and you pick up the morning paper and it's front page. Not front of the Variety section, but on page A1, where somebody at the venue leaked the catering rider and there's a long story about the M&M's in the dressing room. You get off the plane and this is what you look at. And you're like, 'That's my existence they're talking about. They're writing about what I deal with every day. Oh shit—that's weird.' And worse yet, *he*'s gonna read that, and he's gonna call me and say, 'That's not a good look. Are you dealing with that?' "

Mark Brown, who was already resentful of the way Prince had moved Melvoin into the spotlight, was having the hardest time of it. He said that during the making of *Purple Rain*, Prince would tell him, " 'Mark, after this, you're never going to have to work again.' " But now Brown was upset about the band's salary, which he claimed was just $2,200 a week, and he began drinking heavily during the tour. "For me, the whole thing was a little too much at a young age," he said.

Even though he was recording music for himself, Sheila E., the Family, and other side projects along the way, the routine of being on a lengthy tour was interrupting Prince's usual constant flow of ideas. Doing the same thing night after night for six months, so soon after the time spent dedicated to the movie shoot, was aggravating to someone used to complete freedom to pursue his creativity. "I think the process of the filmmaking took so long, and his pace got a little off, so there was no way to quench his thirst again—he needed things fast," says Jill Jones. "He would finish a record, and then he would be on another one. He couldn't sleep, he was just driven, to the point of 'Where is he getting all these ideas? Where's the stimulus coming from?' You can't live like that—because then I think it just became an escape. I think he was having fun, but I think he had to make a lot of adjustments."

In addition to starting to work in some of the material from *Around the World in a Day,* there were other changes happening in the nightly set. The conversations with God were taking up a more prominent spot in the show; some nights, Prince would fall to the ground as if struck down by the Almighty, and the concert would take on the tone of a desperate plea for redemption. "His emphasis was not on sexuality anymore, but on God," said Howard Bloom.

Bloom believes that the onstage psychodrama was about more than just a spiritual struggle—it was something both familial and musical. "He had the voice of God coming down from the very center of the ceiling," he says. "When I hear that voice, I know Prince is going through a wrestling match between himself and his dad—that's a voice inside of Prince. There's Prince the child, the adolescent rebelling against his dad, and then there's the Prince who *is* his dad. Prince who is his dad is not an original musician, and Prince rebelling against his dad is."

Prince also started messing around with the band lineup, most notably bringing saxophonist Eric Leeds into the mix. In

Greensboro, North Carolina, on the second stop of the tour, Leeds was tapped to add a solo in "Baby I'm a Star." Then he was worked into another song, and by midway through the tour, he was practically a full member of the Revolution.

"I'll never forget the day," says Alan Leeds. "We had a benefit at the Santa Monica Civic Center one morning—it was actually a morning show. And Prince did an abbreviated set and he went offstage, waiting for an encore, and he said, 'Tell Eric to go out there and play the introduction to "Purple Rain," instead of Wendy's solo.' She would always start it off and, particularly on these casual shows, she would play sometimes three or four minutes before he'd come back out. But spontaneously he said, 'Tell him—let Eric do that,' without any regard for the fact that this was diplomatically difficult for me.

"The whole crew watched Wendy, and it's all they talked about—'Did you see her face?' Some of the guys on the crew were like, 'Yeah, go, Eric!' and it was, like, a scandal. By then, the enormous success of *Purple Rain* gave Wendy cred with the other guys—because she was huge; you couldn't deny that. It was easy to resent a nobody, but now she's not a nobody anymore. That changed real quick."

On February 21, on a day off between a series of shows at the Forum in Los Angeles (during one of which Madonna and Bruce Springsteen would both join the band onstage for the encore), Prince showed up at the Warner Bros. offices with a group including Melvoin and Coleman, Joni Mitchell, and his father, who was wearing a caftan. They sat on the floor of a conference room while the staff was gathered to listen, for the first time, to *Around the World in a Day.*

"It was so extraordinary for a major artist to have so little label oversight," Susan Rogers wrote in an e-mail. "I don't know if anyone at WB even received copies of works in progress. A single cassette copy of each song made in the studio was handed straight to Prince. It was rare to make copies for anyone other than him or a band member."

From all reports, the album was received enthusiastically (though it's hard to imagine a surprise visit by the label's biggest star eliciting a cool reception). But the project certainly raised a number of questions. It must have been clear on even a first listen that the album was a left turn from *Purple Rain,* with none of the flashy guitar and few of the pop hooks. "Raspberry Beret" and "Pop Life" gave the label some radio-friendly fare to work with, but tracks like "Tamborine" and "Temptation" were experimental, cerebral. Not that potential singles mattered for now, anyway, because Prince made it clear that he wanted no advance promotion for *Around the World,* hoping that fans would listen to it as a whole. ("This has got to be the easiest album I've ever worked on," Warners creative marketing chief Jeff Ayeroff told the *Los Angeles Times.* "In a way, it's very refreshing—it's merchandising anarchy.")

Most critically, of course, was the fact that shifting his focus to a new album meant that Prince was winding down *Purple Rain,* even as it remained the center of the live set and continued to sell by the truckload. "The promotion director was very concerned that we would be putting a stop on *Purple Rain*," says Bob Merlis. "It obviously could have been bigger if the next album held a little while—and that became the ongoing struggle between Prince and Warner Brothers."

"I guess *Around the World* was a smart record, all things considered," says Alan Leeds. "Anything too obvious might've been more successful at the time, but in the long run, it would not look good. Later, when I came off the road and was running his label, we would talk on almost a daily basis about how to get material to the market quicker. He told me once, 'I look at these songs like newspapers. They're obsolete tomorrow. It's not stimulating for me to play, my head has moved on, so I need a machine that's more immediate.'

"So I think the answer is yeah, he was over *Purple Rain*. And he also realized that the most important thing was 'How do you follow this?' and whether you like *Around the World* or not, smartly, there was no consideration of doing *Purple Rain 2*."

Well . . . maybe not as an album, but Bob Cavallo was certainly looking at Prince's options in Hollywood. Though *Purple Rain* had turned out to be a blockbuster, Warner Bros. had been so unsure about the project that they had no rights to his next film. Cavallo claims that he negotiated a deal with the studio that would give Prince a deal comparable to what a star like Dustin Hoffman would have commanded at the time, with a significant percentage of the box-office gross.

"So I tell him, 'Here's what we should do,'" says Cavallo. "'Warners wants a sequel. I know you won't do a sequel'—I understood that—'but we could do *Purple Rain 2: The Further*

Adventures of The Time.' That's my title, whether or not they would call it that. I said, 'The movie starts with the night of the show where he sings "Purple Rain," and in the audience are some guys from Vegas. Prince wins; the Time get second prize, and that's a month in Vegas in some lounge.' Basically the story I tell him is 'the Time go to Vegas, you come to play Vegas—so we'll have one scene with you—they come backstage and ask for your advice because they're in trouble with the cops, they're in trouble with the Mafia, and their only friends are the show-girls.' So you know the movie I'm envisioning: a big, monster movie, like a Martin and Lewis film, with a lot of great-looking broads and caricatured mob guys, whatever. He said that was, like, insulting to him.

"Morris Day came out of *Purple Rain* such a superstar," he continues. "I wanted to make a movie with him. He said, 'I'm not working with you anymore. You turned me into a clown.' I said, 'Well, you're a comedian; is Richard Pryor a clown? What are you talking about? And secondly, do you really think that you'll be a superstar with your music career?' As soon as he started getting high, instead of thinking that Prince was helping him, he thought he was using him. The Time came out of that movie big; they could've had their own movie deal and made a series of films. That's what I believed."

Day may have been the most visible disappointment, but he wasn't the only one to come out of the *Purple Rain* project with a distorted sense of his own standing. It was as if the confidence and fearlessness that Prince had drilled into all the musicians around him had become a liability. "The one thing that changed in me was a certain sense of stardom, almost an ego-boost thing," says Fink. "I wouldn't say I became snooty or arrogant—'Look at me, I'm the greatest keyboard player in the world'—but Prince used to like to tell us how great we were. 'How does it feel to be in the greatest band in the world?' It was almost like a Muhammad Ali–esque bravado, that kind of attitude. I never wanted to give in to that, I didn't want to get that thing that happens. And then all of a sudden, I found myself doing it and really believing it."

Alan Leeds has also said that the Revolution "had an enormously inflated sense of their importance to the project. . . . They pretty much felt they were the second coming of the Beatles as a band." Elaborating on these remarks, he seems to lay blame equally at the feet of the musicians and at those of their leader for building to an unsustainable set of expectations.

"The whole subplot," he says, "was Prince basically convincing everybody that they were a self-contained band—'It's not Prince and his backup band anymore, it's the Commodores. Yeah, I'm Lionel Richie, but we're still the Commodores.' And, amazingly, they bought it. I would just sit there and say, 'Be careful, okay? I know you've got people screaming your name because you're in a movie, I get it, but Scorsese isn't calling you. Your film career—it isn't a new career. Don't stop playing guitar.' But they really bought it, so when that ended and he got bored and the security blanket was gone, they really felt dissed. . . . It was like a wife who had been cheated on. That's how they behaved. It was just mind-blowing. And I was like, 'What planet are you on?' "

Sometime in March—probably right around the time I saw them play at Nassau Coliseum—Prince took the band aside for a pre-show meeting and told them that the tour would be ending after the April 7 show in Miami's Orange Bowl. They would not be continuing on to Europe or Asia or anywhere else around the world that was clamoring to hear them play.

"He had no interest in it," says Fink. "I asked him why, and he said, 'I've just had enough. I just don't want to do it.' And I went, 'So what's gonna happen now?' and he goes, 'Well, I'm gonna take two years off, and you guys can do whatever you want, as far as solo projects, or you can chill out, go be on retainer.' And that's it.

"And then within three months of the tour ending, he had *Around the World in a Day* ready to go. He gave us a little bit of a break, and then he was ready to jump back into another project, even though he had said it was going to be a much longer hiatus. Personally, I was hoping that we were going to do Europe with the Purple Rain tour—at least do a European leg of the tour, but he didn't. So in that sense I was a little disappointed."

While his band may have been let down, his managers were frustrated that he didn't take advantage of the opportunity to extend the once-in-a-lifetime success of *Purple Rain*. "I said to him, 'If you want to be Miles Davis and do whatever work you want, fine,'" says Cavallo. "'But if you want to be a pop strategist, you can't put out this fucking record now. It doesn't make any sense.' I never won the argument, but it impressed him. I said, 'You can't be both Miles Davis and Elvis Presley.'"

"His management was like, 'You're missing it here; there's something missing,'" says Coleman. "'Why are you doing this hippie thing now?' They were really pissed that he stopped the tour. And I was a little confused by that, too."

"Why are we shifting so quickly?" Melvoin remembers thinking. "This doesn't feel right. You're gonna alienate a lot of people. I mean, I love the stuff, but wait a minute. Slow down."

Mark Brown claimed that at end of tour, each band member got a $15,000 bonus. "It was a slap in the face," he said.

Before the final show, Steve Fargnoli issued an announcement stating that the Miami date would "be [Prince's] last live appearance for an indeterminate number of years." Fargnoli would say that when he asked Prince why he was taking time off, he explained that it was because he was going to "look for the ladder." When he asked for further clarification, Prince replied, "Sometimes it snows in April." These deliberately—some said annoyingly—cryptic responses both turned out to tease song titles from his next two albums.

In the end, the Purple Rain tour played to nearly 1.75 million people in thirty-two cities and grossed an estimated $30 million on ticket sales alone. While Prince pulled the plug after less than six months on the road, Bruce Springsteen kept on rolling; the Born in the USA tour went for fifteen months and more than 150 shows, following a run of U.S. arenas with dates in Australia and Asia, then Europe, and then returning to the States for a lap of stadiums before finally wrapping up on October 2.

Prince also courted controversy up to the very last date,

when religious leaders in Miami expressed their disapproval that his Orange Bowl show, for an audience of 55,000, was taking place on Easter Sunday. Whichever promoter gets the credit for that booking, the fact that Prince ended the tour supporting his greatest triumph on the day symbolizing the resurrection of Christ seemed particularly resonant (think back to that first attempt at a movie project, *The Second Coming*). Almost two years to the day after the end of the 1999 tour, when Prince turned his full attention to the unlikely, seemingly impossible creation of *Purple Rain,* it was all over.

"This has been the happiest season of my life," Prince said from the stage. He ended the show saying, "I have to go now. I don't know when I'll be back. I want you to know that God loves you. He loves us all."

After the show, he and Sheila E. turned up at an after-party at a Miami club. They both had very short haircuts, and Prince would only speak to *Miami Vice* star Don Johnson. There would be one final sour note to the tour, as well, when it was discovered that $1.6 million was missing from the accounts, and one of the promoters was charged with defrauding and misappropriating ticket revenues.

Just two weeks after the Miami show, with minimal warning or fanfare, *Around the World in a Day* arrived in record stores and quickly shot to number one; *Purple Rain* was still selling steadily, and while it started to fade after the release of the new album, it hung around the Top 200 until late 1985. Still, Prince did no interviews and no appearances, but later in the year, when he resurfaced for some unexpected press, he told MTV, "I don't plan on touring for a while. There are so many other things to do." But it wouldn't be too much longer before he was back on a stage, playing a series of one-off shows throughout the U.S. in the spring and summer of 1986 before kicking off a full-blown tour in London on August 12, 1986, to promote not only his next album, *Parade,* but also his new movie, the self-directed debacle *Under the Cherry Moon.*

In that same interview, he was asked if he was worried about a backlash after the astonishing popularity that he had attained with *Purple Rain.* "I don't live in a prison," he said. "I am not afraid of anything. I haven't built any walls around myself, and I am just like anyone else. I need love and water, and I'm not afraid of a backlash because, like I say, there are people who will support my habits as I have supported theirs.

"I don't really consider myself a superstar," said Prince. "I live in a small town, and I always will. I can walk around and be me. That's all I want to be. That's all I ever tried to be."

ELEVEN

Thank U 4 a Funky Time

The success of *Purple Rain,* Prince once said "in some ways was more detrimental than good. . . . It pigeonholed me."

There will always be one big, unanswerable question that lies behind Prince's decision to end the *Purple Rain* cycle so abruptly, and in one form or another, it looms over the rest of his exhilarating, baffling, unparalleled career. Did he choose to rescale things and allow himself to operate with more freedom than a stadium-filling, twenty-million-album-selling artist can have, or did he believe that anything he touched would automatically be that big? Was his ambition to be the world's biggest cult artist, or to be a global superstar—as Bob Cavallo put it, to be Miles Davis or Elvis Presley? Or had it become impossible for him to resolve this conflict?

In some ways, it's the classic artist's conundrum of creativity versus commerce. But there's a hubris that must come along with having the bestselling album in the country for six months and with pulling off a movie project that even those around you—much less the Hollywood establishment—had absolutely zero faith in. But did that kind of adulation scare Prince, causing him to run from it so quickly, or did it warp him to the point that he really believed he could now do no wrong?

"You could look at it as, '*Purple Rain* got me to the stardom I want, and I'm done with *Purple Rain*—I'm that star now, and that's gonna be maintained,'" says Wendy Melvoin. "To me, it feels more like that than 'I'm too nervous to keep that going.' That doesn't sound like Prince to me."

"And that's sad to me," continues Lisa Coleman, "because as a kid, growing up, you wonder about these stars or famous musicians—how many are noticed because they're great, and how many are great because they're noticed? How much do you put into promoting yourself, and how much do you put into being really great at what you do? And a lot of the time they don't go together. I think Prince is such an amazing musician, and why can't that be who he is? I think he's never made that decision, and that is still what gets in his way now. That seems to be his Achilles' heel. I think after *Purple Rain* he couldn't reconcile intrinsic artistry with promotion and pop stardom."

"At the end of *Purple Rain*," says Matt Fink, "maybe he felt, 'I need to take a break, because this is so oversaturated now; it's so big that I've got to let people absorb it, and I have to let it go away for a while.' People get tired of you and they move on to the next flavor, and that's how it goes, and he knew that. So maybe he thought, 'Okay, now I did it, this is what I wanted,' but then, 'Oops! Now what do I do?' He couldn't rest on his laurels, but he also couldn't milk it beyond that initial part of the tour due to his own impatience and wanting to move on.

"He never expressed exactly how he felt to us. He never sat down and said, 'I'm really concerned that I've overdone it, or maybe going here wasn't so great for our careers because now we peaked and it's all going to be downhill from here,' or whatever. He just said one thing and then did another when he put out *Around the World in a Day*."

With the momentum of *Purple Rain* behind it—or, more precisely, with the momentum still going full tilt—*Around the World* sold over two million copies, and no Prince record has been more commercially successful since. Despite his initial claims that he would not release any singles from the album, "Raspberry Beret" and "Pop Life" both reached the Top Ten. In the *New York Times*, Robert Palmer actually called the album "Prince's finest hour—for now," while a more tempered review by Jon Pareles in *Rolling Stone* said Prince was "still odd enough to be fascinating."

But the album didn't capture the public imagination to anywhere near the degree that *Purple Rain* had. If anything, its lilting textures and cerebral lyrics confused a large portion of the fans attracted by the girls-and-guitars spirit of *Purple Rain*. Then again, that seemed to be his intention. "Record sales and things like that," said Prince, "it really doesn't matter, ya know. It keeps a roof over your head, and keeps money in all these folks' pockets that I got hangin' around here! It basically stems from the music, and I'm just hoping that people understand that money is one thing, but soul is another."

In some ways, this was remarkably savvy. As Bob Merlis points out, attempting to top or compete with a success of *Purple Rain*'s magnitude is a loser's game. Michael Jackson not only set himself the goal of beating *Thriller* with his next album but of reaching sales of one hundred million. As a result, when *Bad* came out in 1987, the six million it sold was considered a huge letdown. In the aftermath of *Born in the USA* mania, Bruce Springsteen's marriage fell apart, and his next album was the more personal, musically modest *Tunnel of Love*; after one more tour, he dissolved the E Street Band for more than ten years.

"A hit like *Purple Rain* is a phenomenon of its time," says Merlis. "The stars aligned. Even if you do put out another record that's just as good, success is so circumstantial, and you really have to build in the possibility of great disappointment."

At the same time, though, Prince's decisions in the aftermath of *Purple Rain* also reveal a sense of invulnerability and grandeur—that since he had been right about the movie all along, when everyone else doubted, it meant that he could now do no wrong. Certainly the next project he took on, directing himself in the film *Under the Cherry Moon,* was a series of disasters. Shot in the south of France in glamorous black and white, the movie included virtually no footage of Prince performing, had lead characters (Prince and Kristin Scott Thomas) who were decidedly unlikable, and ended with the death of Prince's character. The sound track, *Parade,* didn't even have the same title as the film. With a budget of $12 million, *Cherry Moon* was critically lambasted and took in only $10 million at the box office.

"All I know is that it was never good after he got eaten by the fame, which was the success of *Purple Rain* and that tour," says Cavallo.

Lisa Coleman and Wendy Melvoin continued to work even more closely with Prince on the *Parade* album (which, by the way, is a fantastic record that I have overlooked for years, probably because of its association with the terrible movie). Melvoin was even featured prominently in the video for the album's smash single, "Kiss," sitting on a stool playing the guitar part (which Prince had actually recorded) while he danced and preened and basically did everything that he hadn't done in *Under the Cherry Moon*. But this collaboration was not to last.

"We had been thinking that we were gonna kind of become another entity, with us and Prince," says Coleman. "There was something different and special about the way the three of us wrote together and did things together. It was really great. We started looking for a house in Minneapolis, and then Prince suddenly started questioning it. Again, he started just shifting, and then he fired us, saying that he wanted to go in another direction."

Not that he slowed down creatively: in fact, he set to work on multiple albums—*Dream Factory, Camille, Crystal Ball*—proposing a triple album to Warner Bros. before eventually releasing *Sign o' the Times* as a two-disc set in 1987. And to many fans it stands as his single greatest record—not as airtight as *Purple Rain* but sprawling in all the best ways, revealing the full breadth and scope of Prince's talents. Melvoin and Coleman still turn up on a few songs, and the penultimate track, "It's Gonna Be a Beautiful Night" (named by Questlove as his all-time favorite Prince song) is a live recording with the Revolution, plus Eric Leeds and Atlanta Bliss on horns, Sheila E. on percussion, and Susannah Melvoin and Jill Jones adding background vocals—effectively a final farewell to the entire *Purple Rain* crew. But *Sign o' the Times* peaked at number six on the charts and stalled at a million sold.

Within the next few years, Albert Magnoli—who codirected the *Sign o' the Times* concert film with Prince, most of which was shot on a soundstage after the footage from a European tour proved unsatisfactory—had replaced Steve Fargnoli as Prince's closest advisor. "Prince and my group had a falling-out, and we sued each other and he bought me out, and I'm sure I got fucked," says Cavallo. "But I wanted out, and it was enough money to equalize the partnership so I could walk, because I wanted to do it my way. I was an eighties guy, a lot of cocaine—you know, I fucked up."

In January 1989 Magnoli took over as Prince's manager. But as Prince got deeper into his next ill-fated movie project, 1990's *Graffiti Bridge,* Magnoli also walked away.

Maybe Prince was simply too restless, too impossible to tame, to ever again scale the heights he reached with *Purple Rain*. But it's clear that part of the reason he got there was the team around him, from the band to the management, and that as he systematically took all of those people out of his life, he never replaced them with figures of comparable stature who could contribute to his efforts and might possibly say no to him.

"Prince didn't just have any old team—he had a team of fucking geniuses," says Howard Bloom. "What other artist has ever had a team of brains around like that? It's almost like that book on Lincoln, *Team of Rivals*. It wasn't just Prince building Prince in the 1980s, it was a team of people at their creative best who put everything that they had creatively into it, because he deserved it, he earned it.

"At every stage of the game, you need goals that are higher than where you are now. And you need a couple of people around who will tell you truths that you don't necessarily want to hear."

"That team of people were *very* powerful guys at the time," says Melvoin. "They had all the resources to make him what he wanted to be, and I think that's the thing that blew it up, because he does not have a team and he hasn't had a team since then. As a younger guy, he was much more able to say to himself, 'I'm gonna manipulate those crazy, strong dudes. They're gonna make it happen for me.' I think that was his laser beam at the time."

Going back to 1986, the expanded Revolution, including Sheila E. and the horn players, continued the Parade tour of Europe and Japan through the summer. The shows were more funk-driven than the Purple Rain shows, with Prince dancing more and playing much less guitar. And then he sent them all home.

On October 16, 1986, the *Minneapolis Star Tribune* announced, "The Revolution is over."

Morris Day steps out of the car. He cinches his coat closed at the throat and casts a glance around the sidewalk, surrounded by his band—including a "valet" next to him carrying a suit bag. His hair is cropped closer than it was in the elaborate 1980s bouffant, but he seems to be in good shape. The scene is shockingly reminiscent of the singer swooping down his front steps and into his car in *Purple Rain*'s opening montage, with Jerome Benton protecting him from a nonexistent crowd of fans.

This time, though, Day is crossing the sidewalk on Forty-second Street, in the heart of Times Square, arriving at B. B. King's nightclub for the first of two sets by a band now billed as "Morris Day and the Time," and including just two other members—drummer Jellybean Johnson and keyboard player Monte Moir—from the original group. It's a cold January night during the "polar vortex" winter of 2014, and the 550-capacity venue is a little shy of sold-out, at least for the early show. The Time hit the stage at two minutes after eight o'clock and play for sixty minutes on the dot, mostly cruising through medleys with abridged versions of their hits. Day can still muster his trademark cackle, and obviously knows that the audience would be disappointed if he didn't have a handheld mirror brought out so he can check his hair every few songs.

Though he makes only one reference to the movie (asking the crowd to "jump back to 1984—jump in that yellow taxi from *Purple Rain,* you remember the one"), the two Time songs featured on-screen are still, inevitably, the climax of the show. The set closes with an extended rendition of "The Bird," and after a few minutes offstage, the group files back out to perform an encore of "Jungle Love." Thirty years later, those numbers are still the meal ticket.

In the latter half of the 1980s, Day scored a couple of solo hits with "Fishnet" and "The Oak Tree." In 1990, a reunited Time actually had their biggest single with "Jerk Out," which reached number one on the R&B charts. Day's much-vaunted screen career, though, never really materialized: he had small roles in Richard Pryor's film *Moving* and Andrew Dice Clay's *The Adventures of Ford Fairlane,* and had a part in a short-lived ABC sitcom called *New Attitude.* He also appeared in a series of commercials for a Toyota dealership in Atlanta.

In 2001, the title characters in Kevin Smith's cult comedy *Jay and Silent Bob Strike Back* proclaimed that the Time was their favorite band, and at the end of the film, Jason Mewes's Jay introduced "the greatest band in the world, Morris Day and the Time!" and the group materialized, performing "Jungle Love." The Time have reconstituted in various configurations since then, playing on their own and backing Rihanna at the 2008 Grammy Awards and releasing a new album, *Condensate,* under the name "The Original 7ven" in 2011.

Maybe it's not the career Day dreamed of when the Time were going toe-to-toe with Prince at sold-out arenas during the Triple Threat tour or while he was being singled out as the comic highlight of the number one movie in the country. But it's also not as bad as things might have been had his drug use persisted after he and Prince began feuding during the latter days of *Purple Rain*.

The experiences of the other musicians are mostly comparable—*Purple Rain* didn't make anyone but Prince a superstar, but they are all still making a living with their music, even if much of their reputation is based on their time in the Revolution.

Bobby Z hosts a radio show every Sunday night in Minneapolis, devoted to playing "the best in Minnesota music." Matt Fink produces local musicians and does other work for hire in his home studio while playing in several groups, including his Prince cover band. Mark Brown continues to play in the Bay Area; a recent Facebook post announced auditions for a new version of Mazarati, the band he started under the Paisley Park umbrella after he left the Revolution. Wendy Melvoin and Lisa Coleman have carved out the most interesting career path, working in the world of film and television music on their own—even winning an Emmy in 2010 for Outstanding Original Main Title Theme Music for the Showtime series *Nurse Jackie*—not dependent on touring for money, returning in a way to something like the Los Angeles session world of their fathers.

"Wendy and Lisa have worthy accomplishments on their own to be proud of—even if they'd never played for Prince, their résumés are respectable, and they're really good at what they do," says Alan Leeds, who went on to work with such artists as Maxwell, Chris Rock, and D'Angelo after his time running Prince's Paisley Park record imprint. "The rest of the guys were the perfect fit for the band. I'm not hating the least little bit, but none of them have done anything of substance before or since. I'm not judging anybody, but they had the ride of their life and got a big check. In Bobby and particularly Fink's case, the way they played their money, they were set for life. Prince was very generous, and they were smart about it, and now they work for fun."

In June of 2000, Bobby Z, Matt Fink, and Mark Brown attended Prince's forty-second birthday party and jammed with him onstage. The national mega-promoter SFX made a major offer for a Revolution reunion tour. Wendy Melvoin took charge of the band and lined them all up to work, but Prince refused.

There was no communication for several years; in 2004, the Revolution members showed up at a club date Prince was playing at LA's House of Blues, and he proceeded to ignore them, inviting other musicians to join him onstage but not them. But after the show, Prince had his guitar tech call Melvoin and ask her to appear with him on Tavis Smiley's PBS talk show. Apparently the "Steve" side of Prince's personality came out to play that day. "He was the guy I knew when I first met him," she said. "He was the guy who spent that night at my and Lisa's house on our pullout bed."

In 2011, Bobby Z had a near-fatal heart attack in Minneapolis. Almost exactly a year later, on February 19, 2012, all the members of the Revolution gathered at First Avenue for a benefit show to celebrate his recovery. For ninety minutes, guitarists Melvoin and Dez Dickerson, keyboardists Lisa

Coleman and Dr. Fink, bassist Mark Brown, saxophonist Eric Leeds, and drummer Bobby Z played a selection of Prince hits from the '80s to a sold-out room. "We're sentimental and we're nostalgic," said Melvoin from the stage.

"To add to the one-of-a-kind spirit of the fund-raiser," wrote the *Star Tribune*, "each of the Revolutionaries did a dramatic recitation from the movie *Purple Rain*. Good laughs all around." A guitar was set up in case Prince decided to swing by at the last minute, but he didn't show.

In 2014, Apollonia served as the "VIP host" for the now-annual benefit, marking her first trip back to Minneapolis since the movie wrapped. After the First Avenue show, which included Bobby and Fink and various other local artists, she visited Paisley Park, where Prince took her on a tour of the complex, showing her the Purple Rain room and paintings that included her image. He then played a surprise late-night set with 3rdEyeGirl, which did not include a new song he had recently recorded called "This Could Be Us," named for a popular Internet meme that featured an iconic *Purple Rain* photo of the Kid and Apollonia on his motorcycle.

At 4:42 that morning, Kotero put up a Facebook post, which read in part: "Heard new music that was dope! He had a cool chair for me on the stage at his side, and I sat there transfixed on every note, every move, every vocal. After every song I yelled and clapped my ass off. . . . And Prince . . . my heart still skip's [*sic*] a beat." The post was deleted a few hours later.

While the band members have always been able to keep their hands in music over the decades, things have been a bit spottier for Kotero. She had a recurring role on *Falcon Crest* immediately following *Purple Rain*. In 1988, she released a widely ignored solo album, and went on to appear in a number of straight-to-video films and made her own workout video. A highlight of her appearances on various reality shows was an episode of *MTV Cribs* featuring Apollonia and her next-door neighbor Carmen Electra, one of her successors as a bombshell Prince protégée. She now concentrates on her management company, Kotero Entertainment, and when approached about an interview for this book, replied very politely that she is working on a book of her own.

Jill Jones's self-titled 1987 album is considered one of the more interesting side projects in the Prince catalogue, but has long been out of print. Jones released a few more albums, and toured as a vocalist with Chic before moving back to Los Angeles and joining the corporate world.

In addition to his work with Prince—*Sign o' the Times* and the music videos from the 1989 *Batman* sound track—Albert Magnoli directed the *Purple-Rain*-on-a-balance-beam gymnastics drama *American Anthem* in 1986 and a few made-for-TV films, and co-directed Sylvester Stallone's *Tango & Cash*.

The one person involved in *Purple Rain* who might credibly claim that it was not the high point of his career is Bob Cavallo. After parting ways with Prince, he went on to form a management company that handled such multiplatinum acts as Green Day, Seal, and Alanis Morissette, and also a film company that produced hits including *12 Monkeys* and *City of Angels*. In 1998, Cavallo was named to the position of chairman of the

Buena Vista Music Group—later the Disney Music Group—overseeing all of the Walt Disney Company's recorded music and music publishing operations, where he served until retiring in 2012. He sure seems to be living the good life now; during our interview, he excused himself several times for phone calls to finalize details for an upcoming vacation trip across the Atlantic Ocean with his wife on the *Queen Mary* 2.

And then there's Prince. Depending how you count, he has released twenty-five albums since *Purple Rain*, give or take. He made three more films. He has toured the world repeatedly, sometimes as a major, arena-scale operation, and sometimes as a low-flying hit-and-run mission. Most infamously, he changed his name to an unpronounceable symbol (an early version of which appeared on his *Purple Rain* motorcycle) and wrote the word "slave" on his face as part of an ongoing feud with Warner Bros. Records—after signing a deal with them that was reported to be worth $100 million. It made him something of a laughingstock, and in many ways his career has never fully recovered. But as digital rights and distribution became the single dominant issue of the twenty-first-century music business, it is also unarguably true that he helped bring awareness to the complex questions around creative copyright long before most of the world noticed.

"What we want," Prince said to me in 2004, "is the easiest, most efficient way to get the business done, that can be as second-nature and organic as picking up a guitar. In Silicon Valley, they're all coming to work with their jeans on, all cool; it's all beautiful, all life. That's how it should be.

"The cool thing about being independent," he continued, "is you're not handed a schedule and told, 'This is what you're going to do.' Your psyche works completely differently. You're not always reacting to things. You feel you're in a creative mode, and that's what keeps you alive, keeps you young."

It's a philosophy that is easy enough to comprehend, even to sympathize with; but as a fan, it's also easy to get frustrated with Prince. His crusade has been driven by the desire to put out as much music as possible, which would be one thing if his albums were of the consistently excellent standard we know he is capable of. (It's also a lot easier to say "Music should be free, anyway," as he told me back in 1994, after you've signed a $100 million deal.) For so long, though, his releases have been such a mixed bag, so difficult to keep track of, much less to actually decode. It's equally easy to over- or underestimate almost anything he does at this point. Though it slowed down his brain in a way he clearly couldn't sustain, even a fraction of the meticulous editing and unwavering focus he gave to *Purple Rain* would go a long way toward raising his batting average.

But he's not really interested in that. "Shouldn't it be up to the artist how the music comes out?" he said to me in 1994, shortly after he had changed his name and his obsessions were escalating. "They're just songs, just our thoughts. Nobody has a mortgage on your thoughts. We've got it all wrong, discouraging our artists. In America, we're not as free as we think."

It seems as if—much like Stevie Wonder, one of the few artists who can truly be held up as a comparable talent—there came a day when Prince just got tired of writing hit singles, became bored by how effortless his melodic gift was. Since the dawn of the 1990s, his albums have all felt like genre experiments or unfinished sketches, while his real attention was devoted to business matters. Nor has he explored more personal issues, even in the stylized treatment they were given in *Purple Rain,* other than the religious narrative of 2001's *The Rainbow Children* and, most painfully, the songs anticipating his son's birth on 1996's *Emancipation*; the loss of his newborn child, who was born with an extremely rare skull malformation, and the subsequent end of his marriage to Mayte Garcia, may have closed certain doors that might never open again.

"*Purple Rain* was the best part of all of his triggers," says Wendy Melvoin. "He used it well, because he was excited. Now he's fifty-some years old; he's not as excited about it, and he doesn't want to have anything to do with his triggers, and he's shape-shifted into this completely different person who reads scripture and tells you fucking parables."

And then every once in a while, whether inspired by creativity or commerce, he can flick a switch and connect with a huge audience again. Tying in to the relaunch of the *Batman* franchise in 1989 proved a good fit, with a hit sound track and a few big singles. In 1994, the gauzy ballad "The Most Beautiful Girl in the World" was matched with some promotion and touring and gave Prince the first number one of his career in the UK. In 2004, the *Musicology* album demonstrated that he at least understood the kind of sound that casual fans wanted from him and brought him back to the top of the charts and the touring world, and his Super Bowl halftime show proved he could continue to scale newer and bigger heights. But while it still feels like he could resurrect himself as a pop star whenever he chooses to, these resurgences are getting farther and farther apart, and the Top 40 world is a rough place for anyone in their mid-fifties.

It's impossible to take *Purple Rain* out of Prince's history, but if we could, would we still think of him as a world-class superstar? Or would we instead consider him an experimental pop figure, "the world's top indie artist," as *The New Yorker* recently called him, with a million people who will follow him down whichever path he chooses—which sure seems like an enviable position for an artist to establish.

"It's almost a uniquely huge cult he has," says Leeds, "because 'cult' usually implies 'small'—and it ain't small if you can sell out Madison Square Garden three nights in a row. There are guys with a lot of hit records who can't sell out three Gardens in a row. So he has convinced people that he's worth seeing no matter what: no matter what your current record is, no matter who's in your band, because you change that all the time, and nobody really gives a shit anymore.

"I'm hard-pressed to think of anyone—maybe Paul McCartney—who could do three shows in a row, and have three different set lists, and be just as good each night. Here's a guy who you can go in and say, 'I want to hear the hits,' and he *doesn't* do the hits, but you're not mad because what he does is so great that you don't even care."

Thirty years later, Prince continues to make new music, to work with new musicians. Though *Purple Rain* will always stand as his crowning achievement, he has refused to allow it to define him, and has never fallen into the trap of becoming an oldies act. Maybe there's something else—so much else—that his fans still want from him, but in fighting against the powerful siren song of nostalgia he has remained a creative force, and there are still plenty of us who wait eagerly for the next installment.

"I get why he doesn't want to celebrate the anniversaries or any of that stuff," says Chris Rock. "You can't be a legend and a current artist at the same time. You can't be in the Hall of Fame and still play—everybody in the Hall of Fame is retired. I'd rather play, and I'm sure Prince would, too."

So was there a real legacy left by *Purple Rain*? Was it just an odd eruption, a fluky confluence (however well planned and executed) of the right songs by the right artist at the right time, or did it make a lasting mark?

Over the years, the film continues to show up on screens as it has entered the world of Midnight Movies and cult classics. It played at Brooklyn's Prospect Park as a public sing-along screening for thousands of people, and in San Francisco at the Castro Theater for an audience of drag queens who dressed up as the characters. Punk cabaret singer-songwriter-provocateur Amanda Palmer and her band donned Revolution-inspired outfits and played the whole *Purple Rain* album as part of a 2013 New Year's Eve show at New York's Terminal 5 club. In 1984, Steven Ivory wrote a quickie biography of Prince that contained the prescient observation that "years from now, the movie will remain a cult favorite among rock music fans, not unlike the success of the '70s rock musical *The Rocky Horror Picture Show*."

"As big as it was, I think it's the most underrated thing," says Bob Cavallo. "They talk about *The Song Remains the Same* or whatever; all I know is, I've never seen anything like this."

Certainly, it has been imitated on-screen by other musicians, for better and for worse. Mariah Carey's disastrous *Glitter* and Eminem's triumphant *8 Mile* were both essentially the exact same movie as *Purple Rain*—though the movie's classic, formulaic plot (underdog star struggles to be recognized for his unique talent while competing for romantic love) is not exactly original enough to warrant too much credit. And the extent to which the fascination with the movie was dependent on Prince's mystique and inaccessibility is completely out of step with today's media universe, where any sense of mystery has been replaced by rap's ongoing obsession with authenticity and "realness," plus the mandatory social media oversharing from every aspiring pop star.

Yet in the decade after the 1984 supernova, which saw the rise of Spike Lee (who claimed *Purple Rain* as an inspiration) and other young black filmmakers and the successful migration of hip-hop stars and themes—from *Boyz n the Hood* to *New Jack City*—to movie screens, it would seem that the movie's triumph did change the playing field. The music, of course, continues to echo infinitely, through the work of OutKast, Lenny Kravitz, Alicia Keys, Pharrell Williams, Daft Punk,

Beyoncé, and Beck, from their drum sounds to their ballad singing, in more ways than can be imagined.

Alan Leeds notes that in all his work on the road during the last thirty years, there is always an inevitable moment when someone pops the *Purple Rain* DVD into the tour bus player. "If you're a writer or a producer or a roadie, there's some moment as a young person that captivated you," he says. "When you said, 'I don't want a real job—I want to be part of this.' And most of the people that I work with today, the Prince Era, meaning '80s Prince, that's their inspiration, their benchmark. That's what motivated them to want to do this."

"*Purple Rain* showed me that you don't have to do what everybody expects," says Darius Rucker, who has topped the rock and country charts. "That being a black kid didn't mean I had to just sing R&B. Prince was such an influence to not let anybody tell me what I can sing or what I can be. I looked up to him; I wanted to be Prince—this little short kid who was just killing them!"

"Prince has all these kids now," says Chris Rock. "You get older and your influence goes in different ways; it doesn't have to just be in music. So there's Spike Lee, Ice Cube—he has big albums and big movies. *Friday* was a movie that's nothing but an Ice Cube album, the same way *Purple Rain* was. I don't exist without Prince. He might not like that now—he's a Jehovah's Witness, and I'm this cursing comedian!"

"Since then, who has done this?" asks Albert Magnoli. "Nobody. It's really hard to bring a musical individual into a film place. It's hard to transfer; a motion picture reveals too much."

Susan Rogers emphasizes just how different Prince was, especially at his moment of breakthrough, from the other stars at his altitude. "Michael Jackson, Madonna, Bruce Springsteen, the Rolling Stones, Elton John—they all had producers and session musicians. They had the best players. Prince was one guy who was writing and arranging and producing, and he was competing with all of them on that level. One guy.

"Patti Smith wrote that book called *Just Kids,* talking about the New York art scene—there were a lot of artists, it was truly a scene. This was a scene of *one guy* who created his own competition in order to *be* a scene. Who does that?"

One element of *Purple Rain* that has clearly had a life of its own over the years is the title song, which, in addition to solidifying over time as Prince's signature composition and fail-safe showstopper, has been covered by a wide variety of artists in a crazy array of settings. Adam Levine sang it at Howard Stern's sixtieth birthday party, while Phish (who have dropped the song into their sets off and on for years) played it during a July Fourth show at Long Island's Jones Beach Theater before going into "The Star-Spangled Banner."

"'Purple Rain' was basically a challenge," says country singer LeAnn Rimes. "I wanted to explore something new and prove to myself and the whole world that I could do a lot more than what they had heard from me. Through the years, during my concerts, it's one of the main songs fans scream out for me to sing. I've rocked it out, I've performed it acoustic—it changes as I change. It will forever remain one of the most influential songs of my musical journey, and I will forever remain one of the biggest Prince fans."

A young Tori Amos began playing "Purple Rain" in her cocktail lounge set immediately after first seeing the movie in 1984, and it has consistently turned up in her shows ever since. "It was like a hymn, like a religious experience, and maybe that's what spoke to me, growing up in church," she says. "It wasn't filled with guilt but with compassion, taking yourself out of a situation and acknowledging that you might have hurt someone. It was like nothing I had really encountered in that way—a song that could be vulnerable and yet in control.

"Something was opened up in my heart by 'Purple Rain,' especially near the end of the song when he goes really high. It seemed not funereal, but like a requiem to me. I remember bawling my eyes out when I first heard it. It woke something up in me—memories, sadness, deep longing; it touches so many emotions."

"The whole movie blew me away, but when he played 'Purple Rain,' that was really it," says Darius Rucker, who has also made the song a regular feature of his concerts. "I got the album, and by the third time listening to it, I was like, 'This guy has just written "Hey Jude"—he's written the perfect rock and roll ballad.' I wanted to sing it ever since. We talked about it in Hootie but just never did it. One day, the guys in my band came up and asked if I'd ever thought about doing 'Purple Rain.' I said yes, forever, but I didn't think it would work in a country show. And they were like, 'Oh, it'll work.'

"I love playing it, but I didn't think it would be something people would come to expect from me. Now I can't stop—I mentioned on Twitter that I was going to stop doing it, and people went crazy. But every night I just love it; it makes me so happy when I hear those first chords."

"Purple Rain" has also become a popular selection in the world of karaoke. *Rolling Stone*'s Rob Sheffield, whose 2013 book *Turn Around Bright Eyes* is an examination of karaoke culture, says that it's clearly the Prince song of choice, though it poses its own challenges. "Sometimes you'll see somebody attempt it and then they look like a deer in the purple headlights, in those long pauses from line to line," he says. "It's a song that requires you to stand your ground and handle those pauses. It forces you to call upon your reserves of charisma—when you sing 'Purple Rain,' you're spending a lot of time standing there without a guitar to look busy with, so you have to go all the way into the song. You can't do that one casually or mockingly."

Though he says he's seen attempts at "Let's Go Crazy" and a "surprising number" of "Darling Nikkis," Sheffield thinks "Purple Rain" offers more latitude than other Prince songs. "There's really no way to karaoke 'When Doves Cry' or 'Raspberry Beret' without the constant pitfall of imitating the man, because his vocal mannerisms are so integral to the melody and rhythm. 'Purple Rain' is more of a 'standard' in the sense that you can sing it without seeming like you're just copying the original vocal. The song still has lots of his personality (practically everybody who attempts it does the 'that means you, too!' part, often with a bit of air guitar), but it isn't dependent on whether or not you can do a good Prince. It's a song that's kind to a mediocre or ordinary voice (like the voice that most of us karaoke obsessives have, definitely including me)."

In a classroom—with full recording studio capabilities—at New York University's Clive Davis Institute of Recorded Music, two dozen students gather on a Friday morning for a class titled "Topics in Recorded Music: Prince." According to the syllabus, the course will "explore the joys and contradictions of Prince's music and business practices." The instructors are Ahmir "Questlove" Thompson (who has to hustle each week from the classroom to his gig as bandleader on the *Tonight Show*) and Harry Weinger, a Grammy-winning reissue producer who serves as vice president of A&R for UMe, the catalogue division of Universal Music Group (Weinger has long overseen the reissue projects for such soul treasure troves as the vaults of James Brown and Motown Records). Today's subject is "'Baby I'm a Star': Prince Goes Mainstream in the 1980s," and the students are greeted with a pop quiz (sample questions: "Who was the female guitarist and female keyboard player in *Purple Rain*?" and "What's the name of the dance performed by the Time in *Purple Rain*?")

The class watches video of the Time performing on *Soul Train*, and Questlove demonstrates the progression of drum machine technology during these few years. Footage of James Brown during his incomparable performance on *The TAMI*

Show in 1964 is compared with unreleased clips of Prince leading the Revolution on the Purple Rain tour. Of course, it's difficult to show even the official music videos, since Prince has them removed from YouTube as soon as they get put up; at the last minute, Weinger had to order a VHS copy of *The Hits* video collection just to screen the "1999" clip.

The students, all aspiring musicians or music professionals, giggle while watching sultry clips of Vanity 6 onstage and make comments both sophisticated ("How did Prince's business arrangements work with his protégé groups like the Time?") and more innocent (no one in the class can identify a song by the Police). Still, they watch, rapt, when Questlove puts on that very first performance of "Purple Rain" from First Avenue—which, in fact, is pulled down the following week in the ongoing cat-and-mouse game Prince plays with the web.

Purple Rain entered history long ago. Questlove and Weinger's class grants the project the respect that it's due. It is in no way demeaning to the rest of a glorious career to say that it will forever stand as the pinnacle of Prince's achievements. It represents the confluence of so many strands of his own creativity and ambition and of so many cultural trends that it could never have happened before or since. And given the splintering of the music audience that followed its colossal success, it seems likely that we will never again agree on anything the way we agreed on *Purple Rain*.

However often he says or acts otherwise, there is clearly a part of Prince that is aware of his contributions to history. Back in the Rocketown dressing room in 2004, in the early morning hours, he grew a bit more reflective. He was about to pack it in—to pass out some Jehovah's Witness literature to the fans still gathered outside and then jump into his limo and speed off into the Nashville night. But he had one final thought to offer.

"When you're a young man, you think you're the center of the universe," he told me. "Later you see you're just part of it. The world is only going to get harder. Me and my crew, we love having conversations about music, but when we get deep, we talk about the future, about what we're leaving for the kids."

But this side will always be at war with the part of Prince that insists, in the words of the legendary baseball pitcher Satchel Paige, "Don't look back—something might be gaining on you." Even as he shocked and delighted his fans with the news that he had mended fences with his longtime nemeses at Warner Bros. and would finally be revisiting his catalogue, he celebrated in the only way he knows: that night he put out a new song, a devastating ballad called "The Breakdown" that many listeners instantly called a return to form unlike anything he had released in years. The message was clear—the chance to regain control of his master tapes was something he had sought for decades, but the music always needed to keep moving forward. Always.

Or maybe it's all part of the show. As in *Purple Rain*, blurring the lines between fantasy and reality, creating a character that was larger than life but still mysterious, building a life in which nothing and no one could get in between the artist and his music, was all part of what it took for a kid from Minneapolis to conquer the world.

In 1994, at San Francisco's Club DV8, he ordered us both a glass of port and offered me a lollipop because, he said, he didn't think I smoked cigars. Leaning over and whispering conspiratorially, Prince lifted his glass and offered a toast.

"To Oz."

ACKNOWLEDGMENTS

First and foremost, thanks to Prince. Though his adamant, longtime resistance to looking back and talking about his past meant that I had no reason to even approach him about participating in this project, his music has brought me more joy than I can say. My dealings with him over the years—some of them recounted in these pages—have seldom been easy, but have always been a pleasure. And the guy is just so damn funky.

Thank you to everyone who spoke to me for this book, all of whom were generous, patient, and giving. Extra credit to Lisa Kanclerz Coleman for assistance above and beyond the call of duty. The glories of social media made it much easier to track everybody down, but thanks also to Renata Kanclerz, Sharrin Summers, Ebie McFarland, Olga Makrias, Lori Nafshun, and Devon Wambold for introductions and guidance. David Prince, David Brendel, and

Roseann Warren passed along some invaluable links and files.

Love and gratitude to Alice Bezanson, who did all the dirty work as researcher, transcriber, fact-checker, and provider of whatever editorial services were needed. I'm so glad you are in my life, and you will remain so wherever your latest adventures take you.

Sarah Lazin, as always, is a wise agent, friend, and sounding board. Thanks also to Sarah's associates Manuela Jessel and Anna Qu.

At Atria, once again, Peter Borland took a leap of faith and then offered support, enthusiasm, and direction. It's great to have you in my corner on these oddball ideas, as well as Judith Curr, Daniel Loedel, Daniella Wexler, David Brown, and freelance copy editor Polly Watson.

Over the years, I've had the chance to write about Prince for such outlets as *Rolling Stone, Spin, Vibe, Tracks,* Amazon, and msn.com. Thank you to my colleagues at all of these publications for the opportunities, and for making my writing better.

Thanks to my classmates in the CCDS class of 1984 and the Yale class of 1988 for sharing the *Purple Rain* obsession in real time.

For so very many things: Hal Brooks, Mike Errico, Keith Hammond, Mike Paranzino, Dick Schumacher, Dan Carey, Jennifer Goldsmith Adams, Sia Michel, Emily Zemler, Rob Johnson, Charlene Benson, Brant Louck, Johanna Schlegel,

Anji Chandra, Sam Kramer, Elysa Gardner, Anthony DeCurtis, and Joe Angio.

Irwin, Janet, and Sharon Light are the most loving, encouraging family on earth.

Suzanne McElfresh and Adam Light, I love you more each day. And you, too, are just so damn funky.

May U Live 2 See the Dawn.

INDEX